THE MORAL COLLAPSE OF THE UNIVERSITY

SUNY Series
in Philosophy of Education

Philip L. Smith, Editor

BRUCE WILSHIRE

The Moral Collapse
of the University

Professionalism, Purity, and Alienation

STATE UNIVERSITY OF NEW YORK PRESS

Published by
State University of New York Press, Albany

For information, address State University of New York
Press, State University Plaza, Albany, NY 12246

Library of Congress Cataloging-in-Publication Data

Wilshire, Bruce W.
    The moral collapse of the university : professionalism, purity,
alienation / Bruce Wilshire.
        p.   cm. —(SUNY series in the philosophy of education)
    Includes index.
    ISBN 0–7914–0196–0. — ISBN 0–7914–0197–9 (pbk.)
    1. Education, Higher—United States—Aims and objectives.
2. College teaching—United States—Evaluation.   3. Professional
socialization—United States.   I. Title.   II. Series
LA227.3.W53   1990
378.73—dc20   89–4455
                                                                                    CIP

10 9 8 7 6 5 4 3 2 1

To
Rebekah Lott Wilshire
and the memory of
Esther Lott Barth

CONTENTS

ACKNOWLEDGMENTS

This book, so eagerly taken up and quickly dispatched in first draft, has proven to be more demanding than I expected. The ills of the university and my feelings about them all seemed obvious. But when others read my first efforts, and made observations and asked questions which I had not imagined they would, I was forced to dig deeper. I found that the very obviousness and self-evidence of the ills had eclipsed their roots and ramifications in the historical background, some of it, I perceived, exceedingly archaic. Yes, research is conducted at the expense of teaching. But why? Why the opposition? Some questions seemed easy. But with each apparent answer, and the response to it, new material, some of it contradictory, came into view—hence new questions.

As for my feelings, it was so hard to grasp them just because they were so close and constant; as they had become routine they had become "certain"—that constant taste of oneself-in-the-world that no longer seems to require articulation and explanation, *until* one tries to express it to someone else. Then I made discoveries about myself.

So to grasp where I already am in the university, and what, in a sense, I already feel, I have had to rely on colleagues and others to reflect back to me what I have written. Leland Wilshire, Howard McGary, Susan Bordo, Douglas Husak, Renée Weber, Benjamin Barber, Gail Belaief (early retired, her students will miss her) read earlier drafts, in whole or in part, and made fitting suggestions that have been so deeply incorporated in the work that I no longer am sure who contributed what.

More recent drafts have been conveyed back to me and illuminated by still more others. Harry Redner encouraged me, and applied his uniquely comprehensive intellect and helped organize some materials, and Edward Casey blessed me with over thirty pages of astute notes—a gift of mind and self that still warms and astonishes me. My colleague, John Fizer, made acute last-minute suggestions. Gautam Dasgupta and Carlin Romano did likewise. Needless to say, I alone am responsible for the use to which I put these persons' aid.

By way of stimulating words on their own themes, others have contributed directly to my thinking. I mention only Nicholas Capaldi's fine talk on the social sciences at Rutgers two years ago, Quentin Smith's marvelous book, *The Felt Meanings of the World: A Metaphysics of Feeling,* and William Barrett's latest feat of thinking clearly and simply about the most difficult matters, *The Death of the Soul: From Descartes to the Computer.*

I want also to thank Rutgers University for supporting my research with ample salary, reasonable teaching loads, several study leaves, and a year's tenure in the Center for the Critical Analysis of Contemporary Culture, where some of my observations were first articulated. It is a university which understands that the search for truth must be expedited, even if the results are not pleasant.

I also want to thank SUNY Press for the buoyance and expertise they have brought to the production of this book. They have believed in it, and I am grateful.

Now the most important acknowledgment, to my wife, Donna. Without her unfailing emotional support I probably would not have continued my work. But more and more she contributes intellectually to it, and even if the Muses should bless me I could never acknowledge this adequately. I can say, though, that I am particularly indebted to her work on a female paradigm for knowing and for identity (which appears emphatically in chapter 12), for her enactment of goddess myths, and for her introducing me to Frank Jones's book on John Dewey's personal and professional relationship to the therapist F. M. Alexander. Without her, all these basic matters would probably have been masked from my field of vision by professional blinkers.

A last personal word. In this book my concern with history is focused and selective: to discern those secularizing and professionalizing tendencies of the culture which greatly influenced the

modern university from its inception, and to reveal archaic practices of the university concealed by these tendencies. My work
complements and is complemented by more conventional
historical-chronological accounts. For two venerable examples of
the latter, see Arthur Levine, *Handbook on Undergraduate Curriculum,* and Frederick Rudolph, *Curriculum: A History of the
American Undergraduate Course of Study since 1636* (both San
Francisco: 1981). To take but one case, the Land Grant universities, founded in the several states in the later 19th century, generated a tradition quite different from eastern Ivy League
universities, and these differences are not simply expunged in the
crush of contemporaneity. I write directly about what I know
best, and what concerns me most: large state universities and
large, private, not necessarily eastern ones—research universities, so called—and their many, many thousands of students and
professors. Often close parallels exist in all universities, but I
cannot systematically draw them, or qualify each instance.

July 11, 1989
Plainfield, N.J.

We moderns have no memories at all.
                                                            —Frances Yates

Man has had time enough to forget about the
sea and make a universe of a crevice in a rock.
But now you can feel the waters lift and stir;
new currents are coming in, but for those of us
in universities who cannot stand the flooding of
our academic boundaries and definitions, there
will be terror as the mythical future becomes
confused with the mythical past.
                                        —William Irwin Thompson

PROLOGUE

A professor spoke up at a faculty meeting, "We all know what 'research university' means: To hell with the undergraduates." Thus the perception emerged that our largest "educational" institutions no longer educate. A number of widely read books have recently pinpointed this failure and have attempted to disclose the causes. But none of them has dealt with a key cause: academic professionalism, and the overt and covert factors that power this modern thrust for identity. Veiled by scientific research and professionalism are, I believe, archaic initiational and purificational practices which establish the identity of group and individual member through the exclusion of the unwashed and uncertified, for example, undergraduate students.

Today "university" is practically synonymous with "research institution," which connotes a loose political and economic grouping of disciplines and fields, little concerned for one another, each caught up in its own research and publishing interests. "Multiversity," it is called.

In this book I create a composite picture of this twentieth-century phenomenon. Most large universities fit the picture, although there are exceptions—better, degrees of being exceptional. By and large, academic professionalism, specialism, and careerism have taken precedence over teaching, and the education and development of both professors and students has been undermined. There is intergenerational failure, cultural failure. I try to plot the problem and find regenerational possibilities.

INTRODUCTION

Mankind would rather have the void for its
purpose than be void of purpose.

—Nietzsche

An upper-level administrator at the university telephoned me at
home. I had been repairing something in the basement, and my
hand, I saw, left a smear of grease on the phone. The administrator asked me about a fellow professor who was a candidate
for a deanship; he had served for a time as an associate dean.
What did I think of him?

I was unprepared. The call was completely unexpected.
Knowing I had to say something, I began by itemizing his attractive traits. It was not just that this was the civil thing to do, but
that I had a clear picture of what these traits were, whereas the
negative ones, I had never been able to focus clearly. What was
the reservation that brooded like a cloud around my thoughts
but would not coalesce in a definite image?

I went on with the positive traits. Yes, he was a bright person, industrious, well-prepared in his scholarly specialty, got on
well with his colleagues, did not flaunt his power and use it in a
coercive or a condescending manner, and had a certain human
touch—in the sense that he could shift gears when pressure was
building in a situation and relief was needed.

The administrator agreed and paused expectantly.

What was my reservation? I tried to buy time with any
words which might conceivably be relevant. The reservation in
the background would not crystallize into a figure. He waited
expectantly, sensing there was more I wanted to say.

Suddenly the answer came—in the form of an emphatic image: boxes with numbers in them. In the Activity Reports which
we professors must submit at the end of each year, there are

boxes for numbers to quantify our "productivity." For example, following, "How many books have you published in the last five years?" is a box. The candidate for the deanship had a comprehensive and precise knowledge of the numbers in these boxes—but I think he grasps little beyond the numbers themselves, I said. He does not grasp what the numbers in the boxes refer to in the world of human intercourse and activity, what the numbers mean. What does it mean, in human terms, to write one of that sort of thing—book—any book? Then, faced with the question, "How many books have you written in the last five years?" how would he judge the difference between one professor's answer when "One" refers to a slim volume of great imaginative power which may change the course of civilization, and another's answer of "Two" which refers to scholarly, well-reviewed, but pedestrian books? It seemed to me that he does not know the difference between the numbers, because he does not know the difference between the books to which the numbers refer.

The administrator made no sound, so I went on.

I said the candidate was brilliant at assembling "hard data" on personnel, and I talked about other boxes. He knows, I said, the number for "How many citations of Professor X's work by professional peers in that academic field have occurred 'in the literature' in the last year." But why, I asked, do we place confidence in this number? Do we forget that much of the most creative work has gone unrecognized at the time? Some thinkers die unnoticed, others vilified in their lifetimes. How would they have fared in the boxes of our Activity Reports?

The administrator was himself an historian, and I thought that last point would impress him. But he made no sound, and I rushed to say something else. We ought to remember also, I said, that Socrates and Jesus seem not to have written or published anything. It is immensely difficult to find numbers to evaluate achievement in teaching. I didn't think that the candidate had any notion of how to judge important contributions teachers make.

With this a vast and tempting region opened. It contained all the issues we seldom discuss, do not know how to evaluate precisely, and have no boxes for. What is the point of educating people in the first place? Because it is good that we be developed in this way. Goodness? But how could I talk about goodness in the few moments given me to answer his question about the candidate?

I faltered and hesitated, longing to leap into this area, but knowing it was hopeless to try. He quickly interposed, thanked me for my efforts, remained noncommittal, and closed the conversation.

I returned to the basement, and soon a suspicion became a conviction. Probably the administrator was himself only interested in the numbers in the boxes, and would feel that nobody in an administrative capacity or outside a particular academic field could hope to know what the numbers in the boxes referred to, what a book or an article meant—and probably that the outsider ought not even to try to grasp this, for that might derail the fragile coordination necessary for the survival of the many-armed and many-headed thing that the university is.

I became depressed.

This situation cannot be blamed simply on the ignorance or laziness of certain administrators. An underlying reason why business is done in shorthand, the numbers confined in their boxes, is that the university research to which the numbers refer falls into disconnected sectors. All academic fields presuppose truth, otherwise why try to discover anything? Scientists conceive of truth in a narrow, technical sense which is linked to their ability to make quantifiable predictions and to test them with precision instruments. This has proven to be highly productive for science. But what of the claim that there is truth to be discovered also in literature, for example? Typically such "truths" do not involve quantifiable predictions which can be tested with precision instruments, so the single word "truth" cannot hide a disparity of meaning which prevents the different fields from connecting or even contrasting their discoveries.

Yet all us knowers and researchers in our different academic departments are in the business of educating ourselves and our students. Education involves a simple but basic assumption: that the self cannot be divorced from its evaluation of itself. "Where do I stand in the world?" "What has my life amounted to?"

"What might I become?" So if we cannot compare and connect the discoveries we knowers and researchers make, we are hampered, even crippled in our role as educators, because we cannot orient ourselves and our students in the world. With only bits and pieces of knowledge we risk getting lost, unguided by what in truth is good for us to become.

In literature, and in the fastnesses of experience—religious experience, for example—the term good "talks" to us on the inner level of the self. But it cannot be taken in as a whole by science and defined in the required precise and predictive sense, so it cannot figure in the truths scientists discover. Science by itself cannot tell us how to educate, not even how to educate as persons those who are to be scientists. In fact, although science is considered the paramount way of knowing, it cannot establish what nearly everyone assumes: that it itself is good.

If we cannot know whether what we do is good for human beings, we cannot be confident in our evaluation of ourselves as educators. It is understandable that we be captivated by boxes full of numbers floating on a page.

My conversation with the administrator occurred in 1972. Since then the conviction has spread that something is wrong with our research universities as educational institutions. Because we are growing, developing beings we ask questions about who we are and what we ought to become that the highly specialized and partitioned university can find no place within itself to raise and consider. There are university newspapers and magazines. There are also faculty meetings, but these and the printed organs seldom provide a place for communication about education because the vocabularies of those involved mix defectively. Typically, faculty meetings are preoccupied with procedural matters—problems of coordinating modules connected only bureaucratically.

The various parts of the great university stand out, clearly and boldly outlined. But when I search within them (the departments within the colleges, the colleges within the university, the administration buildings, classroom buildings, stadia, libraries, dorms, milling students), trying to find a place within the scene to ask the questions about goodness that seem so essential, I cannot find it. Amidst all the reality of the university there is no place for the reality of the questions or of the questioner. Consequently the components of the university, as I experience them, float away—one at a time or in bunches—like items in a dream, or components of a surrealistic movie set being flown around by a giant crane. Each of the parts has a clear definition and can be picked out, but the university itself, the vital unit, disappears.

There is a cry for change, and interdisciplinary programs spring up in nearly every university; faculty committees are assembled to pick a "core curriculum:" what every educated person should know. We are caught up in transition. But the causes of the university's illness are systemic and obscure, I think, historical and institutional, and tied in with our most obscure assumptions about the nature of truth and knowledge, and of the self and world to be known. Causes most difficult to discover! Why do we now conceive truth and knowledge in a way that obscures sectors of our own selves? As Nietzsche put it,

We knowers are unknown to ourselves.

In this book I delve into occluded causes of our alienation from ourselves in our research universities. I think archaic things are going on—processes of purification ritual in the most "up-to-date" professional-scholarly formation of self—which the professional-scholarly way of knowing, so influenced by traditional natural science, cannot know—a deep irony and self-deception! Roughly, the ritual is: I am purely and wholly myself, and we are purely and wholly ourselves, because we are clearly other than those others—those uncertified by our professional tests. Only when the extent of our difficulties is known can we realistically hope to reconstruct the university effectively.

As directly lived, the world is not experienced as divided into boxes, but as one vast, supremely great whole. Attention abstracts and selects from a moody and vague background, an immediate sense of the encompassing world and ourselves in it—lingering, habitual orientations for living inherited from archaic personal or communal pasts. This background may be vague, but if we are to feel solid and real it must be felt to be coherent. Marginally but potently sensed as background of all we are and do, the world exudes a pervasive, moody meaning and quality: if it is odious and fearsome to me, I will live in a withdrawn and fearful way; if attractive and supportive, I will live confidently. As we form meaning in interaction with the englobing world, present both in the focus of our attention and in the abiding and moody background, we form ourselves.

As if it were a laser focusing attention randomly, the university cuts across and eclipses the human background. It cannot facilitate the education of human beings who thrust toward integrated, vital being within a horizon of possibility. What lies in the background of the university itself that explains its obscuration and pulverization of our experience?

A. N. Whitehead maintained in *Science and the Modern World* that the twentieth-century research university is constructed according to the principles of seventeenth-century physics. He claimed that the revolutionary physics of our century, with its repercussions for reconceiving self and world and for integrating fields of learning, came too late to be incorporated in its structure.

The new human institution which burst on the world scene with such momentous impact, the great research university, *is* old at heart. For it is in the knowledge business, and the conception of knowledge which it accepts largely determines its institutional structure and its conception of the knowers. In a real sense, it finds no room for us as integral beings in an integral world, for as it grasps us it splits us into minds and bodies.

Through a leap of abstraction from the immediately lived world—a leap which is made and then forgotten—the world is divided by seventeenth-century thought into material bodies and weightless minds, objective and subjective. The twentieth-century university is fractured into sciences and humanities, with only the former thought to deliver objective meaning and truth. Thoughts about goodness, or beauty, tend to be reduced to mere expressions of subjective sentiment and opinion. What is abstracted from, the supremely singular background world, is ignored. But only within this can a life be one life, integral, valuable, meaningful as an immediately lived whole opening onto the future.

In a brilliant chapter of his *The Abolition of Man*—"Men Without Chests"—C. S. Lewis points out the split made in persons committed to psycho-physical dualism, and to the historyless view of reality as point-instant—ideas inherited from the seventeenth century. As we tend to conceive ourselves, human reality is located either in the head—in consciousness—or in the stomach or groin. There is nothing in-between, no locus in the chest for the moral virtues, which are neither purely physical nor purely mental, but human rather, the *heart* of a complex creature who must be grounded and rooted in some way in human history and the continuous background of the world. For Greek thought the moral virtues are located in the chest: courage, piety, temperance, wisdom, justice.

Without energy and empowerment the moral virtues are ineffectual, and it is just the heart that supplies this, for it involves us in the immediately lived, engulfing world, bonding us emotionally to others and our common fate. Without heart we are not plugged in to the dynamism of all that lives and endures around us; and the heart does have reasons that the reason knows nothing of. Verbalisms and formulae generate power technologically, but that is not sufficient. We also need directly engaged presence, and the sensuous images of presence which stay embedded in our bodies. The shaman knows something that the technologist forgets at his—and our—peril.

Vaguely and archaically but fundamentally we are enveloped by the world not only spatially but temporally—caught up, empowered, given room in that which is coming from some source and going somewhere. This experience is now threatened by a technologized and professionalized culture in which attention is focused on objects to be manipulated for some immediately understandable gain, rather than on the surrounding world moving us—a fixed and constricted attention in which numbers easily lose their ties to the actuality and presence of what is numbered and float in their boxes.

To put it starkly, modern history begins in the seventeenth century with the death of history as previously conceived: his-story, humankind's attempts to make sense of it all in terms of fundamental feelings, stories, and images—"mythological" accounts—of the ever-recurring order of everything. This pervasive, continuous, emotional storytelling, spinning the fabric of the person's and the group's identity, tended to be equated with superstition, fairy tales, mere myths.

We detect the fundamental irony of the modern world since Newton and Descartes, which affects the university in a crucial way: A sure foundation is supplied for mathematical, mechanistic physics, and on this basis technologies of all kinds are grounded, and in the space of only a few centuries the whole earth and our lives are transformed—the other animals driven into obscure corners or annihilated. Yet, at the same time, persons wonder if they can know themselves, and if they can direct themselves intelligently and achieve meaning, self-respect, dignity.

As seventeenth-century science deposits itself in our lives today, it paves over but cannot replace the common matrix of pre-scientific storytelling and image-making which supplied orientation, moral guidance, energy, and worth for countless generations knit up as integral beings within an integral world. But they were more than stories, since they were not contrasted invidiously to scientific truth. For example, Penelope's faithfulness in waiting years for Ulysses, or David's courage in facing Goliath. These images of faithfulness and courage, taken in habitually, inform and gird the self, imparting to it solidity and continuity.

Along with this perpetual storytelling was the practice of the traditional healing arts, which involved the most intimate and trusting contact between the individual and the community. However defective these arts might have been—understood scientifically—they imparted continuity and meaning to the community and its members. And in some cases they may have produced cures we can no longer imagine.

Human reality, self-knowledge, truth, goodness? These are philosophical questions. Don't we have professional philosophers ready to handle them? It is symptomatic of the university's malaise, its distance from the common concerns of humans to build lives for themselves, that philosophers tend to be isolated in highly technical, verbalistic communication with professional fellows. The complexity and expertness of their language is the problem. Engrossed in it, questions about its scope and competence are masked out. Truth tends to be construed as a property of accurate statements, ones that can be manipulated in complex arguments. But is self-knowledge and self-direction mainly a matter of making true statements about ourselves and arguing? It is preposterous to think so.

To be educators is to seek some minimal community and aim, some shared practice and basic vocabulary, and to require of philosophy some special contribution to this.

At the end of the last century, coincidentally with the formation of modern universities along scientific lines established since the seventeenth century, William James wrote of the "scientific nightmare:" In the ordinary nightmare we have motives but no power. In the scientific nightmare we have power but no motives ("Rationality, Activity, and Faith," 1882). That is, we now have great power and can work technological wonders, but why do anything when we cannot know whether the ends to which we direct our power are really good? The danger is to fall either into compulsive, frenzied effort or into paralysis and boredom. James's observation did not deter university builders.

If we cannot make sense of the world and our place within it and find something good and joyous about being alive then nothing else matters. All desires pale beside this one, and if the price for meaning is the relinquishment of subsidiary desires we will pay this price, won't we? At least it is a question. For we possess the capacity to freely suppress desires if necessary, and ego and wishful thinking on occasion, and to stand-by whatever truth we discover—no matter how strange or repellent it may seem—which is pertinent to being fully alive. To exercise this capacity to freely seek truth and to take responsibility for holding to it is making sense of our lives, isn't it, is self-respect, is being fully alive? How can we respect ourselves if we find nothing that takes us out of ourselves—nothing we revere for its wholeness, inclusiveness, greatness, and to which we might belong? Mustn't we know in our hearts what goodness is? But can we? We have powerful means of altering the earth and ourselves, but only a fix on goodness could give our means their aim, support, and meaning—give us meaning. What can we reasonably expect of the university in this time of need?

I believe that education is a moral enterprise and that the contemporary research university lacks moral direction. Amidst all our stunning discoveries we have forgotten, I think, what it means to be a human being in the world—also of course what it means to be a good one. We tend to treat ourselves and our students abstractly, as if we were divided into bodies and minds. With this goes a heartless bureaucracy, modules of the university boxed up in themselves: the administration takes the body—it houses, feeds, shuttles bodies about—the faculty takes the minds—it pumps into them information and techniques, and spends much of its time looking beyond the university altogether, seeking authorization from professional peers nationwide.

Split up, unrecognized as whole persons, many undergraduates feel alienated from their professors. In a survey of 5000 conducted by the Carnegie Foundation 52% stated that they were "treated like numbers in a book," and 42% did not believe that their professors were personally interested in their progress.* I believe that this poll underestimates alienation, for many students have never known a good educational experience—imaginative, supportive, stimulating, crackling with intelligence—so that they have nothing to which to compare their experience. And students cannot be alienated from professors without professors being alienated from students.

If we would restore the university to its educational and moral course we must rethink what it means to be a human being. We must plot the course that science and technology have followed—and professionalism and bureaucracy (even in the university)—this drifting belief that we cannot achieve meaning and truth about the human condition as a whole, that we can tell no life-forming story about what we are and what we ought be that is compatible with truth (we are not talking about fairy-tales, but a way of knowing that can be image-inative). This means that we cannot make sense of ourselves as beings who can freely form ideas and take responsibility for whatever truth we find; that we cannot make sense of our selves sucked into the vacuum of possibility—that vacuum essential to our substance. If Nietzsche is right, this is unfaithfulness to ourselves, a wild "creativity," an urge for destruction.

---

*The Chronicle of Higher Education, Sept. 4, 1985

In sum I argue that the self's identity is formed through basic engagements and bondings in the world, whether these are acknowledged or not. The recognitions professors get from professionalized academic authorities, model knowers, contribute crucially to the matrix formative of self. At the same time, they conceal the depth and scope of the matrix. Behind "current standards of professional competence" archaic energies of identity formation are at work. When professors are accepted into professional groups, primitive initiation and purification rites are performed unacknowledgeably which establish individual and corporate identity by contrasting members invidiously to outsiders. But to be cut off from others, especially those whom we generate, our children and students, is to be cut off from ourselves as adults and teachers, and from a possibility of our own regeneration. Evading awareness of what we are doing is evading responsibility to our larger ongoing community, and this is unfaithfullness both to others and ourselves. It is destructive.

In the last section of the book I offer some ideas for rebuilding the university.

PART ONE

The Academic Professional: Problems of Self-Knowledge and Education

Alienation

Two of us professors sat in my office at Rutgers on a winter's day and enjoyed a rare moment of calm. We had finished our committee work, at least all of it we could accomplish; other members had not appeared. Unexpectedly, we had a few moments with nothing scheduled to do. As if we were ships that had idled their motors, a current, usually overridden, began to move us slowly in a strange direction. My colleague in the philosophy department reminisced, recalling wistfully a book he had read years before, *The Professor's House.* The professor in this story was accessible to visitors in his home which lay close to campus. Students went there when the impulse moved them. Singly, in large groups or in small, they discussed at leisure the items that concerned them as human beings.

We lapsed into silence. Finally, becalmed and drifting oddly, I mentioned that when I had gone into university teaching I knew that the pay would not be high, and that both the status and the power would be problematical. But I had expected that this would be compensated by a measure of freedom and tranquility, a life allowing untrammeled reflection as well as human contact on agreeable and significant terms. I would be "my own man." He nodded ruefully, uttered some amenities in a sigh and walked out.

Then a very peculiar moment occurred. It resembled the situation in which a sound that has been going on constantly suddenly stops, and only then does one become focally aware of what had been going on unpleasantly for so long. Except now it was not something external that flooded my awareness, but my own life. An habitual, thrusting, unspeakably close and intimate rhythm or pulse had suddenly stopped, and as my life rose before me, I saw something frenetic, haggard, and grey. Not a pleasant spectacle, yet I felt enormously relieved, as if a great weight had been taken off my chest.

I seemed to float in my chair, finding myself looking out the window, noticing students passing by on the sidewalk nearby. And I really saw them! Which startled me, for I realized that I had gotten in the habit of not really seeing them—I a professor who was supposed to be a teacher in this university. I could now be aware of how they had appeared to me previously. That was spectral, and it recalled Descartes' description of a world in which the devil may be deceiving us in everything we think we perceive. Are those real people we see, or are they "hats and cloaks which might cover ghosts or automata which move only by springs"? Only in the driest, thinnest, intellectually correct but vacuous sense had the students appeared to me to be human beings.

I did not like what this told me about myself and my situation. Classes in the university met on time, lectures were delivered, tests and grades were given, learned papers were prepared and delivered by faculty members to each other, my salary was received. Everything was under control, tightly interlocked, but I detected a deep alienation which isolated things, people, and programs. I had been caught up in a machine, I feared, removed both from the life of ordinary human beings and from the life of the untrammeled mind. So everything was also out of control.

Is *this* what I had wanted so much and had worked so hard to get? Is this what my parents had raised me to be? Would I want my own children to attend an institution such as this one?

It is the State University of New Jersey, Rutgers, fall 1983, and about 150 undergraduates, largely freshmen and sophomores, are spread out before me, as if arrayed on a large funnel. I look up at them—vestiges of the Greek theatre. We occupy a new building and the chair backs are bright red. Students are vividly outlined against them: one leans her head on the chair top in front of her; others converse—faces close, animated, absorbed; one, nearly recumbent, lolls his head on the chairback and seems to sleep; several drink furtively from straws or eat as they look at me; one peeks out at me from behind his upraised newspaper; some persons whom I cannot see laugh loudly.

These are instants of first contact. I have slipped in and walked down the steps to the semi-circular base of the room nearly unnoticed. Or was there a drop in the noise level? The chance to sit behind the desk presented itself. Immediately it was rejected. It felt as if it would place me at an impossibly great distance from them, as if I could only gaze out across a gulf at another world, handcuffed, unknown. I elect now to deposit my briefcase gently on the floor, very slowly take off my coat, lay it across one side of the desk, and with the greatest deliberateness, hike myself up on the front of the desk and, with legs dangling, arrange my clothes slightly.

Quietly I survey the class. Not one face—of those I see— looks familiar. Perhaps none of them recognizes me either. Each instant is drawn out, pregnant with possibility, and slips beyond recall. If four instants have elapsed, then this instant is fully a fifth of our relationship. A round stone teeters on a ridge. Which way will it run down? A small thing, if one could see it from a cosmic perspective, but I could not look at it this way at that instant. The trajectories of 150 or more different histories meet at this point in time and space. Will the class which begins today amount to anything?

Disturbingly, some students still rustle, read, or loll, although some of this dissident group look away from me as if they want me to see them looking away. It is almost quiet enough for me to speak. What if it will not get any quieter? I am a little frightened. I must somehow enlist them in a joint effort, interweave our trajectories, rather than smash against them and deflect them in who knows what directions. At this point it could go either way. If it gets noisier, I may have to do something that simply imposes my authority, and their old habits of apparent compliance and inner resistance will be reinstated yet again.

The noise remains at a plateau. To abort the possibility of runaway increase I decide to begin. I read, in a fairly loud but matter of fact voice, the single description of this course as it appears in the university catalogue—one description to cover the ten or more instructors who, at one time or another, teach the course, each of whom has his or her ideas about how it is to be done:

Philosophy, 730:105, Current Moral and Social Issues: Examination of such issues as abortion, contraception, sterilization, capital punishment, sexism, racism, censorship, privacy, drug abuse and drug laws, consumption and scarcity of resources.

It is quieter. I ask them if this is what they signed up for and expect to study. Most of them look at me nonplused. It had never occurred to them to question this; they could count on some minimal reliability in the institutions in which they had been students.

I then ask them if they had read the more specific description of courses which had been distributed by the philosophy department to advertise its offerings. Only a scant few raise their hands. This was to be expected, because the distribution of these sheets was limited; each instructor was asked to distribute them at the close of the prior semester to each of his or her classes, and a pile of them was left in the departmental office, three miles from where we now were. I read from these sheets:

For section #5 of Current Moral and Social Issues—Prof. Wilshire— We will be concerned with the question of lying. What are its consequences for the self and its relationships with others? Is lying increasing in our consumer society? Does our work in the university presuppose a commitment to the supreme value of truth?

It was completely quiet now. Puzzlement appeared on some faces or wry amusement, blankness, anger. I told them that the general description, with its "such as" clause preceding the examples of topics indicated a broad, ill-defined area of subject matter, and that the topic of lying overlapped in any case with those of "censorship" and "privacy" which were listed in the general description of the course. I added that if they did not want to stay they could drop the course and add another.

"You mean you are not going to talk about sex, drugs, and abortion at all?" someone spoke out.

"Not hardly at all," I said.

A dismayed silence settled over the class. One student's sidelong glance at me and furrowed brow suggested, however, that it was not so much the absence of sex, drugs, and abortion that bothered him, but that he had been deceived. I hesitated. A new path suddenly opened up. Instinctively I took it. The silence was palpable and magnetic. "I have them, *this* concerns them, they're thrown off stride and believe they have been lied to," I thought.

"Do you believe you've been lied to?" I asked. "What can a person believe nowadays—right?"

I paced before the students and swelled with power and confidence. "This will bring the issue of lying home to them." Yet as I walked about in the silence, this emotion was soon joined by another which vied with it for control. Another student's disgruntled face touched it off. My only recently laid plan buckled slightly beneath me. The plan, of course, was to interest students in lying by suggesting that they had been lied to. But on the periphery of my consciousness, a question encroached: Could anything justify a university professor in allowing even the suggestion that lying to students was going on? The question had not dawned on me in the prior instant. Suddenly it was upon me. [Now I would handle things differently than I did then.]

As they sat, somewhat stunned, and I continued to pace, looking at them, I brushed the encroaching question aside with what seemed to me at the moment a brilliant thought: "At an opportune time in the course, I will discuss this issue of my own conduct and they will become deeply interested in *that*." Besides, a student sitting on the side aisle still read the newspaper and drank from a can of soda which he tilted to his mouth so as to leave one eye clear.

I pressed on, maximizing my advantage.

"How do you know that I'm Professor Wilshire? How do you know that I'm a professor at all?"

They remained quiet.

"How do you know that I'll teach a bona fide course even in lying? Why couldn't I be an actor paid by a group of social psychologists to participate in an experiment to determine how gullible students are in the university?"

One student spoke out without waiting for her hand to be acknowledged:

"We could take your picture and go to the chairman of the department and ask him if you are Professor Wilshire."

"But what if he's in on the act, in on the experiment, and lies to you that I am Professor Wilshire?"

She had no answer to that. She began to retort, mentioned something about the dean but broke off, for it probably occurred to her that to go to the dean would be no help, because he too might be in on the act.

"How do you know that I am Professor Wilshire?"

I called on a student who looked at me sullenly.

"My friends and I could pin you and take your wallet and see if you have the right papers."

The question stopped me for a moment, but only the merest instant. I had not been a professor of philosophy for over 20 years for nothing.

"But, surely, you see that we might have mugged Professor Wilshire and taken his wallet. That's not so hard. Or, that we counterfeited an I.D. Card. But you students wouldn't know how that is done, would you?"

Great laughter broke out.

I was immensely pleased. Not only had they become interested in the question of lying—many of them at least—but they were being led to an involvement in the question of identity of self. To ask about the consequences for the self of the practice of lying presupposes that we know something about the self—or think that we do. And a little further questioning disclosed their belief that they are owed the truth just because they are persons or selves, and not because of any particular merit, social standing, or racial characteristics. So what *is* a self? I pointed all this out to them in a quiet, didactic way, and they seemed to see. I paced for awhile again in silence.

"But what if we pinned you, took your fingerprints, checked them against Wilshire's—assuming Wilshire's are on file someplace—say on his birth certificate stamped by a hospital?"—a young woman blurted out.

Quietly I praised her, indicated how the discussion might continue, and the class was in the palm of my hand—at least for that day. [But I had won their attention at a cost I will no longer pay.]

At intervals during the course I brought up the questions of my identity and my intentions. This came in handy when we tried to describe just how we feel when somebody lies to us, and why we feel this.

"Isn't there a difference between reasonable and unreasonable anger?"

"Isn't it reasonable anger we feel when somebody lies to us and we find out?"

"What if the chairman and the dean came into class on the last day, instead of me, and informed you that—much to their shock—your "professor" had been a fraud, the real Professor Wilshire had not appeared, and that therefore, since the course was not genuine, no credit could be given to you for taking it?"

This evoked the defensiveness, the fear, the sense of things falling apart. [Later I concluded that my performance contributed to this unwittingly.]

We read a little Aristotle and very little Kant. We read all of Orwell's masterpiece on lying and violence, *1984*. I hoped I had weaned them from talk to reading, but soon it became clear that they found it difficult to read anything with any comprehension, even *1984*. I experienced the truth of what others have observed: that most students have sat far longer before TV, video, and movie screens than they have in classrooms, for untold thousands of hours. These screens communicate through flashes of images which may exhibit a kind of continuity, but not the kind possessed by the written word. Short, evocative spans of attention are cultivated, rather than the protracted ones necessary for following the narratives and reasonings of trains of words on a page. TV in particular instills a deep passivity: a spectacle produced by merely pushing a button—consumption at practically no cost. Not even the presence of the viewer is required at the scene which is viewed (and unlike the movies, no presence is required at any public place). The actors are unaware of those looking; I sometimes see students looking at me as if they thought I could not see them, as if I were just somebody on their screen. Students are no longer trained to work hard reading books. The words in their school books do not coalesce with the flashy images before their eyes.

Because of this they do not live in history and inherit the past in the way my generation does. When I first saw TV in the 1940s it looked unreal, strange—the images playing fitfully on the little screen in the big box. Now, to a generation that has never known anything else (and many of whose parents have known nothing else), *I* must look unreal, strange—I with my lecture notes in hand, or reading from a book and speaking in a loud voice in this cavernous room. Where are they—where are they as body-minds that must interpret themselves as coming from somewhere, I thought, and going to somewhere?

To face a group of 150 undergraduates in a typical state university, and to try to communicate something from the history of civilization, is to confront a lumpy, heavy incoherence that nevertheless seems to float: it is temporally without depth, rootless, like a cloud—better, like an image in a dream. Until recently the primary educator was the home, and the stock of books, large or small, which it contained. TV is today an intrusive presence in the home, glamorizing the values of consumption and display which hold in the present "epoch"—"epochs" succeeding, eclipsing, and burying each other every few years (and we should not forget that some of the students now in our classrooms come from homes that are illiterate, analphabetic, or nearly so). In most families the grandparents are off somewhere, and the parents, when at home, typically spend little time seriously conversing with their children (unlike a radio, playing as we speak, TV leads us not to look at each other). By this time the parents themselves may have little of the cultural tradition to communicate, but even if they do, its transmission is impeded. Though they may bring a "B" or "B+" average from high school, the majority of students emerge from home and the "lower" schools and appear in universities intellectually and personally impoverished, their reading, writing, and conversational skills appallingly poor.

It is certain that there is a breakdown in the fund of common knowledge and abilities deposited by history. I could not assume that most students could answer questions such as these: Lincoln was President of the U.S. before Jefferson—true or false? The Mediterranean: (a)animal, (b)vegetable, (c)mineral? Christianity is fairly ancient, but Buddhism is fairly modern—True or False? A galaxy is (a) a group of moving picture executives, (b) a system of stars, (c) a flock of sea birds? The Song of Solomon is (a) a Rock group, (b) a book in the Bible, (c) the confession of a mobster? Many did not know that Mexico, with its masses of impoverished and desperate people, bordered on the United States. They could not learn much of what I wanted to teach them, because we shared no basis from which to begin. They are "culturally illiterate," and I see many graduating after four years who remain such.

In a real way, students are lost, both in space and time. Good instruction in geography and history, which builds cumulatively over the years, would help, and this they seldom get. But the problem is larger. Students live in a society so rich and powerful technologically that most of us need only "punch in some numbers" to get what we demand. We merely look *at* things—a few things at that—to satisfy some obvious needs or whims; we need not look *around* us. But, as John Dewey pointed out repeatedly, we are organisms and cannot escape our surround. To be uninvolved emotionally with that, not deeply coordinated with that, is to lose vitality at a primal level. The educational task is to draw students out into the world so they perceive that there are difficulties in living well, and so that they freely take up the challenge. This I was *trying* to do.

But it is not just the students' problem. I wondered: has our society lost its ability to retain its past and keep itself oriented in the world? Has the university any chance at all of rectifying this? Haven't all previous societies had some way of preserving their basic traditions? How could we grasp securely any possibilities if we rattled around in a disconnected present—a Cartesian point-instant? Although we seldom notice any longer, the very money in our pockets bears witness to a commemorative dimension even in our commercial dealings. The coins and bills are engraved with the images of our nation's past leaders (as they used to be engraved with Liberty, the goddess). This "mere" piece of paper can be exchanged for that valuable piece of goods because the near-numinous force and value of our whole tradition backs the transaction and makes the two equivalent. We trust our history to empower our dealings with each other. But even our most recent history is barely audible or visible to us. Plastic credit cards threaten to expunge the images, to make money obsolete, and economics a purely quantitative study. But what does this do to our image-inations, our sense of the depth of time, our directedness, the substance of our lives?

The numbness and stasis and disconnectedness so often seen in students are palpable and need to be explained and addressed.

There seems to be no sense of being part of history, of sharing a common venture with humankind—at least no sense of sharing a venture with those in power. The disintegration of a sense of historical community is amazing. It is not just that key dates are missing, hooks upon which prior generations have hung a panoramic and coherent view of time and existence, however skewed or biased. Missing is any sense that anything is missing. Few students have a clear awareness that there might be segments of human development which, when laid down, lead up to themselves and point beyond, and for which they have responsibility as the group of living human beings. Few students have any sense that they are missing empowerment and stabilization which comes from identifying with revered persons in the past; as if there were a constant voice which said, These are our sources, our very substance, and we can count on them! The erosion of trust is nameable and nameless.

To sustain an interest in a project presupposes one's belief that something good will come of the effort, and that there will be a future for us. A group of psychiatrists reports that many young people do not believe they will live out their lives, for there will be the ultimate betrayal of trust: arsenals of atomic weapons will be fired by the managers of the earth, and will burn and poison our world. One child reported that being given life was like being given a broken toy for Christmas.*

I tried to sort out the reasons for their apathy. How discouraged were they by the nuclear threat? I asked students both in class and out. With the fewest exceptions, they did not seem to think about it at all. The threat had been with them (and with most of their parents) all their lives. I speculated that if they had ever been anxious about it, the effect now was just a dulling of their sensibilities, or a settled search for distractions. As Robert Lowell wrote, "We've talked our annihilation to death."

I tried the hypothesis that embedded in the apathy is cynicism concerning educated intelligence. If so many educated people in the most "advanced" nations have behaved so foolishly that the survival of life is at risk, why take the trouble to become

---

*Helen Caldicott, M.D., *Missile Envy: The Arms Race and Nuclear War* (New York: 1984), p. 310.

educated oneself? Most students seem to sense that beneath the veneer of argumentative speech and nicely arrayed information exhibited by most authorities—East and West—lie raw, uneducated emotions: fear, confusion, chauvinism, selfish ambition, fragile self-love, foolish pride, childishness. Why study for future benefits when our most brilliant thinkers—or so it would appear—our technocrats and professionals are marching lock-step toward annihilation? Why listen to adults with the emotional age of ten-year-olds? And I was not sure that most of the students had much confidence in their professors either.

I thought more about the ideology of consumerism as a reason for their numbness and detachment. After spending their lives barraged by images equating buying with goodness, they seemed deeply to believe (if they believed anything deeply) that anything good can be bought, and without ever looking closely at the images on the money. A college education meant a degree, and this is a commodity which can be bought by paying fees and serving time. The possibility that knowledge could only be earned through diligent and at times drudging effort to come up to standards native to the enterprise of knowing itself, had apparently never entered most of their minds.

Faced with those serial rows of usually blank faces I could better understand them, I thought, if I imagined large, drowsy-eyed infants sucking at a copious breast—one which they brought with them somehow to the classroom. It is true that there is activity of a sort, a minimal activity of sucking, of cutting into an infinite flow. As Gilles Deleuze and Felix Guattari put it, "Each . . . flow must be seen as an ideal thing, an endless flux, flowing from something not unlike the immense thigh of a pig. The term *hyle* in fact designates the pure continuity that any one sort of matter ideally possesses."* My first—and perhaps last—job was simply to wake them up. Thus I explained myself to myself and tried to justify my methods.

Overshadowing all the factors which might account for their numbness and detachment was a constant: most students did not

---

*Gilles Deleuze and Felix Guattari, *Anti-Oedipus: Capitalism and Schizophrenia* (Minneapolis: 1983) [*Anti-Oedipe*, 1972].

believe that their work in the university would help them know what was good for them to do and to be. Doubtless, their protracted exposure to advertisers' exaggerations or flim-flam, and to endless accounts of various politicians' and executives' shading of the truth, contributed to their scepticism. In any case, they had no confidence that truth about the human condition could be discovered. Either that or they felt no need to discover it.

As I brought up the question of truth itself I saw that they were utterly unequipped to deal with it intellectually. Asking them to raise their hands if they had ever studied the question in twelve or more years of formal schooling, only one raised his hand. They lacked confidence in their own minds, and the joy that goes with this, to overcome their instinctual tendencies to believe in conventional ways. Most refused to treat my conduct as a game which challenged their wits and kept them on edge. I was probably Professor Wilshire, and that was enough to still their minds. There was some interest in truthfulness—the intention to communicate what one thinks is the truth—for they could feel, again instinctively, the pain and hurt of being lied to, and the reassurance that comes with the conviction that one is being honestly dealt with. But when I attempted to extend this interest to an intellectual level, and raise the question of truth itself, they typically lost interest. Why? Because they appeared to have little intellectual grip on how truth could be possible, so why expend much effort on how truthfulness is either possible or desirable?

Indeed! Perhaps a person seriously intends to convey what's true, but if truth itself is highly problematical, perhaps we're not being given it, despite good intentions to communicate it. Did the students begin sucking somnolently on that immense breast because they believed that all the professor's intellectualizing and arguing and learned references to books had no chance at getting at any verifiable truth, even if he was being truthful? Or, were they just incredibly smug, and believed they had all the truth they would ever need?

I should have grasped this aversion to inquiry into truth more firmly, and I tried to make up for lost time. After endeavoring to fix in their minds the distinction between truthfulness and truth, I kept asking them what truth itself is. It was easy to give examples of persons who desire to communicate truth, but who in fact communicate what's false. Ignoring those students who were somnolent, most of the faces of those who were paying attention were blank.

Was I doing something wrong?

Clutching at any straw, I said, "Take this desk I'm sitting on. To say that this desk *is* a desk is to grasp the truth, isn't it?"

"But that's too easy," a bright student joined in. "We all know that what you're sitting on is really a desk, so it must be true to say that it is. Take something important, take human beings, political systems, or the nature of goodness and badness. Who is to say what the reality is?"

I retorted, wanting to *involve* them: "As you or I or nearly anyone are the ones to say that this is a desk, because we can see those essential features that make it a desk, so the ones who know most about the technical features of this desk are the ones to answer the technical questions about it and to say what the less obvious features of it are—engineers, carpenters, metalworkers, physicists. The ones who are in a position to know most about what it really is are the ones to tell us the truth about it. What is goodness? We must ask those—living or dead—who know most about who we *are*, and what makes our lives vital and meaningful."

The same bright student continued, "You're going in circles. We asked you who is to say what the truth is, and you say the ones who are to say what the reality is. But you've gotten nowhere. Who is to say what the reality is?"

"But are all circles bad ones, vicious ones?" I shot back, proud of myself, putting her down [but I would later rue it]. "The persons who are to say what the reality is are just the ones best equipped to look at it attentively and to mean something relevant about it and to test this meaning through ongoing dealing with it, experimenting with it. And if what they mean about the reality is confirmed through further experience, this meaning is the *truth* about *reality*."

"But they might be wrong. And even if they happen to be right, they grasp only a small bit of truth."

"Sure, they *might* be wrong. But even if they are, they can be only if you suppose that sometimes they, or you, or some

persons are right—or else how could you ever *know* that sometimes some people are wrong? And so let's suppose that sometimes some people grasp only a little bit of truth, given the
whole universe, but they do grasp some truth."

But my slight fit of gloating was cut short. Perhaps ten percent of the class showed any interest.

The vast majority did not care at all about questions of truth
or reality, at least not that I could tell. They must have thought
that even to raise these questions in this public place was needless or futile. I could arouse their instinctive interest in reality,
particularly in their own reality, and in that of others to whom
they were related intimately or practically. But their personal interests did not cohere with any ascertainable intellectual interests. Life in the classroom was unhinged from their personal
lives. They were drowsy in class because it all seemed to them an
uninteresting (or threatening?) dream. This is where basic educational effort should gear into students.

But anyone who looks can see that the university, as presently constructed, cannot make this effort. I was reminded that
many professors have nothing to say about truth, regard the general question as "philosophical"—and therefore to be dismissed—and that many others expend great efforts to knock the
instinctive attachment to truth out of students' heads and hearts
and to inject skepticism about most questions. They will sometimes say that they are trying to narrow students' attention to
questions fruitfully raised in the disciplinary field at hand, but
they do not consider how their attack on the students' instinctual
attachments and convictions may be affecting these students'
ability to live. For these primal commitments are the ones that
orient, root, and empower us in the encompassing, background
world; and it is this that these professors have, perhaps, weak-
ened.

It's as if most students' selves were split. In order to maintain
some vital, instinctual attachment to truth, they isolate their critical intellects from their instincts and feelings. Why? Apparently
because they sense that only skepticism or cynicism could result
from exercising their intellects freely: only undermining of their
grounding—only pain, confusion, and disorientation within the
environing background world. So they drug their intellects and

dumbly accept skepticism on the intellectual level. In effect they say, No contest!, and leave the field; for if they disengage and drug their minds, their minds cannot harm them. Instinctively great numbers shun the laser beam of university specialism and professionalism. And I seemed to have done little to counteract their aversion.

Of course, some of the apathy seems to be smugness: they do not believe that any more truth is needed to get what they want—a professional career with some power and wealth. But I think I detect in many cases a defensive aspect to the smugness, a fear cropping out that what they have may not be sufficient for life's problems; so the question of truth is disturbing and should be suppressed. That must be why they suck on the immense tit.

I think that many students come to the university with at least one dogma firmly ensconced, and it shields them from disappointments: "When asked about serious matters of moral concern, one can only think, There is no truth about them." (At least this holds in public, when they must defend their beliefs intellectually.) One can point out to these students that this is a contradiction, for to hold it is to believe that it is *true* that there is no truth. But, alas, it is such a life-denying and self-stultifying position that it numbs the mind which holds it. That is, it incapacitates the mind's ability to reflect upon its own activities and to discern that something is wrong.

When a few select students get a glimmering of the difficulty that their protective skepticism lands them in, most of them attempt to disguise their instinctive aversion to mental effort. Some even suggest that any claim to know truth about any controversial matter is vaguely reprehensible. Why? If they can be prodded into articulation the answer seems to be, "Because it is undemocratic, totalitarian, intolerant of others' beliefs, both in our culture and out. We must try to understand others' points of view."

" 'Understand'?—but then you mean that you try to grasp the *truth* about others' views of things."

But the undermining of self-reflection recurs, as do the rationalizations, such as, "You're older than I and better with words." In effect: "You're a bully." [I now see there was a grain of truth in that.]

I have found, as I said, that the response of fellow professors in the university is often on the same swampy, bleary level. Skepticism about truth, tacit or manifest, mindless or half-articulated, is widespread (although there may be tacit over-confidence in the powers of *one's own* field to discover it). This skepticism about truth—nihilism—occurs particularly, but not exclusively, in English, comparative literature, and various fine arts departments. The typical response of fellow members of the philosophy department is to lose themselves in thickets of technical thought about truth—epistemology—and to lose a sense of the human significance of the philosophical problem of truth that surrounds them everyday: people wander about without moral guidance within cramped or empty horizons, a lived-world which is anaesthetizing, stifling, or falling apart. Outsiders typically lose all sense of the significance of the philosophy department—and of philosophical thinking itself.

The problem for professors today who are educators is that nihilism, cynicism, and mindlessness are most rampant in the university itself. To evaluate our efforts we resort to arrays of numbers in boxes, but the numbers contact the human realities at stray points only. In the main they float detached, because we do not believe that we can discover the truth about what we ought to do and be—about what education should be. We cling to the floating boxes, for they seem to be better than nothing.

The course, Current Moral and Social Issues, is now over. How would it be evaluated? Good? Bad? Indifferent? What would the standards be? Against what background would the judgment emerge? How could anyone tell ("Who is to say?") what each—or most—took away as the trajectory of each life continued in some way, perhaps feebly, or sputteringly. Something had been appropriated from the course, I supposed: a joke of mine? an expression or shrug? the issues of truthfulness and truth that I wanted to be central? Surely the true/false and multiple-choice test which I gave to the large class told me pathetically little. Their notebooks which I had read until my eyes smarted—that invitation to speak personally about their experience with lying? Were they being truthful in those notebooks? Maybe they were just trying to arouse my interest?

Did they grasp some truth about their lives? I had to suppose that they did know something, and that also truthfulness was exhibited in some of the cases. The archaic background demanded this of me.

The course is now over, the classroom empty. How fast it has all come and gone! Along with some quiet satisfaction are feelings of regret, confusion, and suspense. As I sit behind the desk, a gulf between me and the students threatens to open to an impossible width. I summon them back into my mind, and think, so as to convince even myself, "I have made mistakes, but I have not been merely an image on a TV screen which you could wipe away. At least I have been as real as I can be, and concerned in my own way, and we have tried to figure out a way to live sanely!" And there were those gratifying moments in which their urge to form and transform themselves was touched, moments I thought belonged with real education.

But the actual impact of all this? Are the trajectories of their lives any more lively, sustained, directed, hopeful? How can I tell? I will walk outside to a world-politics, a university-politics, and a field of professional philosophy that have shown little interest for most of the century—all of them—in asking educational questions of educators; they are weirdly removed from the human work we professors are paid to do. It is a world unhinged from the young and the unborn that seems to have gone somnambulistic in its tunneling vision and constricting concerns.

And behind all these questions, on the dim margins of my consciousness, I sensed others—just enough to make me deeply uneasy. Why did I have to continually "bomb" students with stimuli to keep their interest? Trying to counteract the passivity of their TV watching, had I become like a TV performer myself? Why did I still feel so alienated from the students? Was it the sheer size of the class (might I have occasionally broken it into smaller groups and encouraged initiative)? Or did I not want them to get any closer to me? Was I really as interested in those students as I told myself I was? Was I deceiving myself? Was I really a good teacher?

I had questions about the structure of the university, the state of the world, and myself. I felt a twinge of hopelessness.

II

What is the Educating Act?

The unexamined life is not worth living.

—Socrates

In his lucid way, Harold Taylor points out what many are aware of—in some fashion—but do not point out: that educators in universities seldom talk about education.* Administrators talk about administrative problems, professors talk about problems in their special fields of study, and those who do talk about education, professors in education departments, are generally despised and shunned. Besides, even if one does listen to this latter group, one usually hears education talked about as if it were just another special field of study, not as something that vitally concerns us all just because we are human.

Is the underlying reason that we simply despair of education and believe discussion is futile? Or do we believe that the topic is threadbare and self-evident?

I want to see the educating act as if for the first time. Imagine that we have been willed a grand house we have never seen and we go and see it. We do not park and survey just one side of it. Nor do we spend all our time with the plans of the house, if we have them. We circle around it rapidly, go in one way, out another, stand back, stand close, get a sense of its overall shape, its site, and the overall shapes, sites, and interconnections of its internal world, its rooms. In a similar way, let us sketch the salient features of the educating act. This before we inquire why the professionalization of academic fields has had such a questionable impact on the act itself.

A feature of the act which strikes our attention immediately is its engagement. How does one reach across the generations and subcultures and touch students' interests so that they parti-

---

*On Freedom and Education (Carbondale, Ill.: 1967), pp. 16, 129, 142.

cipate willingly in a joint venture? There is genius in the Latin word *educere*—to lead out, or draw out. It contrasts richly with *instruere*—to build in. The educator leads students out to confront basic questions, while the instructor merely builds in information and techniques, answers to questions that each person need not ask anew in that thrusting transcendence, that personal energy that builds identity. We are talking about *education,* to lead out or to draw out by exciting students so that they freely initiate the learning process, at least at some stages, and bring to bear their own energies and responsibilities. "This is what it means to others—what might it mean to me?" Ultimately, "Who am I going to be?"

The teaching task is somewhat similar to the actor's: to make the material appear as if for the first time. But then at some points hospitable and inviting room must be left for the student to take the initiative. Although theatre can be an important learning opportunity, learners outside the theatre have responsibilities not shared by those in the theatre-house.

Let us conduct a thought experiment. Imagine as many different varieties of the educating act as we can. Push our imagining to such extremes—and along all the salient axes—so that situations begin to appear that no longer present themselves as cases of the educating act. If we mark the various points at which the educational phenomenon breaks down, points at which it no longer presents itself as itself, we will be marking the outermost reaches, the boundaries and shape of the educating act.

Now, within the domain of possible educating acts which we have staked out by the imagination can we find one in which the free participation of students does not appear? I do not think so. Admittedly, there is an arbitrary element in this initial mapping of the territory. I have assumed that there is genius in the Latin term *educere,* having committed myself to an initial valorization of education at the expense of instruction. But I do not think this is badly arbitrary. There is room in the world for both instructional institutions and educational ones, and all universities with which I am acquainted allot a central place to liberal arts, the liberating arts, for they are intended to draw out, to liberate from stifling ignorance and constricting prejudice.

This entails that anyone gaining a university degree in any field other than the explicitly technical or narrowly professional fields has successfully availed himself or herself of the opportunity of *education*.

Let us look at a very extreme case of *educere*. In one case the teacher—a professor of education—comes into the classroom, sits down among the students, and simply says that he is there and will be available to participate in whatever they wish to initiate. He remains seated and quiet. This leads to consternation and anger, for it disappoints expectations that the students have acquired through many years of instruction. They feel cheated. They report him to the dean. Many do not appear in class.

Now, in our thought experiment (which this time employs an actual case) have we pushed student participation and initiative so far that we experience a breakdown in essential features of the educating act? Some might think so. Surely it is a risky thing for the professor to do. He has pushed things perilously close to the edge, and great pedagogical skill is required to bring it off.

But assuming this skill, I think it is extraordinarily effective, at least for those students who do not drop out entirely and forget the whole episode. As the students' consternation grows, he "passively" reflects it back to them, until finally most of them bring themselves into such forceful contact with their frustration that they begin to sense what it is in them that is being frustrated: their desire to learn. Perhaps some had never felt it before, or it had gradually been covered over by years of boring instruction. What could be more valuable and more meaningful for them to learn? Perhaps even some of those who dropped out came to recognize belatedly that their education is largely up to them.

Through this extreme-case experiment one finds that student participation and initiative are essential—are at the core of—the educating act. The next question is: what role, if any, does the teacher play in the educational process?

In pushing teacher involvement to the point of the apparent bare minimum, we expose a correlative essential feature of the educational process. Even when the teacher sat among the students he possessed some special authority. First, any professor is presumed to be an inquirer into knowledge, and so is presumed to possess the integrity that any such inquiry presupposes: e.g., respect for creative and apposite meaning, for evidence, for clarity and sincerity of communication, and for truth. This presumption concerning the inquirer holds until and unless it is shown to be undeserved. Second, there are other more "external" grounds of the teacher's authority. He or she is invested with authority through the authority of the educational institution within which a position of status is held, and to which the students must submit themselves in some minimal way if they are to remain enrolled. Class is in session only when the teacher is present. Evaluations which the professor makes of students are weightier than whatever evaluations students make of the professor. But, to revert to the first grounds of authority, even when a teacher does not occupy a position in an institution of learning, he or she possesses a modicum of authority simply because others—called students—address him or her as teacher.

Of course, authority of some kind is inherent in all human relationships. Let the imagination push out the boundaries as far as they go: simply to be ignored by anyone deprives one of recognition, and this implies that the other has the authority to ignore or to recognize. We cannot be ignored by a lamppost.

But try as we will, we cannot imagine a case in which the teacher possesses no *special* authority as a teacher (assuming differentiated roles of "teacher" and "student"). The only question is how this authority is exercised so as to be most compatible with the first essential feature we sifted out: the educator is one who engages students in a joint project in which all take responsibility for learning.

The emerging ensemble of essential features generates others in a tight and intimate cluster. The educational venture is a communal project of learning. Only the *instructor* assumes there is a finished body of knowledge that must be built into the students' minds some way. Education involves, at the very least, making sense of things together. Otherwise it itself is nonsensical. To enlarge the area of meaningful questions and discourse is valuable in itself, even if the meaning is not in every case formulated into beliefs and assertions which get verified, which constitute knowledge and truth. Meaning is prior to, and is a condition for, truth and knowledge about the world.

Meaning is not created out of nothing. It evolves, often unpredictably and strangely, within civilization, within an inheritance of signs, symbols, images, art-works, and stances and attitudes incorporated unwittingly perhaps. We cannot imagine meaning falling down from the sky ready-made. We feel its source in leaders of past and present—thinkers, artists, scientists, teachers of all sorts. We identify with them in this larger community and, in a way difficult to explain, their substance flows into us. We easily misjudge the force of this influence—or regard it in a desiccated, alienated, merely cerebral way. Many in our culture seem to be losing all articulable sense of the past. This pinches off the human reality of the educational transaction.

The teacher's authority is particularly pertinent here, for he or she is typically older and more obliged to have mastered the cultural inheritance. But the enlargement of meaning is still a joint venture, and in being forced, perhaps, to communicate to the young, the teacher may take leaps—through the creation of image and metaphor—which discover connections in the world not discoverable otherwise. And the students may respond from their vantage point in history and surprise the teacher.

The communality of learning entails at least two other essential features—organically, intimately connected. First, if sense is made of something it is completely irrelevant who makes it. Meaning, like truth and knowledge, can be no respecter of persons—that is, no respecter of special interests, roles, or privileges. We must be vulnerable to insight, no matter how strange or disturbing, no matter from what source it originates, or how imperfect its articulation. This *must* is an ethical obligation, and its observance is essential to our dignity as persons. For each of us holds resources which transcend the self as mere ego, particularly the capacity to acknowledge meaning and truth, no matter how unpleasant it turns out to be, and to subordinate and control impulses which arise from conditioning by society or biology. If the obligation is not heeded the zest and energy is gone: the boiling and buoying sense that I can take charge of my life and make a difference in it. There is deflation, depression, or stifling blandness, despite access to technology.

Not only do all learners have the right to inquire and to communicate about it, but are to learn as well that they have a responsibility to do so. As John Dewey never tired of maintaining, conditions for truth are also conditions for democracy: freedom and responsibility.

The communality of educational *learning* entails another essential feature. There is an unpredictable degree of communality in the *learned* and the discovered. The nature of learning determines, to some extent, the nature of the world learned about. Learning employs signs, symbols, images, and concepts; and no arbitrary limit can be placed on their inter-connectivity or their generality. This is good, since what we want to learn about and discover is a whole world and our place in it. Subject matter areas and fields of research lie open to each other, and exhibit actual and potential connections, because whatever they grasp, they do so within the world; many of the same general concepts must be used in them all—cause, effect, individual thing, context, relationships, truth, meaning, evidence, integrity. Features of an allegedly educational situation which artificially confine learning within fields, departments, and groups of experts must inhibit learning. Only interdisciplinary studies can minimize the risk of isolation in a special field with its special method of inquiry, while the world learned about is broken into bits.

Let us sum up what we have discovered about the essential features of the educating act. No matter how we imagine it occurring, we must imagine it as the interaction of lives already underway, in trajectory. Each educating moment is caught up in each of our life-trajectories, each carrying historically rooted associations, assumptions, and projections of concern which none of us can fully map and comprehend, let alone control. To attempt to confine inquiry is to attempt to confine ourselves, to cork ourselves in a bottle. We endeavor to enlarge the domain of what we can experience meaningfully, and perhaps to arrive at truth. Let us call this a project of interpretation. I pool my interpretations about me and you with you, and you pool your various interpretations with me. We supplement and correct each other. We help each other piece ourselves together, but always incompletely, and always beholden in one way or another to the vast tradition of interpretation into which we have been born, at one time or another.

Our joint venture of interpreting catches us up in time and in our own activities as interpreters. With this, we arrive at the capital feature of the educating act: self-awareness, or self-reflexivity. All the essential features are consummated here. To be engaged in learning is to be freely committed to interpreting ourselves to ourselves, and this is to take responsibility for grasping whatever meaning and truth about ourselves and our world derives from whatever source. Responsibility to meaning and truth is at the same time responsibility to ourselves, since the capacity to seek and to hold to them is essential to who we are. Intellectual freedom is simultaneously ethical obligation.

Because these features are essential to an act's being an educating one, they also function as criteria of performance. To the extent that a teaching performance fails to achieve them, to that extent it is deficient. Well then, judged by these criteria how would my teaching of that semester of Current and Social Moral Issues be evaluated?

It must be given a mixed review. It had its positive side, I think. My prompting students to doubt my identity and my truthfulness did rivet their attention upon me, and upon the subject matter, lying. With some this interest persisted through the course and prompted them to take initiatives and to probe questioningly into their own experiences of lying. What does it mean for one's personal life to lie and to be lied to, what are the long-range consequences? Some of their notebooks supplied evidence of this engagement. The course was educational to the extent that it drew students out and engaged them self-reflexively with the questions, Why be concerned about truth and truthfulness? What sense can we make of the world? What can *I* make of my own life?

But that engagement could have been much greater—as subsequent classes of mine on essentially the same subject matter, and with about the same level and sort of student, prove. It was limited unnecessarily by a bad mistake of mine. Whatever else my performance was, it *was* a performance—an ego trip. Their attention was fixed far too much on me and not on themselves. Little sense of themselves emerged; they could not explore what their generation could open up in the way of possibilities and responsibilities for themselves and for us. It was not a fully realized *educational* experience.

What do we mean by "ego"? I think "ego" means that fraction of self that grasps as much of itself as it can in the moment and says "I" of it. We inherit a heavy legacy from the seventeenth century, and the tradition of atomistic individualism which has evolved. Descartes' equating of self and self-reflexive consciousness only exacerbates the tendency to deceive oneself, for surely there is more to the self than it can grasp of itself in the moment and say "I" of it. The sharper and more brilliant is the focus on self in its own deliberate self-consciousness, the more obscured is the archaic background of experience which also comprises it—the background with its primal bodily attitudes, habitual orientations and moods, inherited communal patterns of living.

In particular, to be caught up in ego is to be blinded to one's communal bonds to others, to ethical obligation. Truth about one's relations to others and one's motives with respect to them is vexingly difficult. In following semesters of Current Moral and Social Issues I began to see that my earlier tactics for gaining students' attention were self-serving, egoistic. I think that I deceived myself. In some sparkling and superficial intellectual sense I knew that these were essential features of the educating act: finding where students' concerns placed them, listening to what they sensed or suspected, letting things freely reveal themselves, and the coordinate necessity of being free to let them freely reveal themselves—free from wishful thinking and the compulsion to defend the ego. And, ironically, it is just because this is so self-evidently true that I was deceived.

Let me explain. It is so easy to *say* that the ego must be subordinated, and to find it clearly *evident,* that I automatically pasted shut the possibility that, nevertheless, *I* was not *doing* it. The very self-evidence of truth in my own mind—indeed, self-evident truth about me as a teacher—blocked my ability to apply it to myself as a whole being, blocked self-reflexivity and responsibility. The truth I had discovered about subordinating the ego prevented me from seeing that I was on an ego trip—for *I* had discovered it! What could be more slippery, self-stultifying, and ironical than that?

Engulfed in my body, my body engulfed in the world, can *I accomplish* this subordination of ego which I see is ethically and intellectually required?—the crucial question is masked out. All sharply focusing professional consciousness runs the risk of being a constricted awareness which conceals from itself portions of *ourselves with others,* and *ourselves and the background,* which solicit us. It risks boxing itself in the mirror-lined container of ego. Hegel spoke aptly of history happening behind our backs.

I felt driven to perform in that classroom by motives not fully clear to me. One begins to emerge now. It is our whole hierarchical heritage which prompts us to believe that authority is "on high," drops down into history, intervenes, and enlightens the benighted. The danger is to become obsessed with stunning numbers, words, calculations, evaluations, and performances, to stay confined within our boxes—both those of artificially isolated topics, and those fractions of ourselves, our egos—and to lose touch with the human reality within which we live.

It is common to speak of human achievements in general as performances. It is particularly common to speak of the teacher's teaching as a performance. For there are gross similarities to the "most performing" of all performances, theatrical enactments. One presents oneself in a highly structured and protected situation: lecturing occurs in a well defined space and time; the resemblance to the playing area of a stage and to its performance-time is unmistakable. One presents oneself to a group which resembles an audience. And one presents oneself in only one aspect of one's being, the inevitably idealized "role" of "expert knower," "professional thinker"—like a character which an actor enacts.*

But significant differences begin to appear when we begin to think in a sustained way about the important ways in which the

---

*For more on this, see my *Role Playing and Identity: The Limits of Theatre as Metaphor* (Bloomington, Ind.: 1982).

"performance" of the teacher differs from the performance of the stage actor. Let us say that the department chairman enters the lecture hall and walks up and speaks to me. If I tell him I will see him after class, I am obligated to attend to this in some way afterwards, whereas if we were merely playing characters on a stage I would not be so obligated at the end of the performance. This holds for me in the lecture room even though I am enacting, in *some* sense, the "role" of professor, and screening out other aspects of my being. I am "enacting" a "persona" in some sense, but I am nevertheless addressed in *propria persona,* as my own self, when addressed by the chairman. This is a lecture room in the university, not a theatre, and the ponderous concreteness of that fact figures essentially in the contract we have with each other and with the students.

One might say that there is a certain degree of the theatrical in the professor's professional behavior in the classroom, and yet the difference of degree amounts to a decisive difference in kind. While in character on stage, the actor's behavior is sealed off from the ongoing outside world to a degree that the professor's is not. There is an aesthetic element in what I am as a teacher, but I am directly engaged with others and the ongoing, background, inescapable world which makes ethical demands on me; no artistic frame buffers me from it.

I came to see that the theatrical element in my teaching the course was unduly large, particularly when I cast doubt on my identity, hence on my truthfulness. My performance occurred in a classroom, not a theatre, and the students had every reason to expect and demand truth and truthfulness, not fictions. I came to see that my initial misgivings, overridden at the time, were right: a professor ought not to suggest even the possibility that deception is going on. Too high a price is paid for getting attention. With too many students this wounds trust to the point that vital involvement in the very topic of truthfulness is damaged. In subsequent courses in Current Moral and Social Issues I employed the tactic in a clearly jocular way, and have finally stopped it altogether. The results are better.

As a member of an intellectual community, I have obligations as a professor which I do not have as an actor on stage. If I am not deeply in touch with myself and what is happening around me I will lose touch with these obligations. I cannot merely *say* true things about myself, important though this is, but I must *experience* what they are true about—myself—and live with the consequences of their truth. I cannot merely talk or think about my motivations, but must experience their gritty texture and ambience—otherwise I will be self-deceived about them. The self must encounter itself in a way that leaves a compelling image of it engrained in the body. Truths about myself cannot be kept safely inside their boxes—like numbers on an Activity Report.

This is the crux. What if in all our knowing we fail to grasp ourselves? What could be more foolish? As Goethe's Faust says, "Knowledge tricks us beyond measure." It must be reiterated: Knowledge of self, and of what makes self good, vital, meaningful, cannot be merely knowledge *about* self and goodness, but is an experiential knowledge which *is* goodness in its fullest sense—is an instance of it. The special authority of the professor carries the special responsibility to exemplify personally what every investigator presupposes: the nature and value of meaning and truth. The ultimate educating force is who I am. Since it is the humanities professor who is especially obliged to teach what being human involves, it is especially this person who must exemplify *in person* what self-knowledge and goodness are.*

This, I will argue, is the contradiction in the current mode of academic professionalism: the attempt is made to divide the professional level of self from the personal. The boxes and their numbers float—they promise a measurement of "productivity," but are disengaged from the actual life of meaning-making and ethical commitment which ought to be occurring every instant in every teacher. The numbers are good for so many units of promised esteem and advancement; but if they absorb me they mask out my life as a person here and now. They promise an evalua-

---

*The case for teaching as personal exemplification has been well made by William Arrowsmith in his "The Shame of the Graduate Schools: A Plea for a New American Scholar," *Harper's Magazine*, March, 1966, and "The Future of Teaching," *The Public Interest*, No. 6, Winter, 1967. That these eloquent accounts have had so little effect on the "production" of professional scholars testifies to the vast inertia of the professionalized university (it may also attest to the way that publications get lost in a blizzard of paper).

tion of myself. But am I in touch with my motivations and moods, and with what they open up or close off in the world? Do I really see the students around me? Am I glad to be alive? Is what I am, and what I am doing, good? Behind the frenzy of "achievement" can be inner detachment and boredom, the schizzy atmosphere of unreality.

I try to heed Nietzsche's lines in his "Schopenhauer as Educator:"

It sometimes seems to me that modern men bore one another to a boundless extent and that they finally feel the need to make themselves interesting with the aid of all the arts. They have themselves served up as sharp and pungent repasts; they soak themselves in all the spices of the Orient, and to be sure! they now smell very interesting . . . Now they are suitably prepared for satisfying every taste.*

Isn't it essential for us not to bore everyone by being split off from ourselves and less than fully real? Of course, I realize that the sense of "fully real" is not easily explicated.

Oh yes. In spite of my apparent interest in my students, and the energy I poured into the course, I felt alienated from them at its close. I think I feared a more reciprocal relationship. I, as performing ego, wanted to distance them, perhaps erase them; that is the unpleasant truth from which I split myself, deceived myself about.

The ethical responsibility of the individual professor is inescapable. But it is possible to talk about this—and to tell a story about oneself as responsible—which masks out part of the situation which should be illuminated. So I resorted to precarious theatrical techniques to gain students' attention. At least I could say I was provoked. There were 150 of them. They shared few intellectual interests, surprisingly little knowledge, and were not strongly motivated to learn. Moreover, there was little or no provision for interest generated in this course to be developed in later ones. The class would split up and be deposited in the remotest corners of the university. Given the structure of the university, how could this be a full-fledged educational experience,

---

*Friedrich Nietzsche, "Schopenhauer as Educator", in *Untimely Meditations*, trans. by R. J. Hollingdale (Cambridge and N.Y.: 1983).

even if the professor were the best? We must comprehend both individual responsibility and historical-institutional reality, and how they interconnect.

To grasp the university's malaise as an educational institution we must see how it is deeply systemic, and obscurely and complexly historical. The boxes of numbers float detached because truth about our condition in the twentieth century is so difficult to grasp.

If we would know what the university is, we must know whence it has come and how it has developed. What did those who built it want to become by building and using it? In the next two chapters we will explore the complex phenomenon of the near collapse of the religious (and related) institutions within which persons had traditionally been authorized and formed as selves. Into this disrupted background, this near-vacuum, step science, technology, and professionalism—and, of course, the contemporary university at the heart of this abrupt process of secularization. As the university allied itself with science to provide "useful knowledge" to the masses (or at least the middle class), it was powered by a radical deflection of the traditional religious energies of identity-formation which had determined earlier projects of higher education. It deflected these energies without simply supplanting them.

The immense ironies involved here will gradually emerge. The new university was intended to liberate from religious dogma, and to open the doors of freedom and opportunity for many, many people. On a certain level and to some extent it did this. But implicit within its project of the production of useful knowledge was a conception of knowledge, and of the knower, which was constricted and outmoded (dogmatic) even before it was embodied in the university. It was a conception which housed the knower within machines, within a mechanical body and world, and which tended to invalidate intimacy, freedom, and ethical responsibility. It isolated persons from themselves, others, and Nature.

In brief, I will argue that we need recognition in order to be, but because we no longer feel confident that judgments about our moral quality can be true, we place undue weight on judgments of our professional performance. The impersonality of professionalism is largely deceptive. Archaic energies of identity formation get forced into tight outlets. Involved in the turbulence of these energies are, I think, unacknowledged initiation and purification rituals which keep in check unacknowledged fears and aversions. In effect, "I am I, a mind competent and pure, because I am wholly other from you *others*, you students, for example."

William James's concurrent talk of the "scientific nightmare," and some others' misgivings, did not deter the rapid construction of the modern university, nor did the revolutions in physics, psychiatry, and some sectors of academic philosophy which sprang up early in our century. These offered new conceptions of self, world, freedom, responsibility, and moral vitality. But only now, at the end of our century, do these new conceptions have any chance of altering the massive structure of the bureaucratized institution. Only now is it clear that the university has failed to provide a matrix within which our common concerns for meaning and being, and for humane and ethical knowledge, can thrive. I think we must speak of the bankruptcy of the university as an educational institution. It is a humiliating admission: and this is all the more reason to note that more and more educators are making it.*

---

*For example, some normally cautious educators have declared in print that the bachelor's degree is worthless, and not just as a meal ticket (*The Chronicle of Higher Education*, report of Malcolm Skully, Nov. 24, 1982).

III

Crisis of Authority
and Identity:
The Inevitability of
Professionalism

> The professional responsibility to restrain the
> "dangerous classes," to perfect such institutions
> as asylums and schools, stemmed from a
> growing body of expert knowledge that
> described the universe as it actually functioned.
> The culture of professionalism was for the
> mid-Victorians a modern metaphysics.
> —Burton Bledstein, *The Culture
> of Professionalism*

If we are animals—and can we deny it?—we are nevertheless
surpassingly strange ones. With some exceptions in the case of
the more complex mammals, animals other than human seem
simply to be *there:* they are given their nature in the pre-wired
structure of the brain and the ensemble of instincts.* This holds
with the proviso that the organism function within an environment that opens certain opportunities of behavior and imposes
certain constraints. Some newly born birds "pattern" on the first

---

*The exceptions of which I think include dolphins, seals, and chimpanzees.
Perhaps some "genius" in their company effects an innovation and then trans-
mits it to others, which may count as miniature cultural evolution. And maybe
we should include the octopus—not a mammal. Brian Donovan informs me
that it is not of the phylum *Chordate*, so has no *central* nervous system, no
specialized brain. Yet there is the possibility of real intelligence, for it behaves
in complex ways and can control the coloration and patterning of its entire
skin surface, possibly communicating thereby with its kind.

35

moving thing they happen to see, but then *that* is simply given, and the system of behavior remains closed in on itself.

Humans are not devoid of instincts, and discovering what they are is crucial. For example, Konrad Lorenz has claimed that round-headedness, the image of the neonatal or the infantile, triggers a response of protectiveness in adult humans or related mammals.* If true this is most important, for perhaps we can develop it to ameliorate violence in our world. But whatever the instincts are, they are manifestly insufficient to supply us with a viable identity (and they can be overridden, as any parental abuse of children proves about the alleged protective instinct).

We must also become what we are through socialization. How are we regarded by other humans who are already more or less formed? What do they expect of us, and to what place in the community do they assign us? To become educated is to be drawn out to confront this web of interpretation in which one is caught, but then is led to ask, Who am I as a unique being? Who might I be? To be unable to orient and find oneself is to exist in terror, because one's very identity and reality threatens to slip away. Either that or the questions are repressed and boredom sets in.

To approximate the condition of soundness or haleness of self requires some measure of integration between (1) What I am taken to be by others whom I respect, (2) What I *make of* myself as the degree of my individuation increases, and (3) Whatever instinctual tendencies are inherited biologically. So we are biological-historical and cultural-historical creatures—animals of some strange sort. What we are is not independent of the stories we perpetually tell ourselves about ourselves—how we recognize ourselves.

The professionalization and segmentation of the university into research institution, multiversity, cannot be conceived independently of the rise of science, secularism, and professionalism generally since the seventeenth century. For in this historical shift new terms for recognizing ourselves gained currency, hence

---

*As described in Joseph Campbell, *The Masks of God: Primitive Mythology* (New York: 1970 [1959]), p. 47. Lorenz and Campbell are led to ask, What stimuli release instincts funded in us over a million years of animal existence?

new authority, new ways of building a self, new forms of instruction and education. Since we must become something, and must become this through being recognized as something, professionalism is inevitable; in its alliance with science and technology it provides the criteria and terms in which we are recognized in a largely secular age. The university is overwhelmingly influenced, not only because it is a chief repository of scientific research, and because science is heavily funded and taught to great numbers, but because of how professors tend to conceive of themselves as professional knowers, and what they communicate about who they are.

As Whitehead so adroitly pointed out, it is a seventeenth-century (particularly Cartesian) conception of knowledge—and of the knower and the world known—which largely determines the structure of the twentieth-century university. This conception both reflects and augments tendencies in the culture at large, especially the conception of self as scientific knower, self as self-sufficient individual and as ego, self as master manipulator of objects.

Only the broad outlines of Cartesianism need concern us. As Whitehead tells us, "The great forces of nature, such as gravitation, were entirely determined by the configurations of masses. Thus the configurations determined their own changes, so that the circle of scientific thought was completely closed. This is the famous mechanistic theory of nature."* It required an immense abstraction from the world as immediately lived. The only attributes Nature could have were a machine's: force, shape, mass, motion—Nature as colorless, tasteless, purposeless. Of course, something had to be noting all this, and to conceive of the thinker or observer required a matching leap of abstraction. The thinker or subject was all that the bodily realm was not: non-extended, aware, aware of its awareness, and purposive. In fact, Descartes conceives the self as simply momentary self-awareness or ego, and as possessing all and only those traits which it shares with a Transcendent Deity. Never has the self been conceived more abstracted from the body and from the world.

---

*A. N. Whitehead, *Science and the Modern World*, (New York: 1962 [1925]), p. 51.

It is also abstracted from others and from the past and future, existing in one point-instant after another of pure, individual self-consciousness. Hence the famous problem of knowledge inherited from Descartes. If all I can surely know is my own thinking here and now, I cannot be sure that you, or the rest of the "outer world," or even my own body exists. Hence he must prove that a good Creator exists who would not allow our best thinking to be mistaken, our mathematical ideas of the outer world, and the axiomatic truth of my own existence as a thinking thing ("I think therefore I am" must be true because even if I doubt it it is *my doubting.*). So an internal individual self as consciousness reflecting upon itself—as ego, as that which says "I" of itself—certainly exists (the conception of the already formed self, needing only to be instructed, appears in eighteenth-century portraits of children as little adults). And the "external world" spied and calculated by physics certainly exists also—a vast machine proceeding along a linear track of time, to which we can attribute merely properties of force, not "value." For Descartes, only an all-powerful God who recreates the universe in every point-instant prevents chaos or annihilation. This shred alone of the mythological background remains.

Captivated by his arguments, Descartes loses touch with the single ground of meaning experienced by a single integral being—one's uncritical sense of oneself as *one* self, as this derives from one continuous involvement in one continuous world. Both vague and utterly foundational and fundamental, this experience includes the sacred stories the assembled community habitually tells itself about itself and its history. One is mimetically engulfed, caught up in these stories; in fact, one *is one*—at least in part—because recognized by the authoritative community as one instance of types of beings embedded in these stories—ancestral or totemic beings, etc. One is a single being involved essentially in community and world, and has moral attributes which are as real as skeleton, lungs, heart.

The Cartesian partitioning of minds from bodies is profoundly alienating. Not only does it create a vexing problem of how one can know one's body, and the rest of the world, but of how self as mind can *connect* with one's body so that effective and responsible action can be initiated. How can a non-extended mind act upon an extended, mechanical body? But since to act upon belief and to realize wish or will is the essence of freedom, how can one conceive one's own freedom? To be without the assurance of freedom is to be without the assurance that one's purposes and values determine one's behavior. As both Nietzsche and Dostoevsky noted, this is to feel powerless; to generate libertinism perhaps: the desperate attempt to prove through random acts of destruction that one is free. Another possibility, of course, is that the employment of technology for means and ends that cannot be understood in terms of freedom and responsibility, and justified ethically, will degenerate into the boredom and paralysis of a life of routine. Since the very meaning of education is to be drawn out to act freely, effectively, and responsibly in the world, the whole project of education is imperiled.

It is against this background that twentieth-century life and the twentieth-century university must be understood. Once materialism gained in strength, and Descartes' argument for the self was seen to establish only the thinnest abstraction—and his arguments for God no longer respected—only a remnant of the self could be acknowledged by the self. After his great web of distinctions and his scruples and arguments were forgotten, the self becomes for itself only ego encased somehow in a mechanical body, existing in one point-instant after another, until its last instant ends it. Its existence depends crucially on the recognition it gets from others here and now in proving its power, that is, its calculative and technological prowess in the "real world" as described by mathematical physics. The *meaning* of this for human life—its value—is obscured. This is the crux.

Descartes' rationalism and mentalism finally feed a materialism in which only natural science is credited with powers of truth, and ethical and aesthetic judgments are construed as merely the expression of feelings and preferences of self as private ego. Paved over is that primal level of experience in which we are immediately involved as one self in one community of beings with which we identify, and goodness is effective and vital involvement in the world. Gradually obscured is the nearly instinctual level in which goodness and beauty, evil and ugliness, responsibility and irresponsibility, all are as palpably real as anything could be. The sciences are fractured from the humanities and exercise disproportionate influence in the university. Under the sway of thinking like Descartes' we tend to view ourselves as heads joined somehow with stomachs and groins—"men without chests," calculating and acquisitive animals who no longer rejoice simply for being living parts of Nature. And since we are beings with the capacity for self-reflection, this view of ourselves will tend to become a part of who we *are*.

Without habitually enveloping authoritative recognition in the full gamut of one's life, identity cannot deeply jell; we are left with a state of marginal or ghostly existence vividly stated for our time by Samuel Beckett in *Waiting for Godot, 1953*. When my students in Moral and Social Issues would nod off and swim before my eyes like wraiths, I would sometimes recall Beckett's play. They awaited authoritative recognition.

I am not saying that Descartes' philosophical thought created the modern world. But in an uncanny way it reflects and focuses what was at work, and what was to be at work, in the culture at large. It also anticipates the contemporary research university and its master problem: despite its vast research capacities and its knowledge, it exists in strange detachment from crucial human realities, and perpetuates the implicit dogma that there is no truth about the human condition as a whole (e.g., the humanities merely express communal or personal sentiment, hardly knowledge). The university fails to understand what it is doing, and what it is abetting, because in the dominant conception of knowledge, truth about ethical relations to others is blocked or obscured, as is also our involvement in the moody background world—matters crucial to who we are and to what education should be.

Let us take these two blockages in turn. Of course ethical relationships must be misconceived, if for no other reason than human relationships are in general. In accord with Descartes' technical formulations, the "age of individualism" conceives the self as already formed in its basics, for the assumption is that consciousness is aware of itself as a consciousness, an ego; it must simply be pounded into finished shape and polished through instruction in social conventions. But this is a simplistic, distorted conception which fails utterly to grasp how we are

caught up in involuntary imitation of others in the very formation of the self itself. Professional knowers fail to understand
themselves. For example, in their "mentalism" they fail to see
how they are caught up mimetically as body-selves in mentalism's polar opposite and kin, materialism in multifarious forms.
Burdened with this conception it is easy not to see how persons
today *must*, by and large, exhibit technological skills if they are
to be recognized and authorized. In the university it is easy to
allow the humanities a token role, but to think nevertheless that
the role is sufficient.

Thousands of years ago Aristotle enunciated what had practically been commonsensical: that it is human nature to gain a
second nature through socialization, through recognition by others who are already more or less formed. This recognition is
gained mainly through imitating the authorities who recognize
one, and the imitating need not be deliberate. In the nineteenth
century, Hegel, the "German Aristotle," attacked Cartesian and
other forms of individualism, and founded what became known
as sociology. In brilliant analyses he showed how the self-
conscious self arises through its recognizing how the other recognizes it to be self-conscious.

But there is an optimistic and rationalistic residuum in Hegel, and even he, I believe, failed to grasp adequately the pre-
rational structures of involuntary imitation of others, what I call
mimetic engulfment. Much hinges on an ambiguity involved in
Hegel's notion of recognizing another's recognition. If the other's
recognition is recognized *as* the *other's*, then of course the self
will be self-conscious and highly individuated, because the self
will recognize itself as other from this other.

But why suppose that the other need be recognized *as* other?
Why suppose that the self must be self-conscious? Why couldn't
the primitive human self arise merely as a function of a recognition of its humanness by others—a recognition which that incipient self cannot acknowledge, for it is simply engulfed,
unselfconsciously absorbed in it? If so, we would conceive of a
primitive, pre-ego, pre-self-conscious self. The infant's imitating
is involuntary, not self-aware, presumably.

By Hegel's own account there is a level of consciousness
more primitive than that of self-consciousness. He calls it "sense

certainty": sensuous qualities such as pain or redness are certain, and it must follow that they are certain *for* a consciousness. But he does not, I think, adequately develop the germinal idea that this primitive consciousness must have a primitive center, so to speak, must be a primitive self's consciousness of the crudely given world around it. Hegel is overly-much interested in the self-conscious, highly individuated self. Because of this he misses some of the non-rational or irrational structures in the dialectical involvement with others and formation of self. His notion of consciousness as engaged with others is an immense improvement on Descartes, yet he has not travelled sufficiently far from him to grasp the self as *body*-self. He cannot appreciate how socialization as learned control of bodily functions (expectorating saliva, for example) through imitation of others (not necessarily voluntarily) is essential to individuation of self—a topic we treat below. The imitator gains the recognition of the models imitated by imitating them, but need not be aware that this imitating *is* the means. Nor need the ones being imitated realize what is happening. Engulfed mimetically, whole societies ooze, tilt, drift in history.

Accordingly, Hegel cannot grasp the secularizing force of modern science and materialism, nor the way in which its totalizing ambition pulls away from and obscures a still active archaic background of existence. We are torn by these influences which drag us and pervade us as if by osmosis. Only this oversight allows Hegel to maintain his belief in inevitable progress toward greater autonomy and freedom.

I will argue that the weightiest reason for the lack of self-understanding in the university is a failure to grasp mimetic engulfment. This is failure by professional-scientific and professional-scholarly knowers to grasp the energies of recognition and authorization which compose the professional-scholarly self. Among these energies are archaic mimetic engulfments in one's purified group, and phobic exclusions of potentially polluting others.

This obscuration of mimetic engulfment is part and parcel of a larger problem, generated by seventeenth-century and other earlier thought and embedded in the twentieth-century university. It is failure to see that the formation of identity of self—and education—occurs largely at an archaic level of engulfment in the moody background world of everyday experience. This failure occurs because of another tacit dogma: the *omni-competence* of scientific thought memorialized in seventeenth-century systems.

I think there is an insistent need—but easily obscured by easily secured gratifications—to locate ourselves somehow within a *world*—a need to interpret our experience as taking place in a primal whole which authorizes our place within it. The contemporary secular university is the concentrated expression of the scientific ambition to tell us "all we need to know" of the whole, to totalize, to displace traditional experiences of the cosmos, and to locate us within it. I will try to unpack Burton Bledstein's penetrating observation that science and technology became a "modern metaphysics."

With our strongest need being just to *be* something definite, and with the partial collapse of traditional religious, familial, and royal authority creating a vacuum for formation of identity, we witness one of those pre-rational mimetic phenomena of engulfment which are the groundswells of history. To *be* we must achieve recognition by performing effectively in a technological and professional world.

Mimetic engulfment is not a condition merely of early life. Adults in their own groups typically do not realize the extent to which they are undeliberately modeling themselves upon others around them in the foreground and the background world. I think the typical condition of human identity is one of more or less compromised individuation. This is vividly evident in times of great stress—in mob behavior, lynch mobs, etc. Or there are prolonged mass movements of mimetic engulfment in which whole societies move together along lines of least resistance, because it is directly and dumbly felt that the world tilts in a certain direction.

Descartes released a genie in mechanistic physics which swelled over the centuries to immense, gaseous, totalizing size. New modes of authorizing and structuring self arose through mastery of technology and industry, through marketing, travel, and the various formations of urban life. More and more the self was recognized for its technical and professional abilities, and less and less for its performance of traditional ways and rituals, its attunement to the archaic background of experience and to regenerating Nature. Yet that background remains, in some form, at a primordial level. So the self tends to split between its more personal and its more professional levels.

But despite confusion, distraction, and a strange kind of loneliness, there is a vague but fundamental level of experience in which we directly and pre-critically experience ourselves to be one self, to be in a community, or set of communities, and also, of course, in *a world*. Nothing completely expunges this sense, for it is the deepest, if most obscure, source of authorization of self: the moody and visceral sensing of the background, oneself being and belonging in the world. Vaguely but fundamentally we sense the limits of what is immediately present to us sensuously, and beyond that horizon *everything* else.

Moreover, we sense the world as *having been* such before we attended to it. We cannot attend to all of it—past and present—at once, nor are we foolish enough to think that we can itemize every piece of it and add up the inventory every moment. Hence we must repose some deep conviction about what is *all* there, some vague, deep sense. I speak of the way the world is pre-critically and directly experienced, and leave open the question whether the universe is in fact finite or infinite, unitary or pluralistic.

Only if we grasp the totalizing ambitions of modern science and technology will we grasp the immense power of modern professionalization to mould persons and their behavior—and to leave the rest of them untouched, confused, or ineffectual. "Educated" people came to think that (1) *the* scientific method for producing knowledge had been acquired, and (2) the universe is at bottom physical and amenable to the single method of discovery through experimentation and calculation. It is only a matter of time before we have predicted so much—at least in the environs of the earth—and produced so many instruments and machines that our ability to control what happens will, for all practical purposes, be complete. We will be the masters of Earth and of ourselves. Toward the end of the twentieth century we begin to see the limits of our institutionalized modes of knowing. But remember that I am trying to grasp the background assumptions upon which the university was built.

It is ridiculous to dispute the great accomplishments of science, even mechanistic science within its sphere, but it began to be believed that *all* pre-scientific thought and faith concerning fundamental questions could, in principle, be replaced; it was superstition or more or less inadequate common sense. The new secular faith, that all the sciences and special studies (crypto-sciences perhaps) add up to the whole, exists uneasily alongside the archaic, immediate experience of a background world which could never be a mere aggregate of determinate, objectified states of affairs and individuals, because it is experienced *as* the engulfing, never completely comprehended whole, its parts never finally sortable nor enumerable.

Since it was believed that science is forever complete with respect to basic method and to mastery of all the basic physical laws—and that physical reality underlies everything —it followed that all that needs to be done to know and control the world is to locate each scientific specialty, await the results from each and then, if we wish, add them up. The secular university— the knowledge factory—emerged in the last decades of the nineteenth century within this modern myth. Particular sciences supply "the cognitive base" of particular technologies, and these are modes of producing power and wealth—and identity, at least to some extent, to some depth. Each department in the university guards a domain of expert knowledge, a cognitive base "guaranteed" by a professional association nation-wide. Hence the university stands as gatekeeper on the path of power, wealth, and formation of self—formation of some sort. Burton Bledstein's observation that professionalism is a modern metaphysics is not overdrawn.

No doubt, from the very beginning modern science has produced brilliant analyses and syntheses—and brilliant technologies—but it has always had to presuppose the ordinary background world within which its investigators move and turn and imagine things to pick out. In trying to assemble parts into a whole it must presuppose an immediate experiential sense of the whole that can nowhere appear in its account, and in begging this question of the whole, it throws a deep shadow over ourselves as knowers. For our sense of ourselves is not independent of our sense of the englobing world as we directly live it.

All we could ever get by science's methods of knowing and "educating" would be mere aggregates of some size, not wholes as organically communal and directly lived, directly formative of ourselves. By the metaphor of organism I mean a life in which the members exist in and through and for the whole, and the whole exists in and through and for the members; members as "organs" of an "organism." The archaic sense of the world is organismic: we participate in the domain of Divine Providence, or, more archaically still, in Mother Nature. In our different ways we serve Her and are enhanced, and She succors all of us. The relationship is intimately participatory, mimetic; existence occurs within rituals which are part and parcel of the replenishing cycles of Nature. For example, ritualistic symbolizations of rain are enactments which magically participate in the rain itself. Even moderns who have no faith in divine providence enjoy some residual sense—if inarticulate, suppressed, and threatened—that they participate immediately in a world that somehow makes a place for them.

But since Descartes, scientific knowledge pictures the world as *external* to us, a machine. It cannot complement or reinforce our visceral sense of being at home in the world. It can only pick things apart and trust that all that it understands to be real will be added up and put back together. Meanwhile our lived experience within the ever-present background tends to be interpreted as "merely subjective." Because our feeling life and valuational life cannot be grasped in terms of mechanistic physics, it tends to be devalued. When we no longer deeply trust our basic feelings and valuations to disclose the world, where are we?

To devalue immediately lived personal life is to begin to die at the core, no matter how much power is exercised or recognition extracted from contemporaries for technical or professional skills. If awe in the face of the boundless world is no longer treasured, and rejoicing in being a vital part of it no longer valued, the loss is immeasurably great. If I am merely a set of roles available in a secular culture which recognizes me only when I exhibit professional power and technological prowess—only when I produce an immediately valued product or service (or purchase something)—then I have lost the life which roots fully and freely in the archaic background of inherited feelings, affinities, and regenerating energies—lost the sap and sparkle of the formative imagination which commemorates its sources and creates the new simultaneously, and I am merely a set of serviceable masks. That I am not valued simply for myself must be concealed. Quite literally I am de-moralized. Mircea Eliade observed that the secularization of work is like an open wound. For the university in particular, generation as "productivity" tends to split-off from regeneration through the young.

Again, we see the relevance of mimetic engulfment. Theorists of natural science and technology in the seventeenth through the nineteenth centuries did not understand the pre-rational side of the new secular style of life—personal identity needs which prompt us to be sucked in by whatever march of power and recognition we can fall in with, despite the costs—and did not understand inherited patterns of prescientific mimetic engulfment of body-selves in each other and the world. Scientific method as totalizing ambition was uncritical of its own limitations, and did not grasp the background out of which it emerged, and which it had presumed to replace.

The last decades of the eighteenth century—the period of Enlightenment, so-called—saw a momentous intersection of events: the founding documents of the United States were drafted, as science, secularism, and individualism started to gain official status. The divorce of governmentally sanctioned public life from religion was well underway, a breach continuing to widen to this day. Seen against a background of centuries of religious persecution and unrest, this secularizing and protective move is understandable.

But ethical beliefs and practices had been traditionally enmeshed for most with religious beliefs and practices, and when religion was separated from the official center of public life, it tended to take ethics with it. As religion was to be a private matter, so ethical belief tended to become so as well. Inspired largely by John Locke's individualism as found in his *Second Treatise on Government* (and his Cartesian ancestry), government was legitimized by the founding fathers as, first and foremost, the protector of the individual's personal rights—rights to privacy, private property, individual initiative. More and more the public sector was dominated by marketing ventures and values, debates over legality, and the role of expert—typically technological and professional—knowledge in managing the affairs of the nation. The retreat of ethical discussion into private sectors was slow but inexorable, despite Victorian moralizing and the real role that ethical debate played, for example, in the Civil War debates. The Cartesian drift into subjectivity—the private sector of "merely subjective expression"—was now abetted by the founding fathers' legal codes, their "liberalism" and individualism. Legally sanctioned and protected individualism tended to mask from sight mimetic engulfment in the *group* values of consumption and production and the display of both. A contractarian, market-oriented conception of public personhood could not grasp the full capacities of self, particularly its capacity for moral autonomy. Outside this context the emergence of the modern research university at the close of the nineteenth century cannot be understood.

Today, at the close of the twentieth century, massive federal funding for universities (to a great extent even for private ones) caps a secularizing and professionalizing trend that has been growing for 200 years. It is a pervasive influence, only some of which can be pin-pointed: from student aid to huge grants for scientific and technological research.

To put it precisely: by "professionalism" I mean a way of life which provides a livelihood through the practice of a skill valued by society; this requires a "cognitive base" of expert knowledge which can be acquired only through protracted training in a special field. The term also connotes the discipline necessary to exercise the skill whenever required. Since the skill is valued by society, there is the "public service" aspect of professionalism. A profession may or may not have an official code of ethics.

We must shortly give a precise definition of "technology," for more and more the valued practices and skills of professionalism involve technology, hence more and more the cognitive base is science. It is assumed that the total scientific view of the world is built up from more or less autonomous special fields immersed in particular areas of recondite facts—"nobody can know it all." The impact of technology upon traditional ideals of professionalism is immense. Briefly, for the moment: (1) As technical expertise gets narrowed, and expertise as a source of individual wealth and power gets emphasized, the public service aspect of professionalism tends to erode. (2) As professionals become engulfed in ever more specialized groups, and more and more groups contribute to any given outcome, each specialist's feeling of responsibility for the whole is diminished. (3) In general, ethical judgments tend to be construed in ever more technical senses, imperiling the sense of their broadly human significance, and of how they might be *true* of human life in their own coarse-meshed way.

More precisely, by "technology" I mean instruments for accomplishing work which derive from scientific discoveries in particular fields of inquiry and which produce wealth and power. For example, the profession of medicine is now linked with the technology of producing cures and wealth, because the professional physician possesses expert scientific knowledge of bacteria, for instance. Or, again, the profession of engineer is connected to the industrial technology of steam turbines because the engineer possesses expert scientific knowledge of the kinetic laws of gases which relate pressure, volume, and temperature.

The connection between professionalism, technology, and formation of self is, of course, not far to seek. For a necessary ingredient of identity is recognition from authoritative others, and that recognition can be won by most people only through the exercise of professional skill which employs technology to produce wealth or power. Moreover, even if an audience of authoritative others is not immediately available there still exist sources for recognition and authorization. We automatically imagine others recognizing our secular accomplishments—for we must sense them to be experienceable, in principle, by others. In the skillful exercising of a technology we leave our mark on the world, recognizable by all of us. The world itself bears witness to our power and prowess: a sweeping highway cut through the mountains, a tall building etched against the horizon, a huge CAT scan machine for detecting abnormalities of the brain, etc.

No doubt the exercise of technology can prompt primal feelings of involvement in the world. But, as we have anticipated, there is a problem. Typically, each work-day endeavor is split into many tasks, many technologies, each encapsulating its group of experts, and often employed at different times in the production process. The danger is that workers are cut off from the historical and human impact of the endeavor and do not feel a vital part of history—do not feel that throbbing contact which is the sense of individual responsibility for the larger community. Typically there is no *story* which knits them into the experienced world-whole and articulates and justifies the endeavor, and while power is generated there may be no empowerment, no sense of "myself as a vital part of the world-whole."

Enter bureaucracy. By this term I mean a system for organizing human activity so that persons become almost totally absorbed in the welfare of their particular module, and are only dimly aware of the role this plays in the whole, or the way in which the welfare of the whole affects the part. It is inorganic and desiccated connectedness.

Technology is the pivot connecting professionalism with bureaucracy. It has instrumental value only: the means of realizing impulse or desire. It need not be desire yoked to common concerns for meaning, and for humane and ethical knowledge and behavior; technology is centrifugal. Hence a form of governance not determined by such common concerns arises. Bureaucracy: modules which push for their own immediate ends through employing techniques and technologies which define a group of experts, a group of professional academics, say. University administrators are masters of the procedures by which the modules are kept more or less in political balance; they are master technologists. The multiversity is born.

The faith that any whole can be broken into manageable units, and the units reassembled in thought or in deed to fulfill predictions and maximize benefits—their interactions all calculated—is the myth of modernism, and it permeates nearly everything in the culture. But the calculative intellect cannot by itself determine the grand unit which is the condition of all life and all calculation: the situations experienced immediately as wholes in which humans form themselves and become *one* in some complex, difficult sense. The quality of these situations can only be perceived, lived through, undergone—whether beautiful and invigorating or tedious and debilitating, whether valuable or worthless. Because the calculative intellect cannot claim the whole lived situation as its province—cannot "break down to it" and then calculate with it, but must presuppose it—the great danger is to ignore it. But this means alienation from the overarching reality of human life itself and what makes it good. Our technological means of control go out of control.

I believe that professionalism in its typically modern guises is an inevitable development, an inevitable response to the modern shift in authority from the sacred to the secular. More and more the earth's population is pulled into this orbit as pockets of peasants and "primitives" are exposed to technology and western secularism. The movement toward professionalism is inevitable because the movement toward individuation of self is likewise. Even the "pure" scientist who achieves recognition just because of his or her purity as a professional is linked to technology even when it is not clear how the research provides a cognitive base for technology. For science itself can be called the theory of technology: what we must think about the world, given our scientific instruments of observation, prediction, and control of it.

So I submit that professionalization, and the ascendency of science, is inevitable. Because the prospect of becoming a professional will lure multitudes, and because it demands protracted training in acquiring expert (typically scientific) knowledge, the university will be thrown into the spotlight and overwhelmingly influenced.* Expert knowledge is almost always sharply con-

---

*The power and status of the humanities continue to decline. Lynne V. Cheney writes, "Between 1966 and 1988, a period in which the number of bachelor's degrees awarded increased by 88 percent, the number of bachelor's degrees awarded in the humanities declined by 33 percent. Foreign language majors dropped by 29 percent; English majors, by 33 percent; philosophy majors by 35 percent, and history majors, by 43 percent. . . . A 1986 survey funded by the NEH . . . showed more than two-thirds of the nation's seventeen-year-olds . . . could not identify the Reformation or *Magna Carta*. Vast majorities demonstrated unfamiliarity with writers such as Dante, Chaucer, Dostoevsky, Austen, Whitman, Hawthorne and Melville. . . . As . . . a teacher at the University of Illinois at Chicago, observed . . . 'Students . . . do not register to read books of whose existence they do not know.' . . . It is possible to graduate now . . . from almost 80 percent of the nation's four-year colleges and universities without taking a course in the history of Western civilization. . . . In 1988–89, it is possible to earn a bachelor's degree from: 37 percent of the nation's colleges

fined in scope. So the scope of self-reflexivity, that key feature of education, must be sharply confined as well. Our sense of ourselves as ones who have chosen to mark off a sector of research in the englobing world and to pursue it in a certain way must be obscured. Knowledge of ourselves in our freedom and responsibility, our full humanness, humane knowledge, is masked off and threatened.

Certainly, professions existed long before modern science and technology and the bureaucracies which house them: medicine, law, the ministry, scholarship and teaching. We still feel the influence of their codes of conduct, which called for thorough inquiry and skilled procedure, respect for evidence, protection of clients' interests, integrity. But more and more these older professions employ technology—often with marvelous effect—but at the price of becoming dependent upon it. First is the inherent limitation of technology: unaided it cannot discover what is intrinsically valuable, but only goods as means. Captivation with mere power easily results, power for more power for more power—a loss of bearings in the human situation, disorientation concerning what's valuable—mis-education.

The second cost is that dependency upon technology means dependency upon the many institutional structures which promote, regulate, and finance it. Even the most individualistic professions such as medicine are more and more forced to operate in legalistic and bureaucratic structures external to the human subject matter of the profession. The dependency of the lawyer is almost as obvious. A multitude of experts is involved, from ballistic and photo technicians to those who manage the flow of

---

and universities without taking *any* course in history; 45 percent without taking a course in American or English literature; 62 percent without taking a course in philosophy; 77 percent without studying a foreign language." ("Humanities in America: A Report to the President, the Congress, and the American People," report of the Chairman, National Endowment for the Humanities, Sept. 1988, pp. 4–5). But it should also be pointed out that the relative power of the sciences has also declined. In 1971 roughly 425,000 graduated in the arts and sciences category and the same number in the technical and professional. In 1984–85, the latter had swollen to 650,000, the former dropped to 350,000 (*Digest of Educational Statistics*, 1987, U.S. Dept. of Education, p. 105).

work through the courts. Even ministers feel the weight of technologies, in the pressure applied to them to share their authority with psychologists, those who claim to work on the self so that it functions more effectively and efficiently.

As for scholar-teachers in the university, they operate in an institution permeated by the powers, burdens, and implicit values of technological society, and can only remind themselves of standards of integrity and intrinsic educational and scholarly values which technology cannot displace, for—if sanely employed—it must presuppose them. All this tends to undermine the sense of individual ethical responsibility, and immense vigilance is demanded. The university is no ivory tower sealed off from the world. The dominant secular-scientific ideal of knowledge impinges *particularly strongly* on how professional academic knowers narrate their lives and strive to form an identity.

The meaning of "professional" has been so stretched that today it is commonly defined as "salaried member of a bureaucracy." This is dangerous, for mimetic engulfment in fashionable professional modes of existence—untethered to common concerns for ethical behavior and knowledge—can assume an animal-like or worse than animal-like closedness. For we need not be related to persons as persons—need not be ethically related—but can be mimetically engulfed in groups as crowds of objects, or involved in others as material to be manipulated. Objectivity equals objectification, even of ourselves—numbers in boxes expertly used to evaluate us—human presence masked off. This is synopsized in David Riesman's brilliant title, *The Lonely Crowd*.

The self-enclosure of bureaucracy and professionalism has a multiple function. It has some obvious advantages. But as I argue in subsequent chapters, this shiny, contemporary form of organization functions on its shadow side as an archaic purification ritual: "I am I and we are we because we are purely ourselves and *other* than you." The combined force of these explicit and implicit functions is tremendous. I am mainly interested in how they twist and turn the university—and the students within it who plan a professional career of some kind. The university bureaucracy placed 150 undergraduates from very different backgrounds and with very different aims, and with sketchy preparation, into a room for fifteen weeks, two and a half hours a week, and had the temerity to declare that this satisfied a significant portion of a "humanities" requirement. Perhaps a course like Current Moral and Social Issues was better than nothing—even with no follow-up—but must we use *that* comparison? I could only think that the functioning of the university was superficial: unsynchronized with our needs and abilities, and with the development of human identity.

It is not our task to detail yet again the transformation of the world in the last four hundred years wrought by science, technology, and professionalism. Transformed are ways of being human, of having an identity. This includes the fabled "rise of the middle class"—tearing loose from traditional structures of recognition and authorization of self, and "making it" in the great world, rising, being successful. Every young man—and now young woman—a swashbuckling buccaneer, perhaps, or a corporate pirate, leaving his or her mark, piling up a hoard. Of course, some have and will benefit humankind by radically improving living conditions, eradicating disease and unnecessary pain, or perhaps conferring leisure time which will be used for "developing the mind." Technology is an ambiguous legacy.

Control of the means of production is a key concept—regardless of what one thinks of Marx's particular analyses—for control of the means of production (which includes the production of information and its marketing) means control to a great extent of the formation of human identity itself. As the means of production become centralized, life becomes urbanized, radically shifted from the agricultural life and its vital contact with the cycling seasons of regenerating Nature. We are caught in the "mirror" of the other, and in momentary fads, but we have greater choice of those with whom we will associate, if we can generate the will and the means to exercise this choice.

We need not detail all this, but we must get a vivid impression of its tang, pressure, inevitability. The world was shifting, tilting away from the fixed structures of aristocratic and religious privilege—structures within which humans had been forced to seek for power, recognition, identity—and into an horizon of opportunity. We have grown so accustomed to the technological marvels which extend the scope of our bodies and senses, the effective domain of our being, that it is difficult to understand the overwhelming allure that the emergence of these exercised (and do today all over the world). It is mimetic engulfment on a stupefying scale. The American philosopher John Fiske had something like a religious experience watching a railroad steam engine at work. Machines emerged as unquestioning, powerful servants that many could dream of owning.

Serious ambiguities and hidden costs were present but took time to be understood; we still labor with the task. Those who owned machines too expensive or momentous to be owned by any but the richest, effectively owned those whose sole means of livelihood was tending them. Some of the older modes of authority and domination were left behind, but new modes were replacing them. In fact, there were many, many ambiguities, but the new age was so caught up in itself and in its totalizing ideology that it was blind to the background, the old habits which carried over from the past.

I have spoken of an animal-like *thereness*, a closing in upon itself, except now it was an animal caught up in a self-closing domain of calculative, analytical *mind* which masked off a primitive background of minding, of being dimly and feelingly aware, which was still furtively if confusedly at work. It was particularly phenomena of mimetic engulfment, old *and* new, which escaped notice and which moved powerfully—either glacially or mercurially. Lacking was that mode of transcendence and meaning-making which grasps the archaic nether-ground of life, the background world.

Neither the older rationalisms, with their background religious optimism, nor the newer secular rationalisms, with their up-front technological optimism, had positioned themselves to see pre-rational or irrational phenomena of identity formation, particularly mimetic engulfment (irrational, as they must seem to a secularized age). Only very prescient thinkers saw them— for example, Kierkegaard, Marx, Nietzsche, Spengler, Freud, and Jung. Perhaps we should also think of the nineteenth century suffragettes, who could see, from their vantage point below and behind the vanguard of industrial culture, that the most primitive exclusion, oppression, and superstition was continuing into the enlightened new age of science and industry. The march of mimetic engulfment—and all that it dragged behind it—was inexorable. The baggage included the university.

Whitehead's idea that seventeenth-century thought structured the university is correct. Mathematical science deals only with physical objects, and these taken most schematically and abstractly. There is mind, but each is closed in upon itself in tacit or manifest introspection. There is no proper study of mankind in the mass, of history, or even of the individual as he or she is directly involved with other body-selves—vulnerable, porous, caught up—no study of our actual subjectivity, as opposed to the Cartesian misunderstanding of it.

Martin Heidegger has spoken aptly of the nineteenth as the darkest of centuries. Thinkers' lights left completely unilluminated an underside of human history that could not be imagined. Rational calculation became "rational management" of persons and groups understood as objects—the legacy of mechanistic physics and its technologies. How we directly, viscerally experience a world of others and other things was not grasped. The humanities found no generally accepted methods of investigation and self-evaluation. Hence the inevitable emergence of bureaucracy as a way of managing groups which no longer could comprehend their organic intra- and inter-dependency. The university exists in such a world.

We turn in the next chapter to the inevitable rise of academic professionalism. Science and technology are so revered that all fields are influenced; professors are increasingly absorbed in the latest results of specialized fields—the model of science—and tend to think of thought and research as "productivity." But humane knowledge need not be new, nor is the age-old task of stimulating students to grapple with it. The intergenerational task of education, of enticing students to form a vital identity within history, can only dim in importance.

In fact, all the essential features of the educating act are threatened by professionalism unaware of its limitations. Engagement in the classroom or laboratory can be achieved, but for what motives and with what consequences? Wealth and power need not entail well grounded identity. We may elicit recognition and a measure of authorization from the world itself—a highway cut through the mountains, a building etched against the horizon—but nothing like a balanced view of the world and our place within it need result. Truths about this and that pile up, and no doubt this is achievement, but it is no more than mountains of chips if we don't learn something about human life as an integral whole, something about human goodness. Intellectual freedom implies ethical responsibility. Engulfed in the search for recognition and identity within sharply delimited research activities, the implication is easily overlooked. Pursuing the short-range, the ego-self, we can fail of self-reflectiveness and lose touch with the self involved in the background which endures— as burdened with itself, satiated with itself, split off from itself and bored, attuned to the grandeur of the world and elated— whatever.

The danger is to be closeted in contemporaneity, and to grow quietly wild there: to achieve scientific and technological progress and personal tragedy. Can we imagine a more unsatisfying answer to the chief educational question, What shall I be, what shall I make of myself?

Presumptive educational means which are not directed toward ends intrinsically valuable and fulfilling must reach ends which turn into more means, endlessly, restlessly, and ultimately destructively—as Nietzsche saw. Research poses today as the chief means of education. But the means which purport to control education fly beyond the matrix of humane comprehension—are out of control. I doubt if research *must* be conducted in educationally disastrous ways.

Thus the impression so often gotten in university settings: everything is ordered and under control—research is well done (judged by certain measures), salaries are paid, etc.—and everything is also out of control. The unhinged components again. As if an automobile were in excellent working order, the driver settling behind the wheel in good health, his eyes fine, his confidence high. But one thing is amiss: he is ten years old, has no idea of what good driving is, and would not know how to achieve it if he knew it. We blink. Is this actually happening? Surely the child is only playing and will not actually *drive off?*

We turn now to a somewhat detailed account of the professionalization of the university. Fundamental energies of self-formation, previously mediated by religious education and other traditional forms, were quite suddenly diverted into secular channels. The over-valuing of the secular-scientific intellect, which dominates the foreground, risks inciting despair when it cannot cope with certain grave human problems, and my students in Current Moral and Social issues—afflicted with a combination of smugness and fear—are an example of this. Obscure energies of identity formation, of fascinated participation and inclusion or sickened aversion and rejection, seem still to be at work in the archaic background of our lives.

IV

The Professionalization of
the University

The great transformation from dominantly religious-agricultural societies to dominantly secular-scientific and urban ones includes the transformation of institutions of higher learning in the last decades of the last century. At this point the university as we know it today emerged, shot up. Ever since the seventeenth century the impact of science and technology had produced a wrenching of civilization on its foundations. But nowhere, I believe, has the impact been greater than in the abrupt creation of the modern university. Most traditional institutions of higher learning had been under the control of religious authorities. The new secular institutions collided with the older and in most cases displaced them rudely from a central role in the evolving life of the nation.

Apart from records that we can only regard as authoritative, we would be unable even to imagine the state of higher learning before the emergence of the contemporary university. As late as the opening decades of the nineteenth century the structure of institutions of higher learning remained medieval. There were typically only three faculties: law, medicine, and theology. Despite the brilliance and freshness of F. W. J. Schelling's, *On University Studies* (1803), for example, it still presupposes the traditional structure. He writes that a state is perfect only if every citizen, while a means in relation to the whole, is also an end in himself. This certainly seems to require that every citizen be given an educational chance. And Schelling already incorporates a version of the eighteenth-century Enlightenment ideal: fundamental truths are knowable by reason alone, and all persons must be given an opportunity to develop and display their rational powers. This view encouraged the democratization of the university. Yet Schelling cannot anticipate its reconstruction, in alliance with science and technology, which will make possible unprecedented opportunity for the masses—particularly in the United States—and he presupposes the medieval tri-partite division.

In still another respect it is difficult to imagine the state of higher learning before the last decades of the last century. This is, typically, its shoddiness, its makeshift character, and finally and simply its smallness. I will sketch these features of the pre-modern university; by doing so we will better understand the inexorable rise of the modern professionalized institution.

The origins and early growth of higher learning in the United States are part and parcel of its religious life. The learned class was composed almost entirely of theologians. With the fewest exceptions only these men (and *men* is right) were equipped to teach on the higher level, and only these founded and directed the colleges. Teaching and founding were considered to be God's work, for, particularly in a dominantly Protestant set of groups, salvation depended upon the ability to read and understand God's word, the Bible. So one had to read and to understand on a fairly high level.

Another incentive was provided by the doctrine of general grace excogitated from this same Book: The Psalmist proclaimed that the Heavens declare the glory of God, and St. Paul affirmed in the first chapter of *Romans* that God's existence is evident "from the things that are made" when seen "in the light that lighteth every man who cometh into the world." This suggests the cultivation of the natural intellectual endowment, science as an instrumentality within a larger whole, and sometimes led to small-scale efforts in natural scientific research—small-scale, occuring under a larger umbrella, but not insignificant.

Powerful intellects were among those who taught in, or who founded, colleges—Cotton Mather and Jonathan Edwards, for example. The involvement of clergymen was essential, and follows an unbroken line from Rev. John Harvard's role in the founding of that college in 1636 to the establishment of the University of Southern California, for example, by Methodists in

1879. Lower points followed: the gradual degeneration, or squeezing out, of this involvement.

Dominant theologians were typically counted as members of the aristocracy, and if not members, significantly connected. Richard Hofstadter writes, "It was the aristocracy that was primarily concerned with the Colonial colleges, the well-to-do class that gave the bulk of private support, and the ruling group that provided the trustees.* The Colonial college graduated "a handful of gentlemen professionals to serve society's relatively simple needs."** By the end of the eighteenth century, Harvard was graduating 42 students per year, Columbia 15, Princeton 23. Almost without exception, these graduates were trained in the traditional trinity of professions: medicine, law, and the ministry. This grouping presupposed a society in which exclusively small professional groups could develop their own standards and amenities and methods of pedagogy relatively untroubled by the generally deferential surrounding world. They also presupposed a stable class structure in which only a few aspired to enter college.

By the last decades of the nineteenth century all this had changed radically. Science and technology had become autonomous, often defiantly so. A large middle class had been created and stood poised, like a flood, before the doors of institutions of higher learning. The university must now satisfy not only established needs for medical, legal, and ministerial practice—and the culturally conditioned and stabilized desires of agent and patient in each field—but naked desire for power and advancement as the possibility of these had opened abruptly in many fields of science and technology for many people. A multitude of professions and professional possibilities—most of them completely secular—beckoned brightly.

What survived as the Colonial college was entirely inadequate to the tasks demanded of it—entirely picayune and shoddy. There were no longer stable social classes and professional roles in which a few physicians train a few physicians

---

*Quoted in Magali Sarfatti Larson, *The Rise of Professionalism: A Sociological Analysis* (Berkeley: 1977), p. 109.
**Burton J. Bledstein, *The Culture of Professionalism: The Middle Class and the Development of Higher Education in America*, (New York: 1976), p. 209.

every year, ministers ministers, etc.—or in which moonlighting
or disaffected clergymen teach a variety of subjects as jacks of
all trades. There were not enough professors, and the university
had to get into the business of producing its own producers of
"usable knowledge." As it geared into the upwardly mobile and
productive society, it simultaneously turned in upon itself and
constituted professional education as a field of expertise.
Through its gates must pass all those who would harness science
to their desires, including those who would be the future gate-
keepers themselves.

Turn now to the degenerate state of most higher education in
the earlier 19th century. The old bond which had connected aristocracy and educator-theologians, and had formed some institutions of high quality, had frayed or broken. With the
impairment of religious and aristocractic authority came disintegrated curricula and unqualified instructors. And all this must
be seen against the background of the ambivalent American attitude toward education in general, which had gained strength as
the ruling aristocracy lost its dominance, and the masses moved
rapidly along every axis: spatially, temporally, culturally, and
sheerly numerically. Vast qualitative shifts in life attended the
quantitative. If renowned historians are to be believed, ambivalence toward education might better be called schizoid contradiction. Richard Hofstadter notes,

The educational writing that has been left to us by men whose names
command our respect is to a remarkable degree a literature of acid criticism and bitter complaint. Americans would create a common-school
system, but would balk at giving it adequate support. They would
stand close to the vanguard among the countries of the world in the
attempt to diffuse knowledge among the people, and then engage drift-
ers and misfits as teachers and offer them the wages of draymen.*

As the frontiers had been pushed westward, schoolmasters
were usually brought along. But in "the real world of men" they
hardly enjoyed high esteem. They tended to be lumped with the
women and children, and, indeed, by the turn of the century
they were being replaced rapidly by women. "Education is im-

---

*Richard Hofstadter, *Anti-intellectualism in American Life* (New York: 1979
[1963]), p. 301.

portant, but. . . ." To be sure, teaching on the college level was a bit more prestigious. President James McCosh of Princeton described the American educational system, composed of the common schools and the college, as a two-story structure without a staircase. Yet, as Bledstein records, teaching was typically in a sorry state—the professorate, if one can speak of it, in tattered disarray.

The lament was universally heard. "It is very hard to find competent professors for the University," Eliot commented in his inaugural address at Harvard in 1869: "Very few Americans of eminent ability are attracted to this profession. The pay has been too low, and there has been no gradual rise out of drudgery, such as may reasonably be expected in other learned callings.". . . As the presidents portrayed the American college teacher, he worked at a second-class activity that commanded slight respect. "Professor" in America could refer to a music-hall pianist, the master of a flea circus, a gymnast, a weight-lifter in a carnival. Every president commented with McCosh upon the "hard-working and under-paid professors, who should be set free from drudgery and world anxieties to give a portion of their energy to the furtherance of learning and science." Insecure and distracted, teachers were harrassed. . . . The American college teacher appeared to be a mediocre talent seeking shelter in the chapel. In 1871, a reviewer in the *Galaxy* described him as "nondescript, a jack of all trades, equally ready to teach surveying and Latin eloquence, and thankful if his quarter's salary is not docked to whitewash the college fence."*

This situation could not last. The rise of professionalism in higher education at the close of the nineteenth century is as inevitable a movement as history can show. Given a vast, emergent middle class, and an increasingly industrialized and secularized society, knowledge was power—and it was secular knowledge and immediately evident power. Seventeenth-century mechanistic physics, and its attendant technologies, stood ready to supply the model of secular knowledge. The power of this knowledge—produced as a commodity—must have seemed miraculous, perhaps numinous. So much knowledge and power had already been attained that its growth seemed limitless. With the basic principles of physics thought to be safely established, secular knowledge

---

*Bledstein, pp. 274, 279, 281.

could be broken down into specialties. The social sciences were born and modeled themselves, as best they could, on the natural sciences.

The trend to greater specialization was not limited to the sciences. A secular ethos of proficiency and expertise created a tidal force that carried the humanities with it. In the 1870s and 80s two hundred learned societies were formed in addition to teacher's groups. Every university divided itself into departments according to the divisions of these academic professional associations. Authority was now vested with master knowers in specialized areas as these knowers were recognized within that sector nationwide. Professional groupings began to shoulder aside local communities. Individual advancement within professions tended to supplant civic duty. The will to power—as Nietzsche put it—became evident, unleashed in its nakedness; the university was the gatekeeper.

The professionalization of academic fields of learning proceeded inexorably and rapidly, with the division of knowers occuring within the broad outlines of Cartesian psycho/physical assumptions. The abstractions of the "objective" and the "subjective" were cemented in place, and the possibility of abstracting differently within the inherited, pre-critical background of experience, and marking different basic divisions, was paved over. The natural sciences explored the outer world of extended, physical nature, and the humanities expressed the inner world of sentiment and mere opinion. The social sciences sparked the hope that the two realms could be bridged (a hope which proved disappointing, as we will soon see).

Within each of these broad, dualistically conceived divisions, particular disciplines congealed and erected themselves rapidly along professional lines. Given the individual's need to form an identity through mimetic engulfment in a determinate group, the various professional associations turned in upon themselves, and there began that monopolizing of "turf," that marking off of distinctive sets of concepts and methods, which would make communication between disciplines increasingly difficult. Although important progress in some fields, especially the natural sciences, doubtless occurred, there was an ever diminishing willingness and ability to attend to basic concepts shared by all disciplines. As a consequence, such concepts as meaning, truth, evidence, cause, individual, integrity, tended to be appropriated somewhat differently by different disciplines (whether treated explicitly or not), and tended to freeze into place and be taken for granted. The ability to compare the senses of terms and the methods used in different fields declined.

The unhappy consequences of Cartesian dualism are particularly evident in the studies which directly confront the human condition, history and psychology, for example. Depending on whether the preferred approach fixes on the mental or the physical "sides" of humans, there spring up methods of inquiry and sets of concepts which find no common ground for communication. It is frequently assumed now that no ground is shared by different "schools" and methodologies in psychology, so it is pointless for an "outsider" to criticize any of them. Whereas in history there are endless debates about the status of the discipline. Is it a social science or one of the humanities? And how are natural sciences relevant to the study of history?—a moot point.

In sum, since no principles inherent in knowing as an intrinsically unifying enterprise, or in the knower as an intrinsically integrable being, are kept alive, only external principles of organization remain to be forced upon the aggregate and to constitute a "university," better called, of course, "multiversity." These external principles are bureaucratic ones. The departments are political units within a huge, sprawling bureaucracy. The insularity of the disciplines, and the awkward ambience of the multi-versity as a whole, are only increased by the generally uncomprehending and vaguely condescending attitude of a society that still imagines itself on a frontier, "in the real world of men," a frontier which has vanished.

In a rough, preliminary way we have framed the historical background against which the Current Moral and Social Issues course can be seen. The great majority of students were deposited there by forces and motives that had little to do with *education*. They were there because others of their social caste were there, and they wished to secure professional careers endowed with power and wealth. Most of them *wanted* to fit into a bureaucratic niche. To be sure, their contact with peers in dormitory, fraternity, sorority was a fundamental educational experience, in the sense that they confronted decisions unshielded by their families: What ought I to do? What am I going to make of myself?*

But education has traditionally meant more than this, for it involves the partnership of the young and old in the perpetuation of the arts and sciences and the cultural tradition. This must involve the contact of professors and students, and it is the dislocation and alienation here that most concerns me. The point of education, as Plato saw, is to foster desire for right conduct and good things; this cannot be neatly packaged and delivered. The teacher's task is to tease or jolt students into the habit of self-reflection, and to cultivate the sense that truth and learning—beside their utilitarian powers—can be delightful and fulfilling in themselves. It is ticklish business: to tap archaic energies of identity formation which are rooted in a generic-religious background, but which could only be identified *as such* at the cost of baffling or alienating most of the students. And the task is compounded by the failure of the university to coordinate educational efforts through four years of cumulative learning, and to reward professors who pour themselves into teaching in a tangible, reliable, career-sustaining way. Indeed, professors can bank on being rewarded only if they look beyond the university most of the time and secure recognition from their national professional associations. The integrity of professors as teachers is sorely taxed.

We must patiently unpack and critically examine Burton Bledstein's brilliant but inadequately developed remarks,

Regard for professional expertise compelled people to believe the voices of authority and unquestioningly, thereby undermining self-confidence and discouraging independent evaluation. . . the culture of professionalism in America has been enormously satisfying to the human ego while it has taken an inestimable toll on the integrity of individuals. (p. xi)

---

*The Rutgers anthropologist Michael Moffatt has lived in student dormitories, and the University's press has issued his *The Coming of Age in New Jersey* (New Brunswick: 1989). This is crucial work, and its rarity in this century underlines how removed from the lives of students most universities have become.

Bledstein's remarks refer to professionalism generally, and to apply them to the academic sort requires some qualification. Nevertheless, he grasps brilliantly that professionalism discourages independent evaluation outside one's established field, and that it is great for the ego but takes a toll on integrity.

We have already alluded to the human need to totalize experience in some way, to feel that one is oriented and located within the supremely singular surrounding world. One is *where* one is, and this is read off from the marks one leaves, or where others "who should know" place one on the basis of these marks. One is authorized thereby and formed as a self within cultural-historical time, regardless of whatever instinctual tendencies one brings from the biological-historical past and which complement (or complicate) all of this in some way.

We have also alluded to the scientific revolution of the seventeenth century and the presumption of mechanistic physics to discover all the basic laws of the universe. The various sciences and their attendant technologies spring out of the womb of physics. Even the social sciences model themselves on the physical sciences and various "social statics" and "social dynamics" emerge. The humanities grow ever more desperate in their need to justify their existence, and tend to delve so deeply into fields of study so specialized that nobody else can claim expertise, hence a crypto- or quasi-scientific authority devolves upon the practitioners. (What do *you* know about the English novel from 1838 to 1844 as it relates to the industrialization of the Midlands?)

The structure of the contemporary university follows apace. The presumption of aggregated totality is institutionalized. If all the knowledge amassed by all its component departments could finally be added up, then, in principle and given enough time, there is nothing significant that could forever escape its comprehension. Since the world locates and forms the self, and since the secularized university grasps the world, this university must form the self—"finish it" in some grand sense. This, of course, is typically not *said*, for it sounds presumptuous and unprofessional. But it is believed implicitly, I think, and the numinous, archaic force of the belief—rooted in an eclipsed but still active pre-scientific background with its hunger for identity and for the meaning of the whole—powers the university into a position of tremendous leverage and privilege—for better or for worse.

The power of modern knowledge is entangled simultaneously with archaic powers formative of self; there must be a knower, and this is a person who must use his or her knowing in the service of forming a self. So no wonder this knowledge appears numinous—secular and yet strangely religious too. The vague, engulfing, organismic sense of the background world—*that* sense of totality—can get confused with the aggregated totality promised by the secularized university and its tacit metaphysics.

Presumably, only the university dispenses the knowledge that grasps the world "as it actually functions." Thus it is invested with a stunning authority, a "modern metaphysics," as Bledstein puts it. The presumption of totalization entails polarization. That is, since only the secularized and professionalized university is presumed to dispense bona fide knowledge, all claims to know which arise from outside the university—or from sources unconnected with university researchers—tend to be stigmatized as specious and ungrounded. And since knowing authorizes an identity, other forms of knowing must seem to authorize only speciously.

Without the assumption of totality and closure the polarization would not occur. If *all* educating power and authenticity were not implicitly claimed by the university, other claims to educate would not have to be regarded as bereft of value. Undreamed-of vantage points and horizons of possibility would open around us.

The secular-scientific presumption to totality greatly hinders us from coming to grips with the prescientific and archaic background of our behavior, eclipsed but still active. Typically we do not understand the power of the identity needs which fuel research efforts which are only apparently impersonal and detached. Intellectuals in particular tend to think of the self as that which says "I" of itself, as that which exists in one point-instant after another until its last one ends it. This is self as ego, and it tends to think of the world it inhabits as encompassable in principle by the divisions of studies inherited from Cartesianism. I take this to be part of the significance of Bledstein's pungent but incompletely explained remark that professionalism is great for the ego but bad for integrity. That is, it excites the self to pretensions of groundedness and stability, but at crucial points cuts the person's connectedness to the actual background of his or her behavior in the world and compromises stability and integrity. One's ego and one's professional sense of self are fragile, in need of constant defense.

To be out of effective touch with the inherited background of behavior is to lack adequate support and guidance. It is to be torn loose from the pre-reflective matrix of one's life as an occasionally conscious human body, whose full resources for living include willing, feeling, and valuing propensities that fall beyond the scope of one's ability to say "I" of them at any instant, even perhaps of one's ability to acknowledge them. Obscured is the vital domain of mimetic engulfment in which we participate in the ongoing, habitual life of both ancestors and progeny, the depth of time and the possibility of renewal.

I must say more about the generic religious energy of identity-formation which the secular university never adequately acknowledges. In contrasting itself so robustly to the religious domain, it masks out the common ground that makes the contrast possible. All polarities, all contrasts, presuppose a kinship. It is absurd to say that shaving cream is not the number seven, or that listening to the voice of the Lord is not a screwdriver, because the pairs lack all common ground. But while this kinship is presumed when we make sense, it is concealed and distorted in the very act of presuming it. This is ironical! We are kept from recognizing the encompassing background of our own experience. It is concealed behind brilliantly lit dichotomies, divisions, and cemented arrays of alternatives.

Now what happens when the secular-scientific is conceived as contrasting with the archaic-religious—displacing it, indeed— and these two alternatives are conceived as exhausting the possibilities? One is *either* religious *or* scientific. This way of conceiving things prevents us from seeing the larger background which they both share—the generic religious energy that secretly feeds the secular mind and goads it to its presumption of transcendent importance and exclusive validity. The tendency of the religious option is to taboo and shun the secular. But it works the other way too. The tendency of the secular is to taboo and shun the religious, and secularism's obstinate transcendence and meaning-making must be bridled in democratic states by principles of toleration and religious rights.

When we look at what actually happens in the contemporary university, the account I have given tends to be confirmed: professionalized research contracts within itself and leaves unattended a vast stretch of personal roots in an obscure background—the roots of the researchers themselves. Professional, official—acknowledgeable—sources of authorization and development of self are overtaxed, and distortion of the ostensibly educational institution occurs. More of personal development is asked of one's professional life than it ever should be expected to give. It's as if foreign agents smuggled goods aboard a freighter at night. It is not designed to carry this tonnage; the captain does not know what he has to cope with.

Again, the success of seventeenth-century physics supplies the clue. This generated the beliefs that correct scientific methodology had been discovered once for all, and that the basic structure of the universe was already known. From this it followed that research fields could be ever more finely broken down, and that the inevitable progress of science would pile up ever greater discoveries of a detailed sort in each field. Under these conditions history tends to shrink to the recent past of the particular science's great accomplishments—"the state of the art"—and to current models of research prowess. The self tends to shrink to the point-instant ego. Only against this backdrop of assumptions can the faith placed in the boxes of numbers in professors' annual activity reports be understood; for example, "number of citations of one's work by peers in the field per year." It is assumed that intellectual contributions can be quickly and accurately assessed by peers, because it is assumed that difficult-to-grasp theoretical or experimental innovations are not apt to occur.

Against this backdrop of seventeenth-century physics we also see why interdisciplinary studies have not been stressed in the university. Since basic methodology and basic laws were assumed to be already fixed and understood, and the world was assumed to be homogeneous at bottom (at least insofar as it was physical, or "objectively" real), it followed that discoveries in various fields couldn't but fall into place with each other if anyone cared to look. Community need not be stressed, because it could be taken for granted.

Becoming apparent against this backdrop is the relative neglect of undergraduates and of the intergenerational task of passing on achieved modes of humanness and of reconstructing civilization: the never ending challenge of birth, growth, procreation, decay, death, as it presents itself anew to every generation. The professional self tends to be atomistic and egoistic, conceiving itself as existing in one point-instant after another—until its last instant ends it. What is the point of thinking about the endless cycles of nature, culture, the generations, those endless cycles of birth, death, rebirth? With the progress of civilization thought to be guaranteed by science and technology, every difficulty of human life tends to be viewed as a soluble problem. Perhaps medical science can indefinitely postpone or even eliminate aging and death. Once this optimism insinuates itself—on some abysmally precritical level of consciousness, of course—the meaning that all prior education had had is shaken. Why lead someone out to confront the question of what one is going to make of oneself in the few years allotted to one before death, if death itself seems, however dimly, to be eliminable?* Why concentrate great energies on the younger generation if the time may never come in which one will transfer one's concerns to them, live through them—because that it is the only hope for one's perpetuation that one could possibly have? Education searches for the meaning of life. But if life does not decisively end, its meaning is up for grabs.

Of course, for us today this dim faith holds on its reverse side the dim fear that life could decisively end at any instant—the other possibility opened by science and technology. Either way, the meaning of life and one's role in the perpetuation and destiny of the species becomes a highly problematical matter for today's intellectuals to handle. It is tempting to forget it.

---

*Jill Redner, "The Bomb and Cultural Nihilism: A Challenge to the Imagination," *Island Magazine* (Australia), Vol. 20, Sept. 1984.

The assumption seems to have grown that education for the meaning of life need not be one of the university's tasks. The idea sounds either too easy, too amateurish, or too hard. Insofar as it is feasible, it can be done at home or in the "lower" schools, it is thought. Emphasis in university teaching can be placed on one's younger colleagues in the research field, those who are apprenticed to the professors and who assist them, the graduate students. All emphasis is on the vanguard of science and technology as it moves inexorably along the track of linear progress, a track travelled on the graduate level. Undergraduates are to hang on if they can, and a great deal of their instruction can be turned over to graduate students. After all, scientific methods of research and discovery are already known, so we simply *instruct* the young in their use; the older young will pass on these methods to the younger young. Pre-university, or lower, education—insofar as it is thought about at all by university professors—is to be supervised by the social sciences and by their theories of human development (and the principles deriving from these studies are to be applied mainly by women, and by those "intellectually marginal men" in the lower schools).

It will be noted that the features of education I am discussing—and which we will increasingly realize that the university fails to instantiate—are those I have factored out as essential. Turn to that essential feature, self-reflexivity. In "The Will to Believe" (1896) William James lamented that truth was becoming merely a technical matter within specialized fields. Both things and the truth about them were being defined theoretically in terms of what the available arsenal of instruments and observations could turn up about those things. If characteristics do turn up as the theory predicts then this counts toward the truth of the theory. The danger is new provincialism: not to imagine beyond the current limits of theory and instrumentation in particular disciplines. For such inquiry abstracts those characteristics in the experiential field that are pertinent and ignores the rest, and since the rest, by definition, can only be "soft data," they are hardly worth noticing. The tendency is to ignore that they have been ignored—to clap oneself in the nutshell of one's theory, to line it with mirrors, and to count oneself king of infinite space (and even the bad dreams of which Hamlet spoke may be absent). Truth is only what works within one's scientific system. One is locked in a closet of "hard data," alienated from the encompassing matrix of one's very life.

This, again, is the fruit of seventeenth-century physics and its alleged autonomy. James is prophetic: widely in the university now truth *is* regarded as merely a technical matter (although the topic seldom becomes explicit). As long as one's theory is predictively useful within one's field, why inquire about the limits of this usefulness, or about possibilities of research which are eclipsed or occluded by the very success of that research? Or why inquire about the theorizer? Why inquire about his or her choice of method and subject matter, and what this choice presupposes and precludes? Or about what truth implies about our freedom and the sources of our dignity: that regardless of how repellent the truth turns out to be, we must be regarded as free to accept it, free to suppress wishful thinking and ego. What kind of animals must we be supposed to be, and what kind of mind as that in which we are caught up?

The educating act is a joint venture of interested and engaged participants. But given the current constricted vision of truth as a technical matter of crude pragmatic usefulness within a single field, this tunnel vision of what learning and knowing involves, professors must seek for confirmation and authorization within a narrow zone: contemporary peers in the particular profession nation-wide. Since only work which is broadcast nationally within a profession can be communicated to peers and evaluated by them, professors must look beyond the university much of the time if they are to be retained and promoted within it.

Inevitably, then, in large research universities most professors concentrate on publication and on those students who directly aid their research efforts—graduate students. Undergraduates are often experienced as a burden and an embarrassment, a reminder of tasks of personal development left unattended. A close observer notes, "the organization of faculties by academic discipline has progressively clouded, concealed, and virtually erased the faculty's sense of responsibility for the curriculum as a whole."*

Charles Muscatine, "Faculty Responsibility for the Curriculum," *Academe*, Sept.–Oct., 1985.

Quantity of professional publications becomes decisively important. As more professors publish more, what can count as "mainstream" in any of their specialties must shrink. This is inevitable if professors are to stay informed of the increasing volume being published in any given area. More of relevance is published than can possibly be read. As a specialty narrows, the difficulty of appreciating and transmitting a coherent view of the world and ourselves in it increases.

This has grave educational repercussions, for a person is not in the world in the way that a match is in a box. A match is a match wherever it is—in or out of its box—but a person is inconceivable apart from the manner in which that person appropriates, interprets, and makes the world his or her own. The breadth and depth of the person is a function of the breadth and depth of that person's comprehension and appreciation of the world. If this is pinched and mean, the person will be pinched and mean. And possessing a Ph.D. today is no guarantee that one possesses breadth and depth of person. It may suggest the opposite.

The printing press, xerox machine, and word processor threaten to shut down, through splintering and clogging, the very channels of communication which they first opened. There is wild proliferation of publications. Although it is difficult to get exact figures, there are about 100,000 scholarly journals, and about a thousand new ones appear each year. Journals are so numerous that only a few readers in a few fields can keep up with what is published even in their own fields. As a result, the quality of many of the journals and their editors is suspect. So one feels that the only recourse is to publish more and more—an infernal spiral that adds to the problem. Many professors are driven by anxiety to publish perpetually, and find no time for personal growth, for commemoration of personal or communal sources, for family or general citizenship; teaching easily becomes a chore.

Of course, in each field some journals are considered *crème de la crème*, or "mainstream," however restricted in focus most of them are. A few publications in these journals amount to sizable trophies. No matter how the situation is sliced, however, the result is the same: splintering of concerns, blocking of communication, failure of civilized conversation, and the clear possibility of arrested development of self. Gerald W. Bracey, of the Virginia Department of Education, writes in his "The World in Bits and Pieces,"

One of the things I do in my spare time is scan a hundred or so journals and summarize *four* or *five* articles from the hundred for another journal. This is small potatoes compared with the services that use full-time employees and electronic data bases to provide summaries, abstracts—bits. After all, there are now more than 40,000 professional journals of science alone, and researchers in search of truth (and fame and tenure) are pumping articles into them at the rate of one every 30 seconds, 24 hours a day, 365 days a year. How accurate are these abstract services? How selective? How accessible? And who controls access to the bits? Knowledge is power, yes, but in a world with too much information, bitting contracts both the past and the future. The result is hardly a greater appreciation of what Eastern philosophers call the Eternal Glorious Present.*

Teaching graduate courses directly fuels professors' publishing efforts. Class lectures may become publishable articles—or they may have already been published. Never mind that written and spoken communication in any language are immensely different from each other—at least as different as any two Western languages are in their written forms. Graduate students serve professors in many ways. Graduate courses require graduate students, of course, and their advancement as young members of the profession usually involves their teaching many of the undergraduate courses which the professors are too busy with research and graduate courses to teach. These are taught by students whose competence to teach—or even their interest in it—is seldom clearly established. (Of course, they may be better than the professors.) Christopher Jencks and David Riesman wrote in 1969 that no university they knew made a "systematic effort to supervise beginning teachers or give them help in doing a better job."** Today a few offer a practicum in teaching to graduate students. But at least the same number are so oblivious or

---

*Gerald W. Bracey, *Newsweek*, Oct. 28, 1985.
**Christopher Jencks and David Riesman, *The Academic Revolution*, second ed. (Chicago: 1969), p. 538.

contemptuous of undergraduates that no effort is made to determine if graduate student instructors sent into the classroom can
even communicate in the English language at a minimal level.
The very outrageousness of the practice tends to protect it. Who
could believe that it happens? Yet it does, and we can only affirm this and try to understand how it is possible.

Very recently cries of outrage have begun to have some effect. In the past, a few departments made some attempts, usually
nominal, to prepare graduate students for the classroom. In November of 1986 the first-ever national conference on the training
of Teaching Assistants was held at Ohio State University, and a
follow-up conference was held at Syracuse in November of
1988.* But considerable resistance is encountered on some campuses to even graduate-school-wide programs of training. Departments fear that the integrity of their discipline will be
compromised by mixing it with the mere techniques for dissem-
inating it, particularly if it is mixed with the generally despised
workings of the school of education. To assume that a discipline
is a pure, self-standing body of method and facts is to mask out
the human reality within which all research and communication

---

*I am indebted to Dean James Siddens for information on the ground-breaking
effort at Ohio State. In November of 1988, eighty-four representatives from
fifty-eight universities attended a follow-up conference at Syracuse University,
which exhibited its truly extraordinary program for preparing and guiding
teaching assistants. For example, each T.A. is asked to bring a sample lecture
and is video-taped and evaluated by a group of teachers, both senior T.A.s and
professors, deemed to be experts. Special attention is given to foreign T.A.s, and
a dramatic decrease in complaints about their language proficiency has occurred. On August 31, 1988, the first-ever graduate-school-wide program to
prepare T.A.s was held at Rutgers, with problems of the classroom vividly addressed. A follow-up on teaching and grading was held in October. A comprehensive manual was distributed, and a newsletter for the Teaching Assistant
Project inaugurated. The first sentences of the first edition attack the root
problem, "In a large university like Rutgers, life is often compartmentalized
and . . . can be very isolating . . . Even when departments share the same building, T.A.s in one department know very little about T.A.s in any other."
U.C.L.A. also has a substantial program for them. U.S.C. has distributed texts
and suggestions to departments, but has encountered resistance to a university-
wide effort. Such departmental parochialism is old and still widespread—an
aversion to mixing disciplines, or, more simply, "There's nothing to teaching—
there's nothing to be taught."

occurs, and the severity of this exclusiveness can only be explained if we postulate unacknowledged and archaic purification ritual—an inquiry I launch below.

Teaching undergraduates is required of most university professors at least some of the time. In no other profession is the training for, and the evaluation of, an essential function of professional life so slighted. Typically no systematic guidance in learning how to teach is *ever* provided. It is a hit or miss proposition, with some being naturally gifted, or others able to reproduce mimetically the skills of the talented professors they may happen to have had in their own student days. To read off a lecture to a class presents the same difficulties of comprehension—magnified—which the students have in reading any substantial material. Usually they need to be monitored constantly for the blank face, frequently motivated, their attention caught, reviews provided. Teaching skills are required—a working sense of what education is.

When professors teach undergraduates they are typically thrust before classes so large and polyglot that it is practically impossible to learn students' names, let alone what would move their hearts and minds. Literacy is gained by speaking and writing and getting intelligent response. But how much of a student's work can be seen in a class of 150? (The classes could be smaller, but there would be more of them, and less time for research.) The temptation to give students the tag-ends of one's energies is alluring—to read off a hastily prepared lecture (or a publishable paper), to *instruct* in some minimal way, not to work up a sweat in trying to *educate*.* That is, the professor is not motivated by the system to *try* to be a good educator. One is not typically hired or tenured for teaching, and the reason is that it is not evaluated and authorized by one's role models in the nationally based professional organizations—The American Historical Association, The American Chemical Society, The American Philosophical Association, etc. The very identity of one's

---

*President Harold Shapiro of Princeton asserts that faculty members "have to correct those papers . . . not just hand them back with [a letter grade] and no explanation." What should be taken for granted can no longer be. *Sunday Star Ledger,* Newark, N.J., Feb. 5, 1989.

scholarly life is involved here. Only published research can be authorized on the national scene, and only authorized research is real research. While teaching the Current Moral and Social Issues course I realized that I would not be rewarded, in any crass or measurable sense, for my pains. In the sciences, advancement depends as much upon securing grants to finance research as upon publication, and this may so consume a professor's time that teaching becomes a merely occasional or incidental activity, even for those on "instructional lines."** In most universities, the lighter the teaching load, the greater the prestige.

I imagine the reader gets the point. Professional certification by one's peers is only part of the university teacher's task. For most professors there looms also a mountain of work with students. And why do it when the university will probably not reward the scaling of the summit? Ah, you may say, teaching is intrinsically good and should not be thought valuable merely as a means to a reward conferred by others. True. And many of the best young university teachers are torn to psychical pieces in this double-bind: teaching well produces intrinsically good results, but this may make it impossible to publish sufficient research to achieve another intrinsically good result—his or her very life as a teacher in the university. It is a conflict of goods, a tragic and reprehensible situation designed to reduce normal, conscientious, intelligent adults to schizoid process.

The structure of the university is determined fundamentally by the specialized research projects of the senior professors and by the graduate programs of studies in their departments which are associated with these projects.* How this specialization of function affects undergraduates we have begun to see. Composing the great mass of students, they are the initiates in the

---

**The dwindling percentage of classes taught by full-time, presumably well prepared teachers, is revealing. In 1986 the portion of part-time teachers in colleges and universities was projected to be 58% (*Digest of Educational Statistics*, 1987, U.S. Dept. of Ed., p. 158). When teaching assistants are added, about two-thirds of the work force is either part-time or irregular, and, it is safe to say, receives less than half the total remuneration.

*See William Arrowsmith's classic articles, "The Shame of the Graduate Schools: A Plea for a New American Scholar", *Harper's Magazine,* March, 1966, and "The Future of Teaching", *The Public Interest,* No. 6, Winter, 1967.

mysteries of higher education. Not only are they not graduate students, but in most cases never will be. The effect is predictable. Implicitly and typically, they are treated as if they were preparing to become graduate students, specialists, young professional academics.*

Gestures—no more than that usually—are made toward a "balanced education." These usually take the form of "area requirements"; for example, six units of social science, six of natural science, six of humanities, and perhaps some smattering of foreign language; the old fashioned Chinese menu, a little of this, a little of that. The vast majority of students in my course were fulfilling humanities requirements, and took my class because it was classified by someone or some group as a humanities course, and because it met at a time and place they could fit into their schedules.

This is a great challenge to the teacher. And it is particularly young teachers who accept the challenge, for they are more energetic, and above all, more drawn to identify with students. They tend to pour themselves into teaching—often a fatal mistake, for they do not publish enough and are discarded by the universities in their middle or late thirties.

Teaching, understood as education, cannot be a fundamental value in the university as it is presently constituted. It cannot because a teacher's accomplishment *as* teacher in the classroom cannot be "replicated" nation-wide or world-wide (the ideal of science); it is not confirmable or authorizable by authorities "in the field." Young teachers who have identified over-zealously with the undergraduates placed in their care will sink into oblivion along with many of their students.

---

*There are some exceptions. Columbia University has maintained a substantial mandatory course for undergraduates in the history of civilization. There are other examples, but they remain exceptions. As Clifford Geertz writes, "The question of where the 'general' went in 'general education' and how we might contrive to get it back so as to avoid raising up a race of highly trained barbarians . . . is one that haunts anyone who thinks seriously about the intellectual life these days" (*Local Knowledge* [New York: 1983], p. 160.) Many first-year graduate students in *philosophy* appear already committed to a speciality, having assumed they already know what they need to know; as if they were post- rather than pre-doctoral; as if the history of philosophy and civilization were easily mastered and left behind (this the *mythos* of scientism).

The undergraduate moves as quickly as possible to that sec-ular bar mitzvah which is dubbed "declaring a major," which amounts in most cases to becoming hangers-on in the research activities of a department. After this watershed event, little time is left for "dabbling" in other fields. Although students may hear the words "the need to achieve a balanced education," may even be required to take some courses in different "areas," as I've said, typically no convincing rationale is supplied to them as to why this is so. The curriculum appears to be a game, a per-formance requirement, with no more point than has a balancing act in a peripheral ring in a circus. No convincing rationale is offered because the university has in fact adopted the structure of managed organization necessary to integrate functions in the newly interdependent, but utterly inorganic and dried-out tech-nologized society—it has adopted bureaucracy. There has been no analysis of knowledge which has discovered principles for or-ganizing the "knowledge factory" itself and the knowers who do the investigating and knowing within it. There is no place within the university to gather to discuss the concepts and presupposi-tions shared by all disciplines—about the capacities and obliga-tions of the knower, for example. As Michael Novack once put it, the university has been de-corticalized. Since the "substan-tive" fields cannot connect with each other, there must be an-other specialty called administering. "Procedural" matters pull away from "substantive" ones, and faculty meetings must be mainly concerned with procedural matters, for they are fear-somely complex and difficult—as if an organism *had* lost its brains, and each joint and muscle had to be coordinated with every other by a battery of computers hooked up to it from the outside. And I might add that the beast's chest, heart, and lungs have been eviscerated. There is little sense that the university is an educational institution, that education is a moral enterprise, and that its current practice lacks moral direction.

It is not just the teaching of undergraduates that is frag-mented, but the whole university community, a failure of orien-tation, of guidance of feeling and decision. The ultimate absurdity is that philosophy becomes just another professional specialty—the field that should provide the open space within which specialties can cross-fertilize, the field that should provide connective tissue. Philosophy occupies a small corner in a division under a dean. Typically the hard sciences fall under another, and the fine arts under still another. Ancient philosophers thought that theatre, for example, is more philosophical than is history, for it deals with what might happen, our possibilities, given that we are creatures of a certain sort, while history deals only with what has in fact happened. In theatre the community gathers to experiment with its own feelings, insights, problems, to discover perhaps what is good for us to be and do—truth about goodness. There is no open place within the university to raise this possibility, and even mentioning it seems vaguely preposterous. The university is filled with discord and dismay, a background noise so abysmal and constant that it is hardly noticed at all.

As with all bureaucracies, each department becomes so absorbed in its own immediate operations and their proliferating detail that it cannot try to comprehend the whole of which it is part. For the same reason, administrators become absorbed in their bailiwick of "procedural" rather than "subject matter" concerns—thus the putative scientific totality polarizes itself blindly in this case. But, of course, none of this can be said. The result is that nobody speaks convincingly for a balanced curriculum or an intellectual community (although someone at graduation ceremonies may do so).

There are a number of reasons for this silence. No academic willingly admits to being a bureaucrat; he or she is a professional who allegedly serves disinterestedly the end of the academic field in question, which is knowledge for knowledge's sake—at least in that field. Guilt is another reason for not facing things. Non-academic bureaucracies have some excuse for not trying to comprehend the whole system of which they are a part. After all, a distinctive body of knowledge forms only the cognitive base of their work, and they are busy in discovering the empirical detail of their superstructure and in employing it in trade.

But the university bureaucracy has no excuse for indulging in a vague faith in the whole system. We are supposed to be knowers. Guilt, as I say, prevents us from facing our situation—as do some other primitive psychological states which I discuss below. Since knowledge is the product, the superstructure and not just the cognitive base of the endeavor, an attempt ought to be made to comprehend—at least in sketch—the whole body of growing knowledge. For knowledge is intrinsically conceptual, and concepts tend to interrelate with other concepts, even if impediments to this growth are imposed from without; coherence and comprehensiveness are essential features of conceptual life—essential in some way to all mental life.

Even when knowledge can be said to be cumulative, it is not added *partes extra partes,* externally, as marbles to marbles, saucers to saucers. True, this may appear to be the case today. But consider: truths are asserted meanings which get verified. Truth can range only as far and as deep as the available meanings (we speak of concepts, but we might also speak of meaningful symbols, beliefs, images). And meanings imply or suggest one another. They ramify in many ways, but always internally. The concept of cause in twentieth century physics exhibits unique features and variations, but it overlaps at points with the concept as it is employed in other domains. Likewise with concepts of truth, individual thing, meaning, etc. However irregularly placed, changing, or tenuous these meaning-connections between different fields turn out to be, they operate at such a fundamental level that they constitute a sustaining webbing, rootage, matrix. Even striving for a unified view would produce already a degree of unification on the human level of fellow-feeling, collegiality. We must tone down John Henry Newman's totalizing rhetoric in *The Idea of a University,* but nevertheless the gist of it is fundamentally important:

An idea, a view, an indivisible object, which does not admit of more or less, a form, which cannot coalesce with anything else, an intellectual principle, expanding into a consistent harmonious whole—in short, Mind, in the true sense of the word.*

And referring to a new breed of academic administrator he adds, immediately, "they are, forsooth, too practical to lose time in such reveries." The conceptual structures of various academic departments, the webbings and rootages of meaning and sense,

---

*John Henry Newman, *The Idea of a University* (New York: 1947 [1852, 1859]), p. 393.

must tend to grow together to create a view of the world. To oppose it is to oppose the life of the mind. As we have seen, however, seldom is this rudimentary self-reflexivity achieved in university discussion. Because attention is confined to sharply circumscribed ideational zones, the necessary level of human concern and conceptual generality is not reached.

The life of the mind is inimical to the efficient functioning of the contemporary university. The contradiction goes that deep. How things might be changed will be discussed after the historical baggage which still burdens the university is detailed.

Let us look for a moment at "the new breed of academic administrator" Newman observed beginning to emerge in the newly formed secular university, the University of London, in the 1850's. This is the "manager," the one who no longer feels confident that the enterprise of knowing can generate within itself principles for guiding or governing the knowers. For many administrators today, this insecurity is disturbing conflict, for they are genuinely interested in scholarship, and in scientific and artistic creation. Some would like to be patrons of the arts and sciences. The bureaucratic splitting of functions in universities relegates them to being little more than fund raisers, accountants, custodians—or manipulators. This hampers their ability to function as educators and may blight their lives.

On the other hand, there is a growing body of administrators who have no idea what a university as an educational institution is or ought to be. They are wholehearted adherents of "rational management" and the manipulation of humans as if they were objects. They actually prefer the external relations and foreign modes of governance which have filled the ethical vacuum of the university: modes from the openly commercial, political, or military worlds. The ethical vacuum demands such persons, pulls them in. They are those who prefer to manage, manipulate, push and intimidate rather than to lead by moral or intellectual example—assuming they could do so. They are those who might operate in military or overtly commercial hierarchies, but—wary of the larger world—prefer to crack the softer wood of the academic personality. This sub-set of manager-administrators can be called thugs in tweeds, and when one thinks of the mind-

boggling frustrations of running an institution so rife with dis-
locations and contradictions, it is surprising that they are not
more numerous than they are.

Nietzsche was right, I believe. Typically we academic knowers do not know ourselves. By now we should begin to know
why. The university was old before it began, for it is organized
according to the dualistic principles of seventeenth-century physics. This science, and its offshoots, presumed to supply an explanation of the totality of experience. So we must believe that who
we are is to be explained by some field, or set of fields, within
the aggregated totality of scientific life. But eclipsed by the totality as it is enshrined within the university are archaic needs to
become an individual self through participating vitally in the
world, and these urges to transcendence move at a level of background experience more primitive and engulfed than the neat
abstractions of objective and subjective, matter and mind, culture and nature. These urges cannot be acknowledged within the
framework of thought inherited from the seventeenth century, so
acknowledgeable fields of learning and activity must be overtaxed in the formation of self. For beyond these fields what else
could there possibly be? (Can we place much trust in the humanities and their "mere expression of sentiment and opinion"?*)

This polarization of the acknowledgeable and the unacknowledgeable entails, I believe, that thinkers' professional activities are powered in significant part by unacknowledged energies

---

*Some professors construe the expression of opinion and sentiment in the hu-
manities as the will to political power. Lynne V. Cheney, chairman of the
N.E.H., writes in September, 1988, "Some scholars reduce the study of the
humanities to the study of politics, arguing that truth—and beauty and excellence—are not timeless matters, but transitory notions, devices used by some
groups to perpetuate 'hegemony' over others. . . . The humanities are about
more than politics, about more than social power. What gives them their abiding worth are truths that pass beyond time and circumstance; truths that, transcending accidents of class, race, and gender, speak to us all" ("Humanities in
America . . .," pp. 4, 7, 14, cited in chapter 3). One can insist that sometimes
ideas about what is human do involve deep cultural biases that do oppress
other groups (and also that the concept of "timeless truths" requires explication), but still agree with her major point that exclusive preoccupation with the
will to political power obscures the crucial question of truth in the humanities.

and burdened by hidden freight. Nothing like a viable identity is establishable by professional means alone, but the urge to establish it must be unleashed, so there must be something else at work which is not professional, but which cannot be acknowledged by the professional mind—given its totalizing pretentions. In addition to somewhat obscure socio-economic factors, there are very obscure archaic tendencies to form a viable individual self through purification ritual. We are not quite ready to focus on these primitive phenomena.

We must prepare ourselves for such an encounter, however. Each person's urge to comprehend the one world experienced through one experiencing of it springs from the strongest urge, which is just to be and to endure as one real individual. This urge is not satisfiable once and for all during infancy, or even during pre-university years of formal schooling. Gulfs do not divide stages of education. It is convenient to believe this, however, for then university professors need not dirty their hands with motivating students to learn difficult material or nursing them through emotional crises attendant upon reaching new levels of experiencing and comprehending the world. That can be left to the "lower" schools, or to the younger, deeply involved university teachers who "probably won't make it anyway."

Above all, it is convenient to believe this, for then we senior professors can convince ourselves that our own identity needs have already been met. It is lamentably easy for a "professional knower" to rationalize away and conceal his or her stunted personality and emotional infantilism, insofar as these hang on behind or within the professorial persona. When one thinks of it, what could be easier? We are professional rationalizers, and the power can be used for good or for ill.

The organizing center of the university ought to be the organizing center of the developing human person. The only viable form that university organization can take is that which facilitates the never fully predictable growth of human knowing and being. Since seventeenth-century philosophy and physics it has been impossible to speak of the organizing center. A person is split in two: the extended substance of the body, conceived to be like a machine, and the so-called non-extended substance which is the mind. As I've pointed out, the structure of the university reflects this dualism. It is the province of the administration to house and shunt about human bodies (as Robert Hutchins observed, the university is a collection of departments held together by a heating system), while it is the province of the professors to inform students' minds through such techniques as lectures. Almost inevitably this will be instruction rather than education—building-in rather than leading-out into self-confrontation—because, again, it is just the organizing center of the person—professor or student—that is no longer conceived.

The corollary of this is obvious. Since there must be some organizing principles of the university—in addition to the heating system—they must be those which are foreign to the educational process. Since even private universities are now dependent upon state or federal funds, account must be given of the money funneled to them, and in terms that accountants outside the university can understand: fractional numbers of human units processed per dollar spent. But these external standards of calculation imposed externally could never have carried the day so quickly without the collusion of external standards within.

A subliminal mood of conflict and disorientation pervades the university. Recall James's mordant words about the scientific nightmare: In the ordinary nightmare we have motives but no powers, while in the scientific nightmare we have powers but no motives. If intentions, emotions, and valuations are "merely subjective," uncertain events which cannot be measured and precisely located in the extended domain of objective Nature, then how can we have any confidence in them? But if we can have no confidence in them, what is to direct the use of our powers? But if we can have no confidence in the use of our powers, how can we have any rational motive to use them?

This is the schizzy atmosphere of unreality which hangs like a fog around contemporary materialism and our secular institutions. It is the feeling that beset me when I looked out from my office and saw what I took to be students but felt as if Descartes' devil might be deceiving me. In periods of slight derangement—in depression or extreme exhaustion—we may objectify a person's body in a certain way and wonder if there is any consciousness inside that body or behind that face. But it is not so much a rare phenomenon in one's personal history to which I wish to draw attention, but to an attitude and atmosphere taken for granted and unnoted, which pervades the whole society, and particularly the university.

We can be fairly precise about the dream-like contradictions and incongruities in our experience of the university. Elements which we think cannot coexist nevertheless do—for example, control and lack of control. Primitive drives for realization of self, the hunger for this most valuable of the intrinsic values, co-exist somehow with an ideology of impersonality and detachment, and the professed ability to know scientifically only about objects, not minds or subjects. On this latter view "self-realization" is a mere subjective feeling.

So everything is under control, perhaps, but because the person cannot give scientific credence to the experience of intrinsic value—and the excited willing of this value—which could give guidance to the control of one's life, everything is out of control. There you have it, the unhinged components of a dream.

Nietzsche is right about us knowers being unknown to ourselves, because so many of us have gone out of touch with the heart of ourselves—almost literally the heart, as the Greeks knew—our willing, valuational, and valorizing life, particularly as this links us in solidarity to the cycling generations and the cycling seasons of Nature. To fail oneself at one's heart excites the generalized desire for destruction. Nietzsche would "shoot out a shining star" to capture our devotion and striving. Yes, even the most constricted research shows tacit devotion to the ideal—to meaning, truth, integrity, responsibility. But its constriction belies the magnitude and openness of human beings, our ability to respect ourselves. We *are*—in large part at least—what claims our devotion.

Remnants of Cartesian dualism remain in contemporary popular and semi-popular consciousness: self cut off from other, mind from matter, present from past and future. If our primitive urge to comprehend the one world and to find our place within it were acknowledged, the underlying kinship which makes the dualistic contrasts possible would be evident. That is, scientific ambition would feel no need to take over tasks beyond its ability, and it would not be clogged with unacknowledgable generic-religious drive and affect. It would not be fanatical and obsessive, but more scientific. The self would not be isolated in a subjectivistically conceived present instant, the "closet of contemporaneity," cut off from the regenerating world, and our intergenerational opportunities and tasks.

This is hardly a bright prognosis for that inquiry with the young which is education, is it? For the ultimate assumption of all learning is that we must be free in principle to suppress ego and wishful thinking and to accept the findings of inquiry no matter how repellent they may happen to be. (And free to have patience, free to accept that some inquiries seem to be interminable.) This is the ultimate task of self-reflection: to fix us in that ideal which most fully develops us. But if ego is all the self can acknowledge of itself, how can it suppress it?

In "The American Scholar" Emerson gives a classic description: the scholar must "relinquish display and immediate fame," and in creating and discovering endure "the self-accusation . . . the frequent uncertainty and loss of time . . . the state of virtual hostility in which he seems to stand to society, especially to educated society." To control the ego more is demanded of the scholar than ego, but professional fields and associations offer merely equivocal help. Chances are that only if what is discovered is recognized by professionals already ensconced in an established "mainstream" will it be recognized at all. But the most creative insight and discovery consists precisely in daring to mix what has been kept separate, cutting across disciplinary lines, and then the failure to suppress ego and to endure solitude and rejection means the failure of scholarship itself.

It is natural to expect that the social sciences will explore the social and personal assumptions of all inquiry, those norms and ideals, those constraints upon ego, which knowers employ in their knowing. We would like the social sciences to supply a bridge connecting the purposeless realm of physical nature and the purposeful realm of consciousness. But Cartesian dualism is not so easily patched up or replaced, and the results of the social sciences must disappoint anyone who grasps the conceptual problems involved.

Why? The natural sciences are often able to isolate factors within their domains of study, and to discover necessary and sufficient conditions for a phenomenon, e.g., for the growth of a plant, a given degree of pressure in a steam boiler, the escape of a missile from Earth's gravitational field. Universal truths about necessary and sufficient conditions of very general phenomena are regarded as laws of nature. The social sciences have sought to emulate this undoubted accomplishment. But they encounter a grave problem which they are reluctant to face. Their subject matter is ourselves—social phenomena—and they seek to understand the necessary and sufficient conditions of these. But these phenomena include the activity of social science itself. So, to grasp their own activity, they must presume to grasp the necessary and sufficient conditions of the norms which guide this activity. But this grasping must be guided by these very norms. Social science must presuppose something about ourselves and our common intellectual heritage which it cannot prove, something for which it cannot demonstrate the necessary and sufficient conditions.

Let us spread out the argument. The natural sciences also use norms in setting out their subject matter, and these norms must be excavated and exposed at some point by somebody. But the norms do not figure in the subject matter itself. On the other hand, the activity of doing social science, and the norms that guide this activity, do figure in the subject matter of social science. Now, insofar as these researchers tend to emulate the natural sciences, they will try to find the necessary and sufficient conditions for these norms. We get the sociology of knowledge, even, of course, the sociology of sociological knowledge. But the self-reflexive search for the necessary and sufficient conditions of its own activity cannot achieve complete success, because this search *presupposes the validity* of the very norms of inquiry inherent in the activity to be explained—norms of evidence, valid inference, meaning, truth. Hence if the attempt is made to establish the necessary and sufficient conditions of these norms, their validity or necessity, it must seem to be question-begging.

The net result is that the question of the validity of the norms of the social sciences tends to get swept under the rug. All kinds of knowledge of the conditions of people's *beliefs* about standards and norms—how and why they hold these beliefs—may be claimed. But the crucial question of the truth or validity of the *norms employed by the social sciences themselves* is thrown into a twilight zone, a limbo. If scientific knowledge is only of necessary and sufficient conditions, and social science cannot establish the necessary and sufficient conditions of its own norms, then it cannot achieve scientific knowledge of its own norms and activities as a science. This embarrassing shadow tends to be generalized and to fall across the whole domain of human thought, feeling, and activity, as studied by social science. The intimate and integral activity of self which is valuation and responsiblity (and the historical tradition out of which it grows) must tend to be devalued.

The social sciences have fought shy of facing their own presuppositions, and, of course, this includes the ultimate and most troubling of all the presuppositions of all knowing, the master norm, the validity of which we must tacitly assume if we are to inquire at all into anything: that despite our animality and our conditioning—which does exist—we must nevertheless be supposed to be free in principle to accept the truth, no matter how repulsive it turns out to be on occasion—free to take responsibility.

In four hundred years no laws (in the natural scientific sense) of "human nature" have, as far as I know, been discovered by the social sciences. The possibility that the quest itself is fundamentally mistaken must arise in the minds of those who are not ego-involved in the social-scientific venture. We must consider the possibility that human freedom and responsibility do exist, that our subjectivity can transcend itself and escape total objectification and determination. Suggested is an inherent openness in the human condition which distinguishes us from the other animals, without severing all our ties with them.

This leaves a domain for the humanities to explore with some confidence: norms and ideals are the throbbing blood in our hearts, ingredient in our very meaning and vitality. What fields other than philosophy, literature, languages, and history could best investigate the self-reflexivity of consciousness and its implications for freedom and responsibility—the implicit norms and ideals embedded in our common heritage that guide all our inquiries?

What does professionalism—and egoism insofar as it is part of professionalism—mean for education in the university? Let us recapitulate the answer. The intergenerational task of teaching undergraduates must tend to be deemphasized, as we tend to be locked into a sequence of point-instants. Professionalism reinforces the self in its ability to assert its powers as an individual being at a particular moment, for it provides a social and material framework in which minimal competence can be almost instantly recognized and tangibly rewarded (although it may not be); that is, professionalism reinforces the ego. Submerged will be the traditional educational setting in which elders have a responsibility for demonstrating already achieved forms of humanness, and for working with the young so that we all can make sense of the inevitable stages of our lives. Since the professor no longer identifies in his professional role with his own personal ancestors, so he will tend not to identify himself as ancestor of the young or the unborn.

Most academics in research universities are caught up in the need for immediate authorization by established peers in the field. Yes, the professor may contribute to the ongoing body of knowledge, but without a deeply grounded self one must know *now* that one has done so. Caught on the linear track, the self as ego exists in one instant after another, until its last instant ends it. Are there chances for renewal or rebirth after retirement?— for many, a question far too personal. Not identifying with the young means not identifying with what is young and uncertified in one's self, one's own possibilities, and blocks the chance to be renewed or reborn through one's students.

Our ahistorical society compounds the problem in many ways. Obviously, many students are caught up as well in the instant, in short-term gratification, consumerism. They pose a great challenge to the teacher's moral will and personal energies. Can one, as I tried to do in my class, create community on the spot? It will be particularly difficult for the professor to do if identity needs are not acknowledged, and he or she is engaged in a denial of their range and depth, anxiously hoping that professional recognition and authorization will alone form a vital self. In becoming mimetically engulfed in one's authorizing group, one easily loses awareness of archaic attitudes, particularly aversive exclusions of the professionally uncertified, the unwashed. And one goes out of touch with regenerating Nature. In a literal sense, one is demoralized.

Elizabeth Kubler-Ross writes, "There is no more spirituality left. I mean the inner, deep knowing where we come from."* Caught up mimetically in a mentality of egoism and linearity, we are tempted to construe talk of historical depth and sources as merely that which is revealed by records. But those who have accepted the role of educator, of one who draws out students— and oneself—to confront the question, "What am I going to make of myself?" cannot in good conscience accept this notion as exhausting our historical possibilities. For it does not touch our capacities to maintain contact with our "ever present origins" in "mythological consciousness" as Jean Gebser puts it so well—our inner life, if you will, as beings who are constituted in and through immemorial presences.** To be in touch with the "mythological" past is a condition for projecting in imagination a "mythological" future, a compelling story of self and others, a "bright star" upon which we can fix our devotion, and under which we can freely and responsibly subordinate mere ego and become origins ourselves.

In Plato's *Phaedrus,* Socrates expresses fears of writing, because persons will rely upon it and cease to use their memories, their inner selves:

If men learn this, it will implant forgetfulness in their souls; they will cease to exercise memory because they can rely on that which is written, calling things to remembrance no longer within themselves.

Needless to say, Socrates would be doubly or trebly apprehensive if he were alive today, for one's Vita and Activity Report, which mainly are sequential records of one's writings, threaten to replace the person who accomplished what is recorded on them. In sending my Vita, I send a paper surrogate of myself. Indeed, I—Bruce Wilshire—find it difficult to remember what is accurately recorded there as what I have done. And I am not very happy reading it, for this threatens to freeze me in the too recent past or in a tunnel-like present. My thought about life threatens to lose touch with my life.

---

*Elizabeth Kubler-Ross, "Lighting Candles in the Dark", *Woman Spirit,* Spring Equinox, 1982, p. 46.
**Jean Gebser, *The Ever Present Origin,* trans. by Barstad and Mickunas, (Athens, Ohio: 1985 [1949, 1953]).

Over sixty years ago, A. N. Whitehead wrote prophetically of the professionalization of higher education, and warned of an eccentric emphasis being placed on written products:

Mankind is as individual in its mode of output as in the substance of its thoughts. For some of the most fertile minds composition in writing . . . seems to be an impossibility. In every faculty you will find that some of the more brilliant teachers are not among those who publish. Their originality requires for its expression direct intercourse with their pupils. . . . Such men exercise an immense influence; and yet, after the generation of their pupils has passed away, they sleep among the innumerable unthanked benefactors of humanity. Fortunately, one of them is immortal—Socrates. Thus it would be the greatest mistake to estimate the value of each member of a faculty by the printed work signed with his name . . . there is at the present day some tendency to fall into this error; and an emphatic protest is necessary against an attitude . . . which is damaging to efficiency and unjust to unselfish zeal.*

These words recall us to the dateless oral and communal sources of our civilization, and these bind us together intergenerationally. To return to them is to regain what is young and uncertified within us, and to return to the young who are entrusted to us. Whitehead writes, "The justification for the university is that it preserves the connection between knowledge and the zest of life, by uniting the young and the old in the imaginative consideration of learning."

The professional educator cannot in good conscience separate completely his professional role from his personal relationships to students. William James's most considered words for teachers were that they project themselves empathically, so that they could understand their students' lives as the immediately felt ongoing unities that the students experienced themselves to be. Professors must place one foot in the ethical if they would contact the pedagogical. Without this there is no moral guidance for the moral task of education. The ten-year-old child driving the family car is not an overdrawn metaphor.

---

*A. N. Whitehead, "The Aims of Education and Other Essays", in *Alfred North Whitehead: An Anthology*, ed. Northrup and Gross (New York: 1955), p. 135.

There is a delicate balance that must be struck here between essential features of the educating act. On the one hand it is a joint venture which unites the young and the old. On the other hand it involves the special authority and responsibility of the teacher: respect for the student entails respect for the student's roots in the past which the student may not be able to comprehend, and respect for the student's possibilities, some of which may also lie beyond awareness. So the relationship is an ethical one; nevertheless, there cannot be perfect reciprocity. The teacher holds an advantage in power, and can take advantage of the student in ways which the student may not be able to understand. Hence, for example, consent by the student to sexual overtures made by the professor cannot in itself legitimate such practices.

The ethics of teaching at all levels is rooted in the depths of self and in the depths of time. This is the matrix of our common life and the source of worth, and to lose contact with it is to become desiccated and disconnected. To accept a professorship is to accept a caring role—whether one explicitly professes it or not (or even if one denies it). Professional conduct cannot be neatly partitioned from one's personal responsibilities to care for others just insofar as they are persons—not just as housings for teeth, or bodies understood as mechanisms, or as parties to a legal contract, or as minds with bodies attached. For far too long the notion that "the university is a community of adults" has been used to rationalize sloppy and uncaring relationships to students and to demean our role as teachers. The old convention of *in loco parentis* has been abandoned, but no new sense of our responsibility for students (or of their responsibilities) has replaced it.

I believe that the truth—repulsive as it may be to certain professionals—is that there is a parental aspect to teaching, perhaps a maternal aspect. Cries Faust,

Where are the nipples, Nature's springs, ah where
The living source that feeds the universe?

Goethe can be called a classical thinker, for he strove for balance in an age which eccentrically emphasized dissection of experience into controllable parts. He has the paradigmatically modern intellectual, Faust, find remedy for desiccation and disorientation in *das Ewigweibliche,* the eternal feminine. This question will be taken up later.

We turn now to the professionalization of academic philosophy. If this field can be professionalized, any can be. It is a test case for our ability to understand the process. Philosophy had been deeply involved in its own long history. That this was, nevertheless, largely forgotten under the pressures to professionalize signals their capacity to fix us in a suffocating point-instant present.

The university is in crisis, and in significant part because of our proud professionalism.*

That there is a crisis is, of course, not news. Reports of this come from the Carnegie Foundation for the Advancement of Teaching, The National Commission on Excellence in Education, The National Endowment for the Humanities, The Association of American Colleges. "The authors of these reports all decry the lack of curricular coherence, the threat of excessive vocationalism, hyperspecialization of vocabularies, faculty self-indulgence, political self-interest, and fanatical departmental allegiances" which have eroded liberal learning (Calvin Schrag, "Involvement, Integrity, and Legacy in American Liberal Education," International Association of Philosophy and Literature, Seattle, May 3, 1986).

PART TWO

Academic Professionalism and Identity: Rites of Purification and Exclusion

V

A Specimen Case of Professionalizing a Field of Learning: Philosophy

Making sense of things is an organismic activity. Items in any interpretation gain their meaning from the whole context, from the way the whole feeds into the items within it; and, conversely, the whole is meaningful because of the meaning-contributions of each of its parts. We say that the university is a knowledge factory, that is, it produces assertions or beliefs that are proved by some means to be true. But, as we have seen, before truth can be achieved meaning must be created; only meaningful beliefs and assertions have a chance to be true. Another way of saying this is that all the disciplines in a university must employ concepts, and some are so basic that all fields employ them in some form, explicitly or implicitly: again—meaning, truth, context, relationship, explanation, individual thing, cause, effect, self, other, past, present, etc. (this does not commit us to an absolutism of unchanging concepts).

The division of the university into distinct departments, each facing away from the university toward a national professional organization, carries on its face a danger to organismic relationships, and hence to learning (which is not to say that the mainstream never makes important discoveries). If the university today is a whole in any sense, it is that of mere aggregate. Can this be an *educational* institution?

I have not drawn any hard and fast line between teaching and research. The good teacher is simply the good learner or researcher who can communicate the excitement of this to students. Learning is limited in the rigidly departmentalized university because illumination achieved in one area is apt to get sealed

off from others. If allowed to freely propagate, conceptual innovations in physics on the nature of individual realities may trig-
ger breakthrough insights in psychology on the nature of
individual persons, or the influence may be the other way
around. Often this conceptual illumination comes in the form of
innovative metaphors drawn from widely scattered areas of experience. Thus, for example, physiologists could not see that the
heart was a pump until engineers had succeeded in constructing
mechanical pumps. Then physiologists could see that the heart
was *like* a pump. John Dewey employed art and artistic metaphors to prime students to see hitherto hidden facets of natural
processes. Werner Heisenberg recalls eloquently how the great
physicists early in our century employed daring, apparently fan-
tastic means to break out of the conceptual ruts of seventeenth-
century physics and to make new sense of things: outings in the
high mountains, playing music together, writing poetry, etc.*
Perhaps the strange and slippery phenomena showing up in laboratory and telescope could be grasped if the scientists could
imagine likenesses or metaphors hitherto unimagined.

Indeed, a new picture, a new likeness, of reality emerges
from twentieth-century physics: dances of waves of energy replace billiard balls colliding and forcing each other around.
Would it be more illuminating of our situation to picture ourselves as superimpositions of waves—nodes and dances—in a
field of energy?

Now, this is a quick, panoramic view. But it suggests the
danger of professionalizing academic fields, and this danger
should have drawn some attention. That it has drawn so very
little in over one hundred years indicates how tremendously
powerful is the urge to professionalize and to claim a field for
one's own group. A group claims an identity, powers of mimetic
engulfment mold the identities of its members, and before one
knows it the group pulls away from others, and parochialism
disguised as "science" and "scholarship" prevails.

---

*See Werner Heisenberg's *Physics and Beyond: Encounters and Conversations;*
also Elting Morrison's acute review, *New York Times,* Jan. 17, 1971. For the
role of metaphor in scientific discovery, see I. Bernard Cohen, *Revolution in
Science* (Cambridge, Mass.: 1985).

The dangers of parochialism in academic professionalism are particularly manifest, yet they have been little heeded by academics themselves. In the case of other professions, there are usually some means to test their authority. After all, they operate in their superstructures to produce products which either work or not—as this is decided in the everyday world of common sense. Even the medical profession cannot exercise unlimited control on what is defined as health or cure. But the academic profession, as it is professionalized into nearly autonomous university departments, is more nearly impregnable than is the medical, because it defines both base and superstructure. Since the product of the university department is knowledge itself—and knowledgeable persons—the department presumes to define the quality of the product produced, whether it be research or what passes as an educated person. The danger is an aversive isolation from other professional groups.

Of course, science is a worldwide activity and one not limited to universities. Since the natural sciences do make demonstrable progress along certain fronts, one can expect that parochialism will be scotched in these fields at some point. But since neither the humanities nor, I think, the social sciences operate in this self-correcting and progressive context, ideologies will periodically stifle free inquiry. And we know that there are epochs, fads, and "paradigm shifts" even in the natural sciences, which can be construed as phenomena of shifting mimetic engulfment.

Academia creates a façade of self-serving ideology which is extremely difficult to deconstruct and look behind. But we must try to do this if we would discern the hidden background of the academic institution which almost completely controls its operations in spite of its front.

The power of the urge to professionalize looms before us when we confront the professionalization of philosophy. For if the field which has traditionally known no bounds, raised all the questions which humans have wanted to raise about the universe and our place within it, regardless of the apparent hopelessness of answering them—if this field can be professionalized, any can be. How could it have happened? We will find that the confidence in professionalism was so great because we all have been caught up in the new "mental set," the mode of totalizing our experience, or presuming to do so, by analyzing it into an aggregate of discrete parts: any grouping of any desired size can simply be built-up, calculated—perhaps produced by technology— the new myth of modernism. Science can, in principle, replace all earlier modes of understanding the world.

Laurence Veysey writes of the failure of the academics involved in the rise of the university to bring their assumptions to critical awareness:

What one sees as one looks at the leading campuses toward the end of the nineteenth century is a complicated but rather standard series of relationships springing to life before one's eyes—yet practically everyone at the time taking the fundamental choices for granted. The lack of self-consciousness that was displayed over the new organization as it came into being points directly toward a predominance of latent elements, rather than manifest intentions, in bringing it about.*

This, we will see, applies also to most of the philosophers of the time—a momentous fact. For philosophers are just those who are supposed to specialize in reflecting upon their assumptions. We expect them to be paradigmatically self-reflexive, educated. If we can understand how the urge to professionalize overrode the activity of self-reflexivity inherent in the philosophical enterprise, we will grasp how mightily the urge can distort inquiry.

It has been typical of philosophical thought to be intimately involved in its own history (some would say incestuously involved). At least this has been true historically—until the recent decades of this century. The failure of self-reflexivity in the emerging group of professional philosophers is, then, simultaneously, a failure of reflection upon their own history and roots. Our astonishment increases when we realize that this history is directly relevant to understanding the situation in which the modern, professionalized university arose. One might think that

---

*Laurence R. Veysey, *The Emergence of the American University* (Chicago: 1965), pp. 267–68.

when philosophers were faced with the opportunity to professionalize they would have reflected upon their historical situation. Great modern philosophers had made gallant attempts to
do this—Leibniz, Spinoza, Kant, Hegel, even Descartes in his
own way—and John Dewey continued to do it. They knew that
if science could not be integrated in some way with the traditional background, the sacred matrix in which we are linked
with the generative and regenerative energies of the cosmos, we
would become dislocated and lost. Obviously, this has the greatest significance for education.

What Descartes had begun, however, could not really be
stopped or even controlled. He began to split off philosophical
thinking from its traditional involvement in religious, cultural,
and historical preoccupations. His notion of pure reason, technical and mathematical, is a revolutionary departure, and paves
the way for the masking of the background and for secularizing
and "scientizing" thought of all kinds.

This splitting of philosophy from its traditional matrix went
hand in hand with the partitioning of the world into sacred and
secular which was occurring rapidly in Protestant Christianity.
As Alasdair MacIntyre puts it,

Luther, like Calvin, bifurcated morality; there are on the one hand ab-
solutely unquestionable commandments which are, so far as human
reason and desires are concerned, arbitrary and contextless; and on the
other hand, there are self-justifying rules of the political and economic
order.*

Max Weber pointed out, with particular reference to Calvinism,
that this secularizing bifurcation was integral to capitalism and
its conception of the mundane world lying ready to be processed
and exploited—the "invisible hand" of laissez-faire economics,
and "social Darwinism." Before they took the step to professionalize, few academic philosophers reflected upon the explosive
emergence of secularism and specialism and their ethical consequences for ordinary life. At the turn of our century many philosophers were focused so narrowly on technical issues internal
to philosophical "systems" that they forgot the archaic back-

---

*Alasdair MacIntyre, *A Short History of Ethics* (London: 1968), p. 196.

ground of experience, and our mythical and even magical involvement in sacred creative and recreative energies—the obscure connection between the secular and the sacred that had held on for four hundred years and which the great modern philosophers had tried to deal with in some way. For example, they lost touch with Kant's assumption that an ethics of pure, formal reason was possible, a conception of the good will, but always against the silent background of the holy will of God. It was an odd connection, to be sure: one in which the sacred and the secular existed partitioned from each other. Many philosophers, however, could not even imagine this connection, because they were already encased within the secular side, primed for professionalization and specialization.

Only a stray intellectual, such as Nietzsche, could hear the buzzing of the sacred behind the partitions, and he existed in beleaguered and bitter rebellion against academic philosophy as it had fast become professionalized (in a sense) in Germany. William James was also bitter—and apprehensive. However, his response was startlingly ambivalent. For unacknowledged energies of identity formation lie hidden behind the partitioning of secular thought. The new identity of professionalism taps into them furtively. Using them and denying them, it must be ambivalent and out of control. We will return later to James's troubling response.

But let us look first at the easily chroniclable events.

Eleven professors of philosophy, headed by J. E. Creighton of Cornell, met in New York City in late 1901, and decided that a philosophical association of national scope would be formed and called The American Philosophical Association. At its first annual meeting in 1902, Creighton was elected president and stated its purpose. Philosophy, once so important, had been eclipsed by the natural sciences. If it was to compete it would have to make progress, as science does, and for this it would have to find its own standard method of inquiry that could involve philosophers in cooperative endeavor. Scientists cooperated and added measurable increments to their work; philosophers must emulate this.

Over a century earlier Kant had noted the momentous and often startling progress of the natural sciences and had called philosophy's failure to make demonstrable progress a scandal. By the opening years of the century this had become an insuperable embarrassment for many philosophers. But what could the standard philosophical method possibly be? Inevitably Socrates would be recalled. Much of his work consisted in defining fundamental terms. Obvious stumbling blocks for philosophy were the vague and ambiguous terms which so frequently appeared in philosophical discourse. Even when thinkers used the same terms, the meanings ascribed to them were often slightly or very different, and the parties talked past each other.

So it was assumed that good philosophical method must include a procedure for clarifying terms. It seemed self-evident to Creighton and his associates that this method can best be exercised in annual meetings of accomplished thinkers. When a philosopher merely reads another's work, or hears about it secondhand, there is danger that terms intended in one sense will be taken in another, and that the misunderstanding will go undetected and uncorrected. But when the other's views are "reinforced by the living personality" of that thinker—and when exchange on the spot is possible, indeed demanded—these views are not nearly so apt to be misunderstood—or ignored. Thus Creighton put it in his presidential address, "The Purposes of a Philosophical Association."*

To doubt that annual meetings of philosophers in their own professional association is a self-evident good may seem unnecessarily contentious, obtuse, perhaps churlish. No doubt some misunderstandings of some key terms have been cleared up this way. Nevertheless, we should remind ourselves that most of our assumptions are latent and unexamined—unquestioningly secular. This means first and foremost that we simply assume that progress in any field is possible, and that it can be brought about by calculation and measured in immediately applicable and demonstrable ways. We must forcibly rouse ourselves if we

---

*Reprinted in *Proceedings and Addresses of the American Philosophical Association*, Nov. 1986.

are not to be captured by the brilliant focus of our endeavors and lose all sense of the residual and obscure background of human history and mimetic engulfment which haunts all our-projects. Even when we easily recall that paradigmatic philosopher Socrates, we will likely get a jolt. For he tenaciously engaged other philosophers in person, and had masterful powers of clarification of terms. Yet his discussions were often indecisive, particularly those with the professional "dialecticians" and orators, the sophists.

With the greatest emphasis, Socrates and Plato distinguished between kinds of personal exchange between thinkers. There is *dialectic* in the true sense, in which the parties have subordinated demands of ego, and desire to discern what is meaningful and true in what the other says, if meaning and truth exists there at all and can finally be coaxed out. On the other hand, there is *eristic,* in which the consuming desire is to overwhelm the other and to secure what must appear at the time to be a victory of wits and argumentative skill.

The clear implication is that there is something profoundly difficult about clarifying the philosophical terms in any discussion. Brilliance and wit are not enough. Other traits are required: exceptional patience, respect for others' capacities and intentions, and love of meaning and truth. Socrates repeatedly raises the "what is" question. What is justice, truth, substance, self, goodness? No ready and adequate definitions lie at hand, nor can one in good conscience simply make one up, stipulate it. The thinker must struggle and squirm to get inside the topic as it actually presents itself in experience, and to turn it in various ways to get better angles on it, a more comprehensive idea of what its various "sides" and "nooks and crannies" are. And often one must admit inadequacy—even with the best of intentions in a likeminded community.

Not all philosophers at the turn of the century had forgotten the peculiar difficulties of achieving agreed-upon clarity in basic terms, and the ethical demands made upon "pure" theoreticians. Of those invited to join the fledgling philosophical association in 1901, William James declined, responding tersely,

I don't foresee much good from a philosophical society. Philosophy discussion proper only succeeds between intimates who have learned how to converse by months of weary trial and failure. The philosopher is a lone beast dwelling in his individual burrow. Count me *out!**

There is a remarkable synchronicity here. In the very year in which philosophers were organizing into a professional group which aimed to emulate science and set commonly accepted standards of progress, James had, so to speak, fallen out of secular consciousness altogether. On the verge of his sixtieth year, ill and confined to his bed most of the time, James wrote his Gifford Lectures, published as *The Varieties of Religious Experience* in 1902. Trained as a scientist he had gone on to philosophy, for he was vexed by basic concepts and terms which he could not define and get straight. He had conversed in loving struggle with intimates—which included himself—not just for months but for years, and had come to the point of throwing into question all the inherited atomism and psycho-physical dualism.

James was striking into a level of experience that was presupposed by the received modes of scientific objectification and abstraction, but which was covered over by them. Even as religious institutions began to crumble beneath and around him, he was probing into the nearly eclipsed archaic and sacred background of experience—that area in which we cannot be conceived as individual minds neatly and snugly encapsulated inside neatly individuated bodies, nor the bodies conceived as neatly encapsulated within nicely defined groups. It is the area in which conversions occur, and in which we are radically vulnerable and precarious, open to the world around us. The area cannot yet be focused clearly, if it ever can be, and the very meaning of one individual self is thrown into question.

In other words he was into the zone in which professional expertise operating with standard methods of clarification in an atmosphere of personal and emotional detachment was radically premature and obfuscatory; it would produce "premature crystalization." He was well aware of how untimely and unpopular his ruminations were, and at one point in particular in *The Varieties* aimed trenchant words at the heart of professionalism:

---

*Quoted in Edward I. Pitts, "Ideals and Reality: The Early Years of the American Philosophical Association," p. 2. This is excerpted from his dissertation, Pennsylvania State University, 1979, and was delivered as a paper at the Society for the Advancement of American Philosophy, 1980.

Religion, whatever it is, is a man's total reaction upon life. . . . Total reactions are different from casual reactions, and total attitudes are different from usual or professional attitudes. To get at them, you must go behind the foreground of existence and reach down to that curious sense of the whole residual cosmos as an everlasting presence, intimate or alien, terrible or amusing, lovable or odious, which in some degree every one possesses. This sense of the world's presence . . . is the completest of all our answers to the question, "What is the character of this universe in which we dwell?"*

The meaning of professionalism has never been better captured, I think, captured through contrast. The professional is encased in the "foreground of existence" and attempts to mask off "the curious sense of the whole residual cosmos . . . which in some degree everyone possesses." Concealed are sacred or quasi-sacred bondings, fusions, energies.

James was groping in an area quite foreign to Creighton, and it cannot be said that this professor of philosophy from Cornell was superficial. Over and over in his presidential address we are struck by the apparent probity and balance of his views. While he advocates the "inductive method" in philosophy and the emulation of science, he notes immediately that he is not construing this in the narrow sense. Philosophers operate on a peculiarly general level of experience and seek to clarify the terms presupposed by all rational endeavor; their "induction" is not the fruit of experimental intervention into Nature. Notice the sophistication and balance when he affirms,

The abstract view of nature as a whole which the physical naturalist furnishes, has to be humanized by philosophical interpretation, *which construes the facts differently,* finding in nature the congeniality with the mind of man through which alone it is intelligible. . . . Just as philosophy humanizes the physical facts by viewing them in relation to mind, so it also objectifies subjective facts by viewing them as functions through which the individual realizes his unity with nature and with his fellow-men.

This is truly sophisticated. We see in Creighton's views no crass scientism. Nevertheless, he assumes that basic terms—"the mind", "the individual", "the facts," and, above all, the dual-

---

The Varieties of Religious Experience (New York: 1958 [1902]), p. 45.

izing terms "objective" and "subjective"—are detached from a religiously conceived background in experience, and their clarification by "scientific" philosophers can proceed through professional means.

James is beyond this point and into a much more radical questioning of individuality, and of the very meaning of objectivity and subjectivity. He is supposing that our basic topics of discourse must be stabilized and focalized ever anew within the archaic, moody, sacred background of experience—"the curious sense of the whole residual cosmos." This is an immense difference between the two professors, but the extent of it does not show up for decades, not until professionalism has run its course and shown its limits.

The drive to professionalize philosophy was fueled by the belief that there could be a single correct method of inquiry—with clarification of meaning playing a key role—and that science could be emulated at least with respect to a standardized language and measurable increments of progress. A series of specific problems could be identified and solved one by one. It was impossible for this drive to achieve great success before the 1930s, because major thinkers of great individual talent spilled over into the twentieth century from the nineteenth: Charles Peirce, James, Josiah Royce, Dewey, Whitehead, and younger thinkers such as William E. Hocking and G. H. Mead. In a very real sense they were all amateurs. They had been formed outside a professional milieu. Only some had earned the ultimate professional certification through philosophical training—the Ph.D. degree. Peirce, James, and Whitehead had been trained in the sciences or in mathematics. None would have taken the greatest pride in "incontestable expertise" nor in mastering a standard method of inquiry. All were very imaginative, and, as we shall see, a crescendo of creativity in philosophy occurred in the 1920s.

Nevertheless, the drive to professionalize continued in the first three decades of this century and the yearly meetings of the A.P.A. grew. Reporting as a committee chairman in 1917, A. O. Lovejoy stated the professional ideal:

Your committee . . . believes that one of the principal functions of this society is to bring about a genuine meeting of minds upon actually *identical* points of the logical universe, or to come as near to that result as possible; in other words, to promote the coherent, methodical, and mutually intelligible and constructive discussion of common problems.*

Again, it may seem unnecessarily contentious to doubt that this is a self-evident good. After all, there *is* confusion often enough, and why shouldn't we remove it if we can? Lovejoy had detected, he believed, thirteen senses of the word "pragmatism," for example. But note that there is unclarity in the very call he makes for the methodical achievement of clarification. What does "actually *identical* points of the logical universe" mean? Take "logical universe." Does this mean that our systems of definitions and discriminations in our logic can be made to fit precisely the structure of the physical universe, so that both "systems" have the same intelligible form—and that hence the universe can be called "the logical universe"?

Regardless of what Lovejoy himself meant exactly, it *is* this sense which professional philosophers increasingly came to assume. They believed that topics and relationships picked out by analytic thought allied with science—its sorting out—could coincide with the structure of the universe itself, and could do so best when detached from the background, "the curious sense of the whole residual cosmos."** In picking out "actually identical points of the logical universe" we could become certain of exactly what all of us were talking about in the actual physical universe, and how in general to talk about it.

A mathematical logic was created which links predicates, concepts, *sorts* of things—a sort being a set of individuals which share properties necessary and sufficient for membership, each member counting as *one* of that *sort*. Once this logic is set up, it is thought to be autonomous. Its terms are given a universal sense—allegedly impersonal and non-psychological—which correlates them one to one with items in the world. Allegedly, meaning is a purely objective relation between symbols and a

---

*Quoted in Pitts, pp. 2–3.
**See Bertrand Russell's oft-reprinted "Logic as the Essence of Philosophy" (also his "Descriptions" and "What there Is" in, e.g., R. Ammerman, *Classics of Analytic Philosophy* [New York: 1965]). The next few pages will be of interest mainly to philosophers. Those reading primarily for the broader issues of education and the university may prefer to skip forward a bit.

purely objective reality. The philosopher need no longer consider the aculturated body-self's sensuous imagination unpredictably carving out topics for perception—novel sorts and their novel instances. This activity falls beneath the purity and universality of logic.

For thousands of years philosophers have been concerned with identifying things by identifying the conditions which single them out, individuate them. Aristotle developed his theory of the essential characteristics of different species of "substances." For example, all humans share the traits of animality and rationality, and once this species has been sorted out from the rest, all one need do to pick out one individual human is to point at one and only one instance of the species or sort—this one here and not that one there. Every *this* is a this some*what*.

Many philosophers, ancient and modern, have realized that the ability to pick out and perceive individuals is only as good as the ability to conceive or imagine *sorts* of beings which may *have* individual instances. But it is a realization easily forgotten in the press of life, for if sorts are unimagined, but do exist and have instances, these individuals will not, of course, be recognized. Insidiously, as if caught in a hypnotic spell which precludes recognition, nothing is left to disturb the "completeness" of one's mapping of the world.

But philosophers could not simply revive Aristotle's scheme in which philosophy was the master science which superintended and ordered all specialized inquiries. They were separated from Aristotle by the irruption of natural science into dominance in the seventeenth century. They could hope for a *formal* logic merely, with the substance or *content* of findings about the universe to be provided by science. *Which* sorts have physical instances is decided ultimately by science. That is, philosophers could grapple only with problems of how implications between statements occur (how their formal structure, regardless of their content, guarantees that if one or more are true, another must be), or—most important for our study—philosophers tried to determine the most general conditions for terms to refer to unitary topics or individuals of any sort, whether physically real or not.

Philosophers gave up a great deal, but they gained a measure of autonomy; they could claim a special expertise and hope for respect from the public (Creighton was very concerned about that). Philosophers accepted—at least implicitly—seventeenth century psycho/physical dualism and deferred to the sciences. Philosophy would leave to the hard sciences knowledge of the "external" or objective world, and to the humanities the "expression" of the "inner" or subjective realm. But by way of compensation philosophy would have its own domain that no other field would be tempted to steal, not because it seemed so ambitious, but because of its extreme formalism, abstraction, crystalline purity, and Mandarin exactitude. Philosophy would be purely and definitively itself because wholly other from everything else. In its craving for definitiveness and exactness, philosophy was caught up in the atmosphere of science without its substance.

Responding to Descartes in the seventeenth century, John Locke had described the philosopher as "an underlaborer to the scientist." This was taken to new lengths by twentieth-century "analytic" philosophers, those who increasingly dominated the professionalized discipline. Philosophers and scientists would engage in a joint secular effort to break down the universe into its ultimate individual components, and reassemble the aggregate through calculation. This would be completely professional, that is, completely independent of that vague sense of "the whole residual cosmos," the strangely sacred background and its energies formative of human identity.

Philosophy gained something, but it forfeited its role as mediator between special studies of concrete subject matter—the open area of imagination, appreciation, criticism, and recollection in which purity and exactitude are abandoned, and we keep focused "the whole condition of Man," as T. W. Adorno put it, the whole condition of the thinker.

This might seem to be an issue which concerns only a small group of academics, but the answers given to it are of momentous, if veiled, consequence for civilization. For if we can decide "what there is" (in however airy and general a way)—the sorts of topics that can be referred to and discussed intelligently—and can do this independently of the archaic background of experience, then secularization and atomization initiated in the seventeenth century is firmly set in place and becomes sclerotic.

Philosophers will tend to assume that the latest findings of natural science (whatever the "state of the art" is assumed to be) are the best detailed word on the way things are, and on which things actually exist. The philosopher is, then, not set to imagine revolutionary reconceptions of the nature of individuals, coming perhaps from science itself, or from images and metaphors in poetry. Imagination is foreclosed. The buoying sense of possibility is pricked and a suffocating constriction of imaginal space occurs; the self—call it soul if you wish—is confined to a pedestrian zone of reference.* But subjectivity, our feeling, dreaming, and thinking can never be reduced to merely a referring function, nor can it be exhaustively inventoried and referred to. Only evocative language includes the living knower in the world known.

Nobody remains in the university with the special obligation to trace and nourish connective tissue between departments and foster the education of human beings. The very meaning of the ultimate degree conferred—Doctor of Philosophy—is eroded, for it no longer makes sense that there is a conceptual matrix *inherent in concrete subject matters*—changing and incomplete though it might be—which is shared by all fields.

Thus an intensely focused secularism tends to solidify and to form its own "self-evident" partitions and tradition. Only this analysis, I believe, can explain what happened when the acme of professionalism was reached in the 1930s with "logical positivism": it was both dismissive of religion and—despite its professed allegiance to science—blind to many of the revolutionary

---

*Despite the fact that language is the central topic in analytic philosophy, its practical function of denoting and picking out is stressed, even when the supposed richness of language is being catalogued (as when J. L. Austin picks out its locutionary, illocutionary, perlocutionary functions). Woe to the writer who dares to capitalize the big words, such as Nature. The reality of words is reduced. There is a sense in which all professional philosophy is nominalistic, as James Hillman writes: "Nominalism empties out big words.... Words have no inherent substance of their own. From the fourteenth century ... to Wittgenstein and his contemporary heirs, there has been an accelerating decay of large, abstract, polyvalent ideas in favor of small, concrete, particular, single-meaning names. The word has moved from being a power of its own to an implement in the hands of specialists called philosophers." (*Re-Visioning Psychology*, New York: 1975). p. 5.

philosophical implications of twentieth-century physics itself, which were ahead both of the culture and of philosophers isolated in their professional groups.

We have located, I think, the issue which has torn at philosophy—and through it, tacitly, at civilization—in our century, and it is the one which divides professionalizing from non-professionalizing currents: can intelligence be detached from the archaic historical background of human experience? Professionals may concede that this background is inescapable for the persons who do the thinking, but that it need not be acknowledged in their thinking itself.

Those who refuse to go along with this maintain that if the background is left unacknowledged in our thinking, both our thought and ourselves will be impoverished. Any attempt to build up the whole universe as an aggregate of its scientifically and logically denotable parts must assume a sense of the whole that can never appear in the professional account. It must beg the question. This silence about the primal background must also be a silence about ourselves mimetically engulfed in it.

The position critical of professionalism holds that some moody attunement to the surrounding background world focuses and limits what we can turn to, pick out, and individuate, *even in thought*. Each instant engulfs us in a spatial extent and temporal depth in which factors overlap and interfuse, and which cannot begin to be thought unless first felt and lived through. This primitive involvement and sense of depth and the whole is the locus of myth and story. But the professional's cool analytic account must also presuppose it; it must abstract from it, however unwittingly. In its building up of an aggregated whole through discrete terms and linear scales, it is constrained furtively by possibilities and limits inherent in the archaic matrix from which it abstracts. The analytic reference to individual parts must presuppose a primitive sense of the whole, must beg the question *in its thought;* but it cannot acknowledge that it does so, because it cannot acknowledge the full range of our experience and nature *as persons*. Both thought and person are impoverished. If part of a larger venture, the professional's techniques of logical analysis can be valuable; isolated, as they typically are, they are pernicious.

We have used James as a bellwether. In *The Principles of Psychology* (1890) he alludes tacitly to Aristotle and uses the word *essence,* but he puts it in quotation marks. The "essence" of things is just the characteristics we must assign to things of a certain *sort,* given the present state of our inquiry into them. We can then pick out "instances" of these "essences." At this point in his career he had not dropped out of secular consciousness, as I put it, but he was on his way to the much larger—and some would say abysmal—sense of history that possesses him in *The Varieties of Religious Experience.* At this later point the "essence" of "individual self" or "human mind" is thrown wide open and becomes disturbingly problematic. *What* are we pointing out when we pick out a human being in a religious experience of conversion? What are we picking out when we pick out the "same" being alone in his study calmly reading a book? Or when we pick out the "same" being swept up in a lynch mob? Are the conditions which individuate a living human body for the purposes of physiological analysis identical to the conditions which individuate a human self? It would seem too simple to suppose so. And what are the conditions which individuate one group of human selves? Why draw lines in such a way that one particular grouping is made instead of an indefinite number of others? Are we drawing lines as intelligently and fruitfully as possible? We could go on—the ramifications are momentous.

In believing that logic could pick out *one* of anything, the range of denumerable topics to be studied intelligently, and all independent of "the curious sense of the whole residual cosmos," professional philosophers were tacitly presumptuous. The belief that the basic sorts of references and referents, the basic sorts of "units," are grasped by logic (with the concrete instances and details supplied by science) implies that everything is itself and *not* another thing. With this apparently innocuous initial move the world must appear segmented, and directly lived imagination, participation, and involvement must be obscured—particularly mimetic engulfment, the already obscure texture of our existence which demands the intimate mixing and interaction of philosophy and nearly every other field if it is to be seen. The ancient prejudice which emphasizes differences at the expense of similarities (which in chapter twelve I construe as male bias) is perpetuated, and Aristotle's "law of the excluded middle" (something must be either itself or not itself) becomes simplistically understood in most professional philosophical thought in our century.*

A. N. Whitehead had won an international reputation as a mathematician and logician. But by the 1920s and 30s he was exceedingly critical of the attempts to professionalize philosophy by "logicising" it. If mathematics is to be applied to the world— if we are to pick out any single thing to perceive or talk about— we must know what *one* of that *sort* of things is. But what *is* one of those? This apparently simple question is fundamental, and staggeringly difficult. The logician and mathematician turned philosopher writes,

The self-confidence of learned people is the comic tragedy of civilization. . . . There is not a sentence which adequately states its own meaning. There is always a background of presuppositions which defies analysis by reason of its infinitude. . . . Let us take the simple case; for example, the sentence, "One and one make two". . . . Obviously, this sentence omits a necessary limitation. For one thing and itself make one thing. So we ought to say, "One thing and another thing make two things." This must mean that the togetherness of one thing with another thing issues in a group of two things. . . . At this stage all sorts of difficulties arise. There must be the proper sort of things in the proper sort of togetherness. The togetherness of a spark and gunpowder produces an explosion, which is very unlike two things. Thus, we should say "The proper sort of togetherness of one thing and another thing produces the sort of group which we call *two things*." Common sense at once tells you what is meant. But unfortunately there is no adequate analysis of common sense, because it involves our relation to the infin-

---

*It might be objected that the logic of relations can handle human involvement. But this logic requires some specificity in the elements related, and this easily attributes an artificial individuation to the elements. Saul Kripke's "Naming and Necessity," a fairly recent production of "analytic" philosophy, owes its significance in great part, I think, to its reestablishing contact with the everyday, concrete background of human life: the "dubbing ceremony" in which persons are named and remain so named within the ongoing, perpetually self-reclaiming and self-constituting community. Kripke's is a critique of theories of reference exclusively "logicist."

ity of the Universe. . . . The conclusion is that Logic, conceived as an adequate analysis of the advance of thought, is a fake. It is a superb instrument, but it requires a background of common sense.*

We must work within a background that we cannot demarcate and exhaustively analyze. Thus the very notion of philosophy as an autonomous zone of expertise is questionable. Whitehead writes, "there is always the dim background from which we derive and to which we return. We are not enjoying a limited dolls' house of clear and distinct things, secluded from all ambiguity. In the darkness beyond there ever looms the vague mass which is the universe begetting us."** The "dim background from which we derive and to which we return": Whitehead's concern for education as *educere* is immediately understandable. Professing—particularly but not exclusively in philosophy—is an intergenerational venture which draws us out to make sense of our shared humanness, our common careers as historical beings who are born, grow, and die—emerge from an enveloping generative matrix and return to it, give back to it—and who do so in a universe unboundable by any professional expertise.

At this point Creighton's inaugural presidential address to the A.P.A. in 1902 should come as no surprise:

I would like to express my opinion that it would be a mistake to make the discussion of methods of teaching philosophy a coordinate purpose, or even to introduce papers on this subject into the programme of the meetings. Even if the membership of the Association were composed wholly of teachers of philosophy, which will never, I hope, be the case,

---

*A. N. Whitehead, "Immortality", in *Essays in Science and Philosophy* (New York: 1947), pp. 95–96. How quantified objectification over-simplifies gendered existence is shown in Luce Irigary, *This Sex Which is Not One* (Ithaca, N.Y.: 1985). "Woman's body is not one nor two. The sex which isn't one, not a unified identity." See also Jane Gallop: "You can have one or multiple orgasms. They are quantifiable, delimitable. You cannot have one *jouissance* and there is no plural. . . . Feminine sexuality is a '*jouissance* enveloped in its own contiguity'." Quoted in A. Dallery, "The Politics of Writing the Body," in Jaggar and Bordo (See last note in Chapt. XII).
**"The Analysis of Memory", ibid., pp. 122–23.

the meetings should not, it seems to me, be occupied with the consideration of such secondary and subordinate topics.*

Teaching a secondary and subordinate topic for a philosopher! This foretells the course of professional philosophy in this century. Removed is the only sure foundation that philosophy ever had: the cooperative effort of young and old, person to person, to orient ourselves in the world, make some sense of life, and to live sanely. Philosophy concerns the vague background "giving birth to us"—which can be the subject of no special field of professional expertise, for at best we are all *ama*-teurs here, as Plato knew, mere lovers and seekers of wisdom.

With ever increasing momentum professional philosophers defined their group as wholly and purely itself because wholly other from every other professional group—a cleanly defined, self-sufficient topic and entity. The broad assumptions of seventeenth-century psycho/physical dualism were cemented. Only science could disclose detailed facts about the physical world of Nature, and philosophy should not try to rival it. And only the arts and literature can "express" the subjective realm of sentiment, and philosophy should not try to rival them. But there *is* a field for philosophy, and it is tacitly presumptuous: formal logic, that which *seems* to bear no relation at all to any possible content, be it "subjective" or "objective"; formal logic, particularly the rigorous study of the general conditions which allow us to mean and to refer to individual items in the world.

However, a crucial fact is ignored: We may not know what these conditions for reference are, because we may not be able to imagine possible sorts of units or individuals (e.g., incipient individual systems, or strange [single?] fields or rapidly evolving patterns). The emphasis on logic, on the formal manipulation of content, *obscures the possibility of new creation of content—*

---

*Republished in Nov. 1986, *Proceedings and Addresses of the American Philosophical Association*. A counter-tendency to the subordination of teaching is observable recently. In 1975 the journal *Teaching Philosophy* was inaugurated, and the A.P.A. now incorperates a national committee on teaching, offers a bulletin on this topic, and holds a yearly seminar. This all has been spurred by the need to compete for students, but there is more involved than this, and these new directions reveal a significant broadening of interest.

new angles and expectations which conjure up units, topics, organic connections previously unimaginable. What we confidently count as separate units may coalesce in larger units we cannot imagine. Conversely, what we count as a unit may be self-opposed or multiple in important but veiled ways. New meanings can be coaxed out of the background by novel images or metaphor, say, and into the focus of consciousness: a learning and an educating that is image-inative.

Most destructively, of course, the stress typically placed by analytic philosophy on reference, on picking out objects, tends to treat *ourselves,* the imaginers, as objects; it constricts the content we can find in *ourselves* (for the dominant preoccupation this century has been with the "extensional" meaning of concepts). To be sure, minds may be ascribed to us, and thoughts ascribed to minds, but these "attributes" tend to be construed as dimmed-down or echo versions of the "real and objective" world in which *things* have attributes. "It is" has become the paradigm of reality rather than "I am" or "we are." Our being in the world is not understood in its own terms—how we ecstatically and empathically belong to the horizon and to what lies beyond it: possibility, myth, story, the animating presences of the background world. To miss the excited significance open to everyday living is to "miss everything," as James put it.*

In the obsession with formal logic, imagination in its integrity is left behind. Fruitful contact with the body is lost, along with the rest of the world's natural forces, and its particularities and spontaneities. This means a loss of contact with the wellsprings of meaning, the ways in which the body can project its meaning metaphorically beyond literal descriptions of itself, and can gift us with metaphors such as "dances of waves of energy."

Forgotten indeed is the human matrix of philosophy and the primal urge to form an identity which is vital and exciting because growing unpredictably, an urge that cannot even be understood, let alone satisfied by logic alone—or even by logic in tandem with science. Not surprisingly, with the "logical positivists" a sharp division was made between the "cognitive," the

---

*"On a Certain Blindness in Human Beings," reprinted in my *William James: The Essential Writings* (Albany, N.Y.: 1985).

intellectual and knowledgeable, on the one hand, and the "emotive," the merely emotional and sentimental, on the other. Coinciding with this is the division between "facts" and "values." The only meanings which can form truths directly about the real world of objective Nature are those which refer to individual items upon which observers fix their attention, agree as to their defining properties, and make universally testable measurements and predictions. Moral and aesthetic judgments do not refer in this way, it is thought, so they cannot form real knowledge, but merely express subjective sentiment. "Rape is bad," for example, merely expresses personal or social disapproval. The "badness" of the activity is not a testable property of it. Nihilism was afoot, and not merely in philosophy departments, for in this climate we all tend to be split, alienated.

Logical positivism swept like a tidal wave into the universities in the mid-30s, 40s, and 50s, and its influence is still felt, even after most philosophers have abandoned many of its simplistic concepts of the easy extractability and manipulability of pure forms and meanings to produce statements, and the divisions it drew between those which can be true and those which are merely expressive. For example, Willard Quine, professor of philosophy at Harvard, criticized positivism importantly, but its heavy afterglow remains in his work. He poses a spectacle, practically unparalleled in history, of a philosopher feted by his peers who has practically nothing to say about either ethics or art, goodness or beauty. Nothing better epitomizes the alienation of professional philosophy, particularly from the lives of students entrusted to us. As Plato knew, the force which drives learning toward truth is erotic; it cannot be divided from the love of goodness and beauty, for in desiring these—and the truth about them—we desire what fulfills ourselves. The attempt to divide truth and logic from goodness and beauty chops us into pieces, and hangs us out to dry in a tedious breeze of words and formulae.

The progressive purification and isolation of professional philosophy reveals the titanic attempt to break clear of the archaic background of experience and to found an identity as a professional independent of it. It serves as a kind of theatre in which secularizing tendencies of the whole culture are compressed, focused, made visible. We see in miniature the disintegration of the university into multiversity, the divorce of "professional schools" from the liberal arts, sciences from the humanities, and philosophy—which might have supplied connective tissue—from everything else. One may know how to make money, transform the earth and ourselves in indefinite numbers of ways, and not know how to live.

Inexorably, the professionalization of philosophy left behind the thinkers I emphasize: Emerson, Nietzsche, James, Dewey, Whitehead. They were not sufficiently hard, precise, "scientific" in some sense, that is, professional—they were too "literary." As an old man, and almost in desperation, Dewey published *The Problems of Men* (1946). At the turn of the century he had seen that logic cannot be isolated from the background of experience—our ethical and existential depth. He agreed in essence with Whitehead. There is no isolable logical technique for picking out the individuals which are the furniture of heaven and earth, and for producing a definitive inventory of the sorts of things that can *be*. Dewey writes,

"This," whatever *this* may be, always implies a system of meanings focused at a point of stress, uncertainty, and need of regulation. It sums up history, and at the same time opens a new page; it is record and promise in one; a fulfillment and an opportunity.*

This "system of meanings focused at a point of stress, uncertainty," involves our engulfment in history; we cannot demarcate and neatly objectify it, and our conception of the conditions which individuate things is always open to startling revision. What opportunities will emerge for making new sense of things are unpredictable. The "furniture of heaven and earth" change, as our criteria for picking things out change.

One who learns best about the world is one who learns best about how we learn. Whether we realize it or not, each item we pick out "sums up history" in *some* way. To be sure, Creighton, first president of the A.P.A. thought that the history of philosophy should be studied by philosophers "in the light of current problems," and this became the watchword for professional his-

---

*John Dewey, *Experience and Nature* (New York: 1958 [1925, 1929]), p. 352.

torians of philosophy in the last five or six decades. But this is the question that ought to have been asked: is our sense of current problems and our hold on meanings adequate for grasping our history and existence? The right question has yet to dawn on many professional philosophers.

In the half century 1930–1980 professionalism triumphed. The center of the "action," the secular focus, lost all articulate touch with the archaic historical background of human experience. Indeed, so caught up in one form or another of logical expertise ("state of the art") were most philosophers that all sense of history was lost, even the recent history of the development of logical expertise itself—so-called "analytic philosophy." The focus intensified, pure and laser-like, and concentrated in the current leaders of analysis in the A.P.A. Contact tended to be lost even with most contemporary European philosophers, not to mention those living or dead in the Orient, South America, or Africa. The Ph.D. degree was awarded to persons the vast majority of whom could not speak intelligently for five minutes on the thinkers most germaine for grasping our situation, each of whom (with the exception of Nietzsche) had written fairly recently in English.

It is equally clear, to those who care to look, that while all articulate contact with the archaic background of human history had been lost, not all contact had been. The age-old torrent of human energy and human being, bent on forming an identity for itself, still flowed imperiously, but was now forced into narrow, turbulent, wholly secular and contemporary channels for recognition. A few role models, master technicians of prodigious analytical power, seemed to stand above the tumult. Philosophy, a speciality, was broken into clearly defined sub-specialities, and standards of accomplishment in each were so pure and clear, it was thought, that a decisive ranking of ability was possible— and almost simultaneously with the "performances" which were evaluated. Whatever else was achieved, a device was created which measured, ranked, certified intellectual accomplishment, and thereby authorized and molded the identity of anxious professional academics. The hunger for identity was appeased, at least for the moment. The person was authorized and oriented—

but only professionally, only within a limited, aseptic sector of one's life.

All in all, academic professionalization entails criteria of evaluation of one's "performance" in which the theatrical ingredient is uncomfortably large: one submits activity for evaluation from only a limited stretch of one's life. The full consequences, the meaning, of one's thought about life is not brought to a test by one's life itself. In a broad but significant sense, one is "performing." But in the last analysis, one may be boring others, and oneself.

One can't help wondering how Creighton and his associates would have responded to the final triumph of professionalism had they been around to see it. Fifteen papers, written by professors well known to each other, were read at the first meeting in 1902. Today, counting just the eastern division of the tri-partite A.P.A., hundreds of papers are read over three or four days to thousands in attendance (or to that fraction who hear the readings and are not involved in other activities, such as hiring or looking for work, or hungrily socializing). Most do not know each other. What sort of discussion can go on? What does Creighton's prized "personal presence" of "living personalities" amount to under these circumstances?

Some acute observers, such as Richard Rorty and Janice Moulton, have pointed out recently that the actual form of exchange between philosophy professors at these meetings fits no historical model of legitimate philosophical dialectic, but is rather modeled on the confrontation of lawyers in a courtroom. In the half century 1930–1980, they claim, philosophers have attacked each other's positions in the manner of lawyers attacking each other's briefs: the "adversary method in philosophy," as Moulton puts it.* An instant verdict is rendered thereby, and the contestant moves in one way or another in the shifting, breathtaking rankings of "professionals in the field." But the self is not just the professional ego, and it remains burdened with unacknowledged aspirations, aversions, aggressions, anxieties, and various split-off states.

---

*See her article of this title in *Discovering Reality,* ed. by S. Harding and M. Hintikka, (Dordrecht, Holland: 1983).

If all this is true, as I think it is, then there has been a return of what Plato and Socrates stigmatized as *eristic,* mere disputation, something unworthy of a philosopher. It is unlikely that Creighton could have imagined the impersonality of the current professional scene, indeed, the anomie for most of those who attend the yearly convention and are not involved in the anxious race for top honors. It is impossible to know the work of most of those who attend, and so there is a perpetual breaking down into sub-groups and the creation within several domains of "stars"—those few whose work is known to many. Of course, the groups themselves are ranked, and those who believe they are members of elite groups feel no need to lose time in reading the work of those believed to occupy lower ones.

But we are animals caught up in the life of the mind—philosophical animals. The need to make some kind of sense of the world and of our place within it is about as crude and strong as our need to eat and seek shelter. If professional philosophers pinch off the scope of philosophy then others will arise who restore it to its life within the archaic background of experience and our rootage in it.* By 1970 the foundations of the professional philosophical association had begun to shake slightly. In deep discontent Abraham Kaplan wrote in *Change,* early 1970, "The Travesty of the Philosophers:"

Nietzsche once remarked that a married philosopher belongs to comedy; could it be that the notion of a professional philosopher is equally absurd? What are called "professional standards" are, to a great degree, standards of professionalism, not significant performance. They are, to a significant extent, initiation rites rather than realistic assessments of the capacity to contribute to the philosophic function . . . (which) takes place chiefly at the interface between the life of the mind and the arts of practice, on the frontiers of every domain of knowledge and action. Philosophy thus must look outward for its very life; it grows only at the edges. As the profession turns inward, more and more of its work must be done by outsiders. . . by such people as Margaret Mead, Erich Fromm, Noam Chomsky, even Marshall McLuhan. . . .

---

*In this book I cannot trace the evolution of academic analytic philosophy itself. Any such effort would include John Rawls' *A Theory of Justice* (1971). Though encumbered by residues of formalism and naive individualism, it marks a turn to the re-engagement of philosophy and life.

Students of philosophy enter their training with the most admirable philosophical motives. They come with intellectual curiosity puzzled about the foundations of science, disturbed by religious questions, agonized over politics, captivated by literature and art. All that nonsense is knocked out of them.

Kaplan wrote that he did not intend to start a revolution, because on the philosophical scene "There is little to be gained by initiating controversy and inviting confrontation," and he left the country. Despite his insights, I don't believe Kaplan fully understood the depth of aversion which an in-group can feel toward an out-group. If philosophers are considered incompetent and unwashed, they will be shunned, and their grievances not heard. Given a modicum of self-respect their only alternative is rebellion.

The revolution in the A.P.A. was carried out by others in 1978–79, and continues today. The Pluralists, as they called themselves, directly challenged the entrenched group of "analytic" philosophers, electing from the floor of the business meeting in 1979 their own slate of candidates for offices. In the ten elections since then about half the officers elected have been backed by the Pluralists, and the views presented at the yearly conventions radically enlarged. It is a hotly fought battle reported in the mass media (which means that the media thrive on battles—or that the American public is finally concerned with what professors *do*—or some of both).

We are caught up in transition and there is reason for hope. Today, analytic philosophy is still identifiable: an aseptic, "scientific" atmosphere, glowing like a nimbus, hovers about it, excluding anything "literary" or "spiritual." But as articles appear linking Donald Davidson's "holism," for example, with Kant's and Heidegger's thought, we know that venerable currents in the history of philosophy are about to reconverge. Symptomatic of the break-up of the analytic establishment is the recent admission by Hilary Putnam, an important member of it, that philosophy cannot be concerned merely with "logical puzzles," but also with "regenerative possibilities of experience."*

---

*U.S. News and World Report, April 25, 1988, p. 56.

But meaningful, lasting reform will come only when we have exposed the causes of professionalism that lie in the eclipsed, archaic background of experience, as well as identified factors in our technological and commercial world.

Let us look back at the sibilant apprehension which greeted the onset of professionalism in the nineteenth and early twentieth centuries, unheeded at the time. Some of the first misgivings come from the poet-philosopher Emerson before the middle of the last century. He writes in "The American Scholar," "Thought and knowledge are natures in which apparatus and pretension avail nothing. Gowns and pecuniary foundations, though of towns of gold, can never countervail the least sentence or syllable of wit." The true scholar "plies the slow, unhonored, and unpaid task of observation," and "must relinquish display and immediate fame"—must "hold by himself; add observation to observation, patient of neglect, patient of reproach, and bide his time—happy enough if he can satisfy himself alone that this day he has seen something truly."

In the 1870s a stridently apprehensive voice is heard, that of Nietzsche, who as a young man had read Emerson's essays. The Ph.D. was a German invention, and professionalism there took the form of mastery of an elaborate apparatus of scholarship supervised by a master researcher in a university or research institute—an institution typically chartered and funded by the state. Nietzsche had won a professorship as a precocious master of Greek philology at the University of Basel. His first published book, *The Birth of Tragedy from the Spirit of Music,* was a work of genius which defied every canon of professionalism. Not only did he not limit himself to an established scholarly specialty—he ranged over many fields and epochs, including ancient and contemporary dance and music—but he dispensed as well with the apparatus of scholarship, the elaborate litany of acknowledgements and references in footnotes. Moreover, he brilliantly illuminated the Dionysian strand in all creative work. Not surprisingly, he was savagely attacked by some; but most established scholars simply ignored him. Attendance in his classes dwindled, as students, pre-professionals, worried that that association would damage their careers. Ailing in health, disgusted, he applied for a pension after a few years, and at about the age of thirty was "put out to pasture." What this odd horse would do in the pasture, few could have imagined.

He had early identified with Arthur Schopenhauer and that philosopher's similar banishment—and his stoic and, Nietzsche thought, heroic biding of his time. In his "Schopenhauer as Educator," Nietzsche records his anger and foreboding concerning a professionalized professoriate. We increasingly detach our thought about life from our lives, and are consumed by haste, restlessness, and boredom, Nietzsche says. "He who nowadays knows how to open up a new field within which even the weakest heads can labor with some degree of success becomes famous in a very short time: so great is the crowd that at once presses in." In our personal impoverishment we become addicted to acclaim, and forget that the most important matters can be identified and fruitfully explored only among "nearest friends." It is the proper role of the university to protect those who have exposed themselves to possible failure in seeking difficult truth: "the smaller band. . . . which wants the protection of a firm organization so as to prevent itself from being washed away and dispersed by that tremendous crowd, and so that the individuals that comprise it shall not die from premature exhaustion." But the university is in league with the state to produce wealth and fame.*

We have already alluded to James's curt rejection of the invitation to join the A.P.A. in 1901, also to his pointed attack on philosophical professionalism in *The Varieties*. He was not content to leave matters at that. In 1903 he published "The Ph.D. Octopus." We become fatefully distracted by badges and honors, he says. "Human nature is once for all so childish that every reality becomes a sham somewhere, and in the minds of Presidents and Trustees the Ph.D. degree is in point of fact already looked upon as a mere advertising resource, a manner of throwing dust in the Public's eyes." James continues by upbraiding the whole industry of professional academic preferment.

It is of more than passing note, I think, that—nevertheless—

---

*All quotations are from "Schopenhaur as Educator," in *Untimely Meditations,* trans. by R. J. Hollingdale (Cambridge: 1983).

James accepted membership in the A.P.A. in 1904, and in 1905 was elected its president.

This change of mind is the startling ambivalence I referred to, and it can be laid to James' vanity, a vice from which he was not exempt. Two of his younger colleagues, Josiah Royce and John Dewey, had already been elected in preceding years. And it is now fairly well known that his attitude toward his younger brother—the novelist, Henry—was clouded by envy—a harshly ambivalent attitude.

But, in judging an individual censoriously, we may be obscuring fundamental issues in human history and identity which concern all of us. Can most of us today in the "normal" range of mental health afford psychically to decline positions of power in professional or bureaucratic structures, even though on strictly intellectual or moral grounds we disapprove of them? How can we *be* outside these structures? What other power for life can even a powerful intellect have when it still thrusts its roots toward the archaic background, into labile, strangely sacred energies of identity formation, but can only confirm its growth and its reality by being recognized by contemporary, professionalized, secular peers? Are there real alternatives? If the great psychologist and philosopher cannot comprehend or control his own behavior (and I do not think James could), what hope is there for the rest of us?

The consolidation and purification of the secular intellect has been bought at the price of its contraction, and this powers the restless, vulnerable, "point-instant" ego-self. What we get is schizoid disintegration, says Nietzsche, while what we want is "real, red-blooded life."

We will continue to ask what vital and substantial identity of self is, and how "higher education" in an age of professionalism focuses and extends the self in some ways and frets and tears it in others. We turn now to other professionalized academic fields, purified and isolated at crucial points from adjoining fields—as well as from the background of experience—and philosophy, professionalized, in no position to help with a mediating "story" of who and where we are and what we might be. However schematic and evolving this connective tissue is, it is significant.

VI

Eccentricities and Distortions
of Academic Professionalism

Professionalism is a strongly laudatory concept, and to criticize it is, at first glance, as foolish as for a politician in the United States to attack George Washington. Yet I am particularly critical of its academic form, for it masks out crucial educational obligations—especially to acknowledge that the most basic educational force is who the professor *is*. Are ethical qualities demanded by the educating act exemplified in the professor's life? The question is obscured.

This attempt to divide the professional from the personal has at least two dire consequences: professional activity in a secular age tends to be overloaded with unacknowledged thrust for personal identity—a fierce, narrow focusing—and, related to this, professional activity may even damage its own *professed* interests, because overloaded with a narrowly focused thrust it can fail to learn from discoveries in overlapping or adjoining scholarly fields. It defines itself anxiously as *not* the *other*.

Since at least the time of Plato it has seemed clear that persons must specialize in the development of skills. For they differ from one another in their "native" propensities and talents, and a great portion of each of their lives must be devoted to developing one (or a very few) of these. We have only limited time and limited energy, and "All things excellent are as difficult as they are rare," as Benedict Spinoza put it. And only when different persons develop different skills can each person benefit maximally from every other's talents in a community of complementing services and interdependent lives.

But should specialization be driven to the point at which it consumes a life and there is no time to develop the rest of one's person in civil and civilizing activities? Most thinkers have main-

tained that beyond all everyday employment lie the highest intrinsically valuable activities, particularly pure delight in con-
templating the universe and our place within it: "the intellectual
love of God," as Spinoza put it, with "God" meaning the infinitely rich and only partially understandable self-regenerating
universe itself.

It is customary for universities to grant "sabbaticals" to professors, which means, roughly, that in the seventh year of service
ordinary residency duties of teaching and committee work are
lifted. But when we inspect the concept we see how greatly it has
changed. It goes back to early agricultural and Biblical times: on
the seventh year the fields were to lie fallow to replenish their
nutrients. The soil was not to be perpetually forced. Until recently a parallel was thought to hold in human affairs, particularly with the "higher" or more "spiritual" callings, for these
persons must periodically relax, dilate, and regain thematic contact with the matrix of the world. They do not simply forget
their specialized interests, but allow them to be taken over for
awhile by the encompassing matrix into which they root and
seep: those broader and deeper connections which hold us all
and which inform the basic concepts which thinkers share. The
agricultural ground and the conceptual ground are bound metaphorically, and piety consists in recognizing that management,
manipulation, and force are limited. We must speak of the
growth of the mind, not of its forcing itself as if it were a mechanical contrivance driving itself down a path. In its original
sense the sabbatical year for the professor was an instance of the
ever cycling and ever renewing powers of primal Nature.

We have travelled ever farther from this because we increasingly experience our lives mechanistically, and as chronicled according to linear time exclusively. Typically today the professor
applying for a sabbatical year is required to outline a project of
research, and when the year is up to submit a report detailing
"productivity." The numbers which are thought to measure this
are put in their boxes on the activity reports as they are for-
warded up a hierarchy of levels of accountability. This is the "rational management" of human beings in the "multiversity."

Ludwig Wittgenstein thought that philosophy was to provide

timely reminders. I agree; we must periodically interrupt ourselves if we are not to be sucked into a brilliantly "self-evident"
secular focus by stages so small and inexorable that we are
oblivious of where we are carried. By now it is second nature to
be caught up in specialists' critiques of specialism; this is absurd.
Contrary to cliché, the university is not an ivory tower. It is porous and light and carried in the prevailing secular wind of linear
thinking, "rational management," "productivity," modularity,
and bureaucracy. Everything seems to move with this wind, all
standards and norms, so we must perpetually remind ourselves
of what could possibly reveal this drift by contrasting with it.

There is a tell-tale phrase that thematizes this linear and mechanical movement of the culture. It is a quick and smart interrogation frequently heard: "Does it go through?" Tacitly or
manifestly it is asked of everything. Does the application go
through? Does the Activity Report go through? Does the ceramic
vessel sent through various stages of test—fire, vibration, impact—go through? Once put on the market, does it go through,
does it sell? Intellectuals produce arguments before an audience
of professional peers: do these arguments go through? A computer program is composed of yes and no, positive and negative,
at every decision point. The appointed values determine how the
whole thing goes through. The calculation achieves the desired
end or it does not.

Does a human life go through? . . . What? Immediately we
sense an obstruction on our linear path. What could this snappy
question mean in this context? What is to constitute the desired
end of a life, so that the achieving of it would constitute the life's
going through? Almost inevitably the professional thinks of this
in professional terms. The ultimate object of desire might be to
be elected president of one's professional organization. But then
what? We feel the twinge of nausea. For one's life does not end
with the close of the "performance" of one's presidential address
before an assembled multitude of finally outdistanced peers (finally!—no commentator to carp at one's remarks and pick holes
in the arguments). One will have to face death, and now it
comes naked; for while younger, on some ridiculously irrational
level of mind, we may have thought that success would lodge us

beyond the coil of mortality; but now we *know* that nothing we can produce will prevent our aging, our loss of brain cells, and finally our dying.

The secular, linear, calculating culture does not completely conceal this from us. The statistics on those who die soon after retirement are staggering. It's as if there were very little to many of us aside from the professional persona, and when this is taken away we crumple. So there *is* an end concealed behind the avowed ends of professional achievement: it is to stay so obsessively busy with one's current projects, and with whether they go through or not, that one forgets the final end. But this is to forfeit self-knowledge, that which is not only good because it is knowledge *about* what is vital and real in one's own self, but a knowledge which *is* goodness in a particularly vivid sense. Without self-knowledge I can be firmly ensconced within my professional group, but a wandering ghost in the world at large.

Approaching the close of the millennium it becomes ever more difficult to conceal the question of what our ultimate ends are and what their value is. We remind ourselves that the value of some activities and states of being must simply be lived and undergone; all calculation must assume them, for it cannot prove them. These are intrinsically valuable activities, healthy, and vital life—more or less free of obsessions, phobias, and split-off states that render us eccentric, fractured, forever off balance and in motion.

The costs for both the individual and the culture—even for the professions themselves—of staying encased in the customary secular focus of calculation and "productivity" are becoming apparent. Some at least are beginning to see that we have been enticed by merely extrinsic values: power for more power for more power, endlessly, restlessly. Nothing counts as satisfaction. Our ability to manage Nature without limit and to ignore its cycles of birth, growth, death, regeneration is now called into question, for Nature has been so overloaded with the toxic wastes from our "productivity" that at least a portion of it as background must be focused and heeded if we are to survive.

To what *end* our productivity and "control" if as individuals we wake up terrified of our own aging and dying and if as a culture we threaten to extinguish human and animal life altogether? Over the din of our interrogation, Does it go through? can be heard another question, Can we regain the cycles of Nature, and cycle back to our sources and be renewed?

Hans Jonas has written brilliantly of the ethical consequences of the unbridled growth of technology:

Not counting the insanity of a sudden suicidal atomic holocaust, which sane fear can avoid with relative ease, it is the slow, long-term, cumulative—the peaceful and constructive use of worldwide technological power, a use in which all of us collaborate as captive beneficiaries through rising production, consumption, and sheer population growth—that poses threats much harder to counter. The net total of these threats is the overtaxing of nature, environmental and (perhaps) human as well. Thresholds may be reached in one direction or another, points of no return, where processes initiated by us will run away from us on their own momentum—and toward disaster.*

Nature is totalized in modern experience radically differently from the way it was in ancient. Then Nature was experienced as continuous on its boundaries with the stability of Divinity. Contemporary materialism and professionalism conceive it as matter to be manipulated. Nevertheless, behind this vivid contrast lies a hidden kinship: both ages assume that Nature is reliable and inexhaustible. The modern mind holds that Nature is a servant, but an inexhaustible and reliable one, and holds to the lines of the Chorus in *Antigone* (but shorn of their piety). Sophocles writes,

And she, the greatest of gods, the Earth—deathless she is, and unwearied . . .

Since in the face of probable ecological disaster we can go longer simply assume this inexhaustibility—since even great stretches of the waters and the air can no longer assimilate our wastes and regenerate themselves—we are forced to dilate our focus and reconsider Nature as a whole, or at least our Earth and its immediate environs, in a way we have not done for four hundred years.

A new perspective is opened on professionalism, academic and otherwise. Since we can no longer assume we control the

---

*Hans Jonas, *The Imperative of Responsibility: In Search of an Ethics for a Technological Age* (Chicago: 1983), p. ix.

consequences of our deeds, we must redefine human reality itself. Indeed, as we single out topics, we must ask, what counts as *the* human condition or situation? Given the limits of our control of the consequences of our deeds within an inescapable but not inexhaustible Nature, how do we redraw the human condition? Since the university claims to educate human beings, how do we redraw the university?

Once we ask these questions we see how we have hitherto conceived of professionalism: progress through professionalization, in or out of the university, has been conceived like progress in general has been for four hundred years. Professionalism is pressured "to go through" and *pay*—and *pay* in generically the same short-range terms as we evaluate any commercial venture. Older standards of professional integrity are greatly strained, and if professors do not resist, the idea prevails that "education" is merely a commodity to be profitably sold. Human identity must be achieved, and for most within a framework of recognition determined by technology, calculation, "productivity." The value of "education" is largely measured in these terms.

Magali Sarfatti Larson traces both the overt and the covert roles that technology and the money economy play in structuring the university. The connection between the university bureaucracy and the larger society is perfectly explicit at some points. Bureaucracies exhibit not only internal interlocking of their parts, but interlock with other bureaucracies, e.g., governmental ones (however inefficiently). It is not just that the university receives money from state and federal governments. Once a university module, a department, "negotiates cognitive exclusiveness"—as Larson puts it—*vis-à-vis* other professional academic organizations, the bureaucratic state steps in to back this up with its registration and licensing requirements.* In many fields the double certification of university and state is gained. One is a licensed chemist, engineer, accountant, psychologist. Thus a monopoly is enforced through an interlocking directorate of university, professional organization, and state or federal government. We learn that fifty-one accrediting agencies dictate what the cer-

---

*Magali Sarfatti Larson, *The Rise of Professionalism: A Sociological Analysis* (Berkeley: 1977), pp. 23–24.

tification seeker must study as he or she pursues a somewhat incidental bachelor's degree.* In these fields, academic professionalism threatens to narrow to the constricted sense of "professional school"—there is slippage between the senses of "professional." The field of professional chemistry is a vivid example of the control of the "educational" process through controlling the number and sorts of courses that must be taken for a degree.

We experience a culture lag in which the natural sciences outstrip the ability of the other disciplines to criticize them. The grossest evidence for this is the sheer volume of money pumped into the departments of natural science and technology in the university, and of the inability of most universities to generate a forum in which the faculty and student body can calmly assess the implications of this for research that is funded. Mustn't researchers think twice before saying or publishing anything which endangers the source of their income? And isn't this inhibition and dependency a threat to the chief assumption and value of all inquiry, that the inquirer be free to follow his or her research wherever it leads?

If various reports are to be believed, a sizable portion of the income of Johns Hopkins University is supplied by the Pentagon.** As one of the most respected universities, and most highly professionalized (the first to offer the Ph.D. degree in the U.S.), this is an arresting example. We should not be surprised, however, since it is just highly specialized people who easily forget the implications of becoming dependent upon money which must determine their research in some way. As far as most specialists are concerned, the numbers stay neatly confined to their boxes and the question of what they mean is put aside.

I must be perfectly clear about what I mean. It is not the particular source of this money which particularly concerns me here—though it is important. I can imagine the argument that the defense of the United States is defense of academic freedom,

---

*Carnegie Foundation, *The Control of the Campus: A Report on the Governance of Higher Education* (Princeton: 1982), pp. 29, 49, 66.
**See "Hooked on DOD: Johns Hopkins University's Growing Dependence on Military Money," *Common Cause Magazine*, Nov.–Dec. 1986, pp. 29–31.

for the record of our nation on this issue is much better than many others (and I am not about to defend most Marxist nations in this regard). Nor am I unmindful of the fact that individual professors and individual groups of professors have protested strongly against money for research which has strings attached. I am only saying (1) that university faculties have a responsibility as faculties to wrestle with this issue on philosophical grounds, (2) they have great difficulty doing this within the segmented, professionalized university, and (3) the record of accomplishment here is, on the whole, abysmal.

I am trying to map the eccentricities and distortions of academic professionalism. One side of the picture is fairly clear: the direct role of the money economy. At salient points the distorting influence is so obvious that there is no reason to belabor it. Many disciplines have stayed highly specialized and out of touch with what is going on in neighboring fields because it has paid: they have been funded to do so. There is a symbiotic relationship between professionalized fields and sources of funding. It is the same large group of experts who write the research proposals and who serve as the referees for these proposals. *That* way of picking out *one* group is revealing. This is one of the reasons that in the half century 1930–1980 proposals for interdisciplinary research were so meagerly funded.

In a personal communication, William Arrowsmith writes that he served for years as a referee for a famous foundation and "watched genuinely interdisciplinary projects go down to defeat again and again. . . . Education and educational reforms are not, alas, very dear to the foundations, which for the most part profess precisely the kind of professionalized activity you're opposing. Indeed, they seem . . . to exist precisely to impose and police your taboos."

The indirect and more or less hidden pressures on professors to compromise their own and their students' educations are at least as dangerous as the manifest ones. Since we live in a milieu in which recognition is accorded and identity molded on the basis of power and wealth, the pressures to conform to such standards are relentless and come from all sides; it is difficult to pin them down and fend them off. Here, it must be conceded, professional associations—at least in some fields (mathematics, say)—may insulate professors to some extent. This is equivocal, however, for standards of productivity and instant recognition permeate even these associations and can exercise devious influence.

Larson puts her finger on one of the most hidden and troublesome influences of technology and the money economy. The university is the gatekeeper on the road to money and power, and the society supplies most professors with a guaranteed monopoly of clients and a serviceable salary.* So the professor is free to define his or her status through relationships, not to the clients, the students, but to fellow professionals. The dependency on student-clients is masked, but I think that unacknowledged dependency upon them generates guilty and destructive feelings toward them.

Here the insularity of professionalism is especially baneful, and here the indirect influence of the money economy continues into a darker psychological side of the picture which I will try to trace. Foretold is much of the remainder of this book.

Recall that I referred to the "new age" of industrialization and "the great transformation" as so caught up in itself and in its totalizing ideology that it was blind to the background conditions and old habits which carried over from previous ages. We might almost speak of an animal-like *thereness*, a closing in upon itself, except now it is an animal caught up in a self-closing domain of *mind* which masks off a primitive background of experience that is still furtively at work. It is particularly phenomena of mimetic engulfment, old and new, which escape notice.

We must now develop this theme in greater depth. In academic professionalism, mind plays a decisive role in structuring personal identity. Mimetic engulfment in the corporate professional body exerts an immense, frequently stupefying pressure. One *must* be "a formidable mind." And again, Descartes' legacy obtrudes: his psycho/physical dualism (although he failed altogether to grasp the group's mind). Despite the growing materialism of the modern world, mind tends to be conceived as essentially self-reflexive, isolated, cut off from the extended

---

*Larson, already cited, p. 181.

domain of bodies, from Nature; and how mind conceives itself is a constitutive element of what we *are* as minding beings. John Dewey traced a fundamental malcoordination: the tendency of our minding to lose touch with its own bases in the body and the environment. We seriously overestimate our ability to manage our affairs. Unlike other animals, we possess the dubious ability to outrun and to lose touch, in a certain sense, with the supportive appliances which are our own bodies. Except, of course, we remain these very bodies.

What, then, are the ramifications for academic professionalism of this animal-like *thereness,* this closing in upon itself, which nevertheless is very unlike the life of other animals? I will argue that the absorption in the secular world of calculation and "productivity" loses articulate touch with the inherited background of habitual body, quasi-sacred and sacred energies, both mimetic engulfments and recoiling exclusions, but it does not simply escape their influence. Indeed, this contact is furtive and implicit, therefore exceedingly powerful and uncontrollable. In the case of academic professionals particularly, I see attempts to constitute a self by denying the messy and "dirty" body, and all that is associated with it, e.g., all that is not yet purified and certified by authoritative *minds* in the "field"; this underworld includes students and professors' relationships to them. Thus the distorted shape of academic professionalism is immensely complex and radically overdetermined by factors in the obscure background.

Because my whole thesis at this point is radical, I have laid the groundwork painstakingly. We live at a strange time in history, I think quite unparalleled, a period of bizarre overlaps. In the sixteenth and seventeenth centuries, modern physical science emerges triumphant. Through techniques of mathematics and observation, it discerns what it takes to be the features of matter, and on this basis provides the means for predicting and controlling a lot of what happens. This leads to the great transformations of modern life, the industrial revolution, etc.

Yet, at the same time, a very archaic procedure is being perpetuated: the control of dirty matter. Ancient Hebrew, Greek, and Christian purification rituals do not suddenly lose their hold—despite what thinkers of the eighteenth-century Enlightenment and later may have thought. It can be argued that purification rituals rise to a new pitch, but now implicit and behind the scenes. The Hebrew belief in the corruptibility of matter, and the need rigidly to segregate human intercourse with it, has, by the sixteenth and seventeenth centuries, combined with the Platonic Greek influence to produce the distinctly Christian aversion to *this* matter, one's own body (perhaps we should speak of the Pauline-Christian aversion). The Apostle Paul excoriates the body and sets the tone of much of Christian culture. In *Romans*, chapter seven, we read:

For I know that in me [that is, in my flesh] dwelleth no good thing: for to will is present with me; but how to perform that which is good I find not. . . . For I delight in the law of God after the inward man: But I see another law in my members, warring against the law of my mind, and bringing me into captivity to the law of sin which is in my members. O wretched man that I am! Who shall deliver me from the body of this death?

I believe that lingering behind all the triumphs of modern materialism and technology remains the dread of the body and the fearful desire to protect its vulnerable cavities and to control the egress of its spillable contents. Descartes' "new" philosophy *is* new in certain respects, but in its divorce of mind from body it plays into the hands of forces of purification and identity-formation long at work in the archaic background. The presumptuous mind which fancies itself divided from the body which generates it can only be blind to that from which it cannot be divided.

Through our bodies we control, or think we control, much of the world. But how do we control our bodies? Psycho/physical dualism lingers as a tacit attitude, the function of which is to "protect" the self by persuading it that its destiny is separate from the troublesome, corruptible, easily humiliated body. This attitude throws us out of touch with reality, I think, and we overestimate and overload acknowledgeable processes and factors of identity formation and lose touch with others.

We will be entering a domain that a hasty glance may not discern as relevant to our study of the university. But if we recall what it means to be an educator, and that a professor's first task is to educate himself about himself if he would presume to educate others—or to educate herself—then what we will be probing into will be seen to be highly relevant. Moreover, the topics with which we deal in this book are ones which should be taught at some points in the university curriculum. Finally, if we do not see the pertinence of all this, we professors will be caught, I believe, within claims from the personal and the professional which conflict, and which we will not be able to understand and adjudicate—as if attacked at night from many sides at once. Encountered thus, the dilemmas for teachers in the university might be discomfiting; whereas if they were understood, they might be tolerable, even challenging and invigorating.

Since my thesis is so radical, the reader has the right to demand more cases of tacit purification ritual. We saw that philosophers defined themselves so exclusively that they lost touch with the genius of philosophy itself. But it might be objected that philosophers are so out of touch anyway, so cerebral, and eccentric (and in today's culture so marginal) that they are hardly typical of academic professionals. To forestall such an objection, I will offer—briefly—four instances in which professionalized university fields have divorced themselves so obsessively from adjoining ones that overlaps and cross-fertilizations have been foreclosed, and their own vitality sapped. This suggests strongly an unacknowledged drive for identity, purification ritual. The motive to avoid this sapping must be strong, so the motive to conceal that it is happening must be stronger. It is just residual, archaic purification ritual that is sufficiently powerful—and sufficiently easily concealed in a mentalistic, secular mileau—to account for the concealment.

The training of physicians—now commonly associated with universities—is an example of the distorted exclusions and aversions of professionalism. Ever since Hippocrates, the atmosphere of a secret society of the elect has hung over this group.* Questions spring immediately to mind. Was this secrecy and exclusiveness fostered merely to prevent dangerous acts from being

---

*Werner Jaeger, *Paideia: The Ideals of Greek Culture*, trans. Gilbert Highet, Vol. III (New York: 1943–45), p. 11.

committed by those who possessed little learning? Or were the motives merely venal—to prevent income from being undermined through competition? I think that even a short review of the practices of the medical profession will cause us to doubt that these explanations, either singly or in combination, are adequate to explain them.

Contemporary physicians zealously distinguish themselves from homeopathists, chiropractors, herbologists, osteopaths, nutritionists, midwives, and other assorted practioners. Let us limit ourselves for the moment to the attested findings of nutritionists and food scientists. I doubt if the extreme reluctance of the medical profession to confront and test these findings can be explained merely by motives of preventing dangerous practices and of undermining competition. Only in a limited number of cases could ingestion of recognized foods be dangerous (when it was offered as a putative substitute for the medication which would be indicated), and given the very high, or at least adequate, incomes of most physicians it is unlikely that nutritionists or food scientists are seen as serious threats in this sector.

I think it plausible to assume that another factor is at work in physicians' excluding of nutrition from serious study—one in addition to both the factors mentioned above *and* to the factor of inertia and conservatism which can be assumed to operate in all habitual human activities, the reluctance to give up already acquired skills. Physicians seem to be assuming that it is only the materials which *they* introduce into the body which can be efficacious. Or, it is only when they *intervene* in the physiological system that cures result. If this is the case, they are assuming that a special virtue or power exists in themselves alone which is *not to be mixed* with anything or anyone else. That is, they are assuming a *purity;* and doing so in the face of empirical evidence to the contrary, since for decades now the therapeutic power of vitamins and minerals not administered by physicians has been established, and since common sense dictates that the hundred or so pounds of materials we consume each month is a relevant health factor.

Another example is close at hand. At the height of professionalism and positivism—and what we can call scientism—in the 1930s, many physicians advised mothers to feed their infants on a strict four-hour schedule. This practice was fairly widely followed by mothers. Less contact meant less chance of transmission of harmful bacteria. The power and prestige of medical science was sufficiently great to counteract the age-old and nearly instinctive practice in our culture (as in most) of picking up the infant when it cries out for nourishment and holding it near and feeding it. To go against such a powerful urge, I can only assume that medical science had installed itself in an already moving background mystique of something like shamanistic power, virtue, and purity. Furtive and constricted generic-religious energies had merged seamlessly and noiselessly with the latest empirical research.

There is, finally, the four years of residency training which physicians endure after the four years of medical school and another four of pre-medical studies. This is an ordeal in the literal, archaic sense, I believe, in which the individual proves through suffering that he or she can bend to the requirements of the group, can be initiated into that corporate individual. Initiation rituals are forms of purification rites: the purgings of allegiances to other groups, and of the desires and demands of the merely untutored self. Why are young doctors systematically deprived of sleep? As in all such cases, the causes are over-determined—many are involved, any one of which might seem to be sufficient to account for the phenomenon. Inquiry here is particularly tricky, for the more obvious answers tend to conceal less obvious ones. Among obvious answers are, "exploitation of cheap labor," or "the acquisition of the greatest amount of training in the shortest possible time." But if only these factors were involved, they would seem to be insufficient to rationalize the costs of the practice and to maintain it, e.g., young doctors so stupefied from lack of sleep that they commit serious blunders in caring for already endangered human beings, or that they imperil their own health.* This suggests strongly that something

---

*In a historic turn, 1988, changes were made in the N.Y. State Code of Rules and Regulations which limited the number of hours which interns and resident physicians could be on duty. "For decades, the marathon schedules of interns and residents have been considered a rite of passage to the medical profession. But in the last few years, with health officials and a grand jury saying the

more is at work, something not easily accessible to the modern, secular, scientific mind. Health care practitioners imperiling health: it is such intriguing contradictions that invite further inquiry.

The next case in which a professional field defines itself so as to exclude data relevant to its vitality is archaeology, particularly its approach to the vast Neolithic tumuli and stone circles in England and Ireland. The older among these are dated at around 3000 B.C., and some are on a scale with the pyramids of Egypt. They have not attracted the smallest fraction of the interest that the pyramids have, however, in part because there are no written texts known to coincide with them (at least none identified as such and deciphered), and, related to this, because of the narrow approach taken to them by archaeologists—which we are about to outline.

By far the most famous of these structures is Stonehenge, near Salisbury, England. It is one of the more recently built and represents the height of Neolithic or high stone age culture—a pinnacle, at least when measured by "thisses" or topics easily accessible to us. It is now firmly established that whatever else it might have been, it was an extraordinarily sophisticated astronomical observatory. Within the last centuries it was seen that on one morning only of the year, summer solstice—the time at

---

exhausting hours had resulted in patients' deaths, the system has come under fire. . . . The regulations call for the young doctors—who have routinely worked 36-hour shifts and 100-hour weeks—to work no more than 24-hour shifts and 80-hour weeks. . . . Dr. (David) Axelrod (N.Y. State Health Commissioner) said . . . that in the past the exhausting hours had 'dehumanized' doctors, leaving them to refer to some patients as 'gomers,' which stands for 'get out of my emergency room' " (New York Times, June 3, 1988). Another epithet is 'dirt bag,' which stands for demoralized patients, those who fail to take minimal care of themselves (I am indebted to Devra Zetlan of the N.Y.C. Municipal Reference Library and to Gilbert B. Wilshire II, M.D.). Mircea Eliade writes, "For archaic thought, then, man is *made*—he does not make himself all by himself. It is the old initiates, the spiritual masters who make him. . . This is as much as to say that in order to become a man, it is necessary to resemble a mythical model" (*Rites and Symbols of Initiation: The Mysteries of Birth and Rebirth*, New York: 1975, p. xiv). But these rites of initiation by purification and ordeal, only slightly disguised, still prevail.

which the sun rose at the most northerly point in space and occupied the longest time in the sky—the sun was to be seen by an
observer stationed at the center of the circle to clear the horizon
precisely above the "heel stone" on the periphery of the circle.
This functioned as if it were a sight on a rifle to "shoot" the sun
at this pivotal moment of the year, this cusp of time. Disclosed
was space-time.

But this much can be established by the crudest observations.
On the basis of a hybrid discipline called geo-astronomy it has
now been established that Stonehenge was, and is, an observatory of amazingly sophisticated powers (that such a discipline
had to be fashioned to fill a serious gap between existing earth
sciences and astronomy is part of the story I am telling). For
example, its many stones are laid out in such a way that the
complexly overlapping cycles of sun and moon can be plotted
through a cycle of 56 years, thus providing both a lunar and a
solar calendar and the connections between them. It must be
that Neolithic astronomers had discovered a phenomenon that
modern astronomy only fairly recently rediscovered.

But Stonehenge is merely one of the more obvious and more
recently built Neolithic structures. Take the massive one built
around 3000 B.C., standing forty miles north of Dublin, called
Newgrange. It is a rounded tumulus about ninety yards in diam-
eter and forty feet in height, walled in by massive curb stones,
some of them carved in sweeping spiraling designs and intricate
figures—decoration at first sight, but possibly a language which
we cannot read, perhaps a semantics and a syntax impenetrable
to our imaginations. Facing the south-eastern horizon is an
opening in the mound. It tunnels 63 feet into the structure and
culminates in a bee-hive enclosure topped by great stone slabs
compromising a corbelled roof twenty feet high. The stones
which constitute the tunnel are apparently irregularly and randomly placed. But nothing at all is random. The tunnel is precisely constructed to allow a beam of sunlight to traverse its
length and spread itself out on the floor of the inner sanctum on
only one morning of the year, that of winter solstice, when the
sun traverses its shortest route through the sky and begins its
re-ascent into spring, into new life out of the death of the year.
Given our historical and conceptual remoteness we can only

hazard a patch-work identification of this "this": a temple-observatory in which the people participated in the regenerating cycles of Nature.

But not only did professional archaeologists in the last hundred years not indulge in such speculations, they did not even test the oft-made claims that the Neolithic structures had astronomical significance. As startling as this sounds, it seems to be true. Well over a century ago travelers and writers had installed themselves in the circles and mounds at the crucial times and made the sightings, thus confirming legends which have circulated from time immemorial, and in 1909 the noted astronomer, Sir Norman Lockyer, claimed considerable astronomical significance for some of them.*

Professional archaeology had sharpened its focus and specialized itself to such an extent that it operated within the assumption that the circles and mounds were *only* burial sites. As late as the 1960s professional archaeologists were ridiculing the astronomical claims. In a book published in 1964 the archaeologist Glyn Daniel refers to the "legend" of the light beam entering Newgrange, and writes that it is a "strange wild-cat account" which "needs quoting almost *in toto* as an example of the jumble of nonsense and wishful thinking indulged in by those who prefer the pleasures of the irrational and the joys of unreason to the hard thinking that archaeology demands."**

How can an empirical scientist make a claim that is so easily falsifiable, and do it with such contempt for his potential critics? All one has to do to test the claim is to walk into the mounds at the appointed times on fairly clear dawns and either the beam of sunlight strikes the floor of the inner room on the appointed day (and on no other) or it does not.

This must be a case of mimetic engulfment in one's group and unacknowledgeable exclusion of others. Professional archaeologists as a group were simply not in the habit of making those

---

*Martin Brennan, *The Stars and the Stones: Ancient Art and Astronomy in Ireland* (London and New York: 1983), p. 32. The whole book should be consulted.
**Ibid. p. 32. This is a citation from *Newgrange and the Bend of the Boyne*, co-authored with Sean P. O'Riordain.

kinds of observations. On these matters they judged a priori. In the grip of what Francis Bacon called an Idol of the Tribe, they prejudged. The similarity of their behavior to those churchmen and others who refused to look through Galileo's telescope forces itself upon us. But these earlier doubters could protest that anything they would see which contradicted their beliefs would be an illusion produced by the Devil's employment of the instrument. What reason for not looking could contemporary empirical scientists give?

Now, what implicit a priori grounds are so convincing and powerful that an empirical scientist in the grip of them would risk easy discreditation? We must suppose that they produce figures or foci so brilliant and self-enclosing that the motivating background is completely eclipsed, occluded, buried from sight. The fixed idea was that the mounds were only burial sites. We can't help picturing the archaeologist as a body-self, not just a mind that happened to be tethered, rather incidentally, to a particular body. The body-self digs, it excavates, it sees only the earth and the stones. It cannot look up and see the sun and the stars, so cannot imagine correlations which link the molded earth with the sun and the positioned stones with the stars.

This body-self does not even conceive of itself, does not imagine itself as what it is, so cannot imagine that in conceiving of itself as a detachable mind it has thrown itself out of touch with the Earth and the people who live upon it. If this reading is correct, then the implicit a priori basis that moves the archaeologist so unwittingly is a weird sort of spiritualism: there are *pure,* properly trained *minds* which can tell in advance of empirical observations what they can and cannot find in the material world. Like the physician, the archaeologist intervenes from some pure, ethereal place on high into the mechanics of the mundane world.

My research indicates that this is true of the vast majority of professional archaeologists who have studied the Neolithic structures in the British Isles. It did not change until Michael J. O'Kelly awakened on the appointed days in the 1960's and confirmed both the legend and the claims of astronomers. However, he did not publish his observations in any form for two years, apparently wary of giving aid to unscientific "fringe" groups, occultists, etc. But that is rather a minor point. The main thing is that no place in his final, allegedly definitive report of his excavation, his massive *Newgrange: Archaeology, Art, and Legend* (1982) does he explore the implications of his observation of the penetrating light beam. He still speaks merely of "the mathematical and astronomical possibilities which are alleged to be inherent in these structures."* No place does O'Kelly explore the possibility that these were burial sites precisely because it was *here* at this *time* that the dead person could be expected to be reborn, caught up in the regeneration of the world itself. He observes the penetrating light beam and lets the matter drop. And the possibility that the great mound symbolized the pregnant belly of a Goddess—who gives new birth to the sun at each winter solstice—is curtly dismissed, even after he had earlier mentioned that the place was a site for the ancient worship of the Goddess, Danu (cf. the Danube River).**

I believe the concept of purity is fundamental. I do not see how we can understand why professional archaeologists ignored for so long astronomers' plausible accounts of the objects of archaeological research, unless we assume that mixing the fields was experienced by archaeologists as taboo, polluting. Evidently astronomers who built the hybrid discipline of geo-astronomy did not experience it this way. This is encouraging, suggesting the power of hypothesizing, and our ability to follow evidence wherever it leads: not all of us need always be subject to an unacknowledgeable load of purification ritual.

After meeting the ghost of his father, and being commanded to remember him and avenge him, Hamlet says,

     Remember thee?
Yea, from the table of my memory
I'll wipe away all trivial fond records,
All saws of books, all forms, all pressures past
That youth and observation copied there,
And thy commandment all alone shall live
Within the book and volume of my brain,
Unmixed with baser matter. Yes, by heaven!

---

*Michael J. O'Kelly, *Newgrange: Archaeology, Art, and Legend* (London: 1982), p. 79.
**I am indebted to Donna Wilshire for this insight.

Is it particularly the male mind—if we can speak thus—which grasps at purity, wipes away all pressures past, and wants the father's commandment alone to rule in the book and volume of the brain, unmixed with baser matter? And at crucial moments will it forget the commandment? The return of the repressed, the base matter? James Hillman speaks of "the long sharpened tool of the masculine mind," which divides what is "worthy" of investigation from what is not.* We defer this possibility of bias until later in the book.

Take as the third example of academic professional groups related to each other through subject matter, but which partition themselves damagingly from each other, the relationship of two attempts to study the human condition scientifically: sociology and anthropology. It is strange on its face that professional sociologists have tended historically to distinguish themselves from professional anthropologists, and conversely, when both fields represent themselves as the scientific study of human beings in groups. It is true that sociologists usually study the behavior of urban Western populations, and anthropologists that of rural and non-Western populations—a fairly clear-cut distinction.

But why divide things this way? Is it a harmless division of labor based on the simple consideration that there are so many different peoples in the world to study that the job should be divided up? But the more plausible way to do that would be to divide tasks between investigators who belong to a single discipline, for that way the communication of revealing new findings, perspectives, and research approaches world-wide could be best communicated to all who might benefit from knowing—and from testing the claims, etc. Scientific method itself prescribes this.

Instead there are two mainstream professional associations, each with its official organs of publication, a great number in each area. No doubt, many fairly obvious explanations can be offered, such as historical accident and, following upon this, the ubiquitous inertia of institutions once rooted, and of those re-

---

*James Hillman, *The Myth of Analysis: Three Essays on Archetypal Psychology* (New York: 1978 [1972]), 250.

searchers who become established within them. Related to this are considerations of self as ego: the more fields there are the faster a greater number of persons get recognition and form a professional identity.

But instead of simplifying explanations by introducing considerations of the nature of self, we almost inevitably complicate things. It happens in this case, as it did in the preceding examples involving physicians and archaeologists, that the actual practices of those who style themselves empirical scientists fly in the face of what empirical science itself prescribes: open communication to all scientific investigators into the human condition.

Why have sociology and anthropology remained relatively autonomous for so long? Immediately the motive of purity suggests itself along with others: If one is really oneself, then one will be purely oneself, and if one is purely oneself, one will be other from the other. The same reasoning applies to the identity of the group relative to other groups, the group of which one is a member and from which one derives an essential component of one's individual identity.

It could be shown, I think, that on both the theoretical level in western thought—the level at which definition itself is defined—and on the practical level of everyday intercourse, traits which distinguish individuals and groups are stressed more heavily than traits which are shared. Some of the reasons for this are obviously practical: traits which distinguish enable us to sort things out quickly in the face of pressures for fast and decisive action. Despite the exalted level of theory upon which Aristotle, for example, was operating, he stressed the trait which divides us from the other animals—rationality—more heavily than the generic traits we share with them—to take but one instance.

So exclusiveness and purity is involved in the very way we define things, cut things up and divide them and deal with them, and a great topic opens for investigation. But immediately we see that there is a weighty related reason for associating purity with the division drawn between sociology and anthropology. Anthropology deals dominantly with non-urban, non-western, non-technological peoples, those *others*—dare we say it, those primitives. If we, the masters of technology and urban life, distinguish ourselves from *them*, how really ourselves we are, how *very* pure. We urban Westerners must be this even though we have created a new barbarism of technological warfare and electronic savagery in this century.

We might say that we are super-pure, meta-pure, too pure to mention it. For it is just "primitive" peoples by and large who engage openly in purification practices. Things are clearly either sacred or profane, either taboo and to be handled with the super-care of purification rituals, or profane and of little account. Typically we pride ourselves that we no longer make the distinction between the sacred and the profane, and no longer engage in superstitious practices of purification. If my hypothesis is correct, however, the very distinction we make between "us" and "them" is unacknowledged purification ritual. In not being acknowledged it is not a vital, integrated part of ourselves, but it is still operating importantly, I think; indeed, it is out of control. Maybe, at bottom, we modern persons only bore each other, as Nietzsche said.

I have spoken of the crucial half century, 1930–1980, and will have more to say about it. One compelling reason for drawing the terminator line at 1980 (these divisions!) is that roughly—very roughly—at this point partitions between professional fields in the university begin to show clear signs of deterioration. It's as if some ground-swell were beginning to move below them, and they begin to crack and go slightly askew. Serious interdisciplinary movements begin to appear.

For but one example, a book by an anthropologist appears which is sufficiently powerful to breach the barriers and enter the discussion of some sociologists. It is Mary Douglas's *Purity and Danger: An Analysis of the Concepts of Pollution and Taboo*. It is published in 1966 and it takes a while for the word to get around, but by the 1980s it is feeding some sociological discussion in serious ways.* We must say much more about this book, but let us turn now to a discussion by the sociologist Andrew Abbott and see how Douglas's concepts are applied by him to our sophisticated western urban life. He seeks to explain the curious fact that prestige of professionals among themselves, for their

---

*Today one finds with some frequency departments or programs of urban anthropology in universities. This, I think, is a hopeful sign.

peers, often differs markedly from prestige of professionals for the public. The explanatory key is found in the striving for purity in both cases, although this striving is consummated in different ways. With regard to intra-professional rivalry, Abbott writes,

Intraprofessional status is in reality a function of professional purity. By professional purity I mean the ability to exclude non-professional issues from practice. Within a given profession, the highest status professionals are those who deal with issues predigested and predefined by a number of colleagues. These colleagues have removed human complexity and difficulty to leave a problem at least professionally defined, although possibly still very difficult to solve. Conversely, the lowest status professionals are those who deal with problems from which the human complexities are not or cannot be removed. . . . Thus, problems that fundamentally challenge basic professional categories are impure and professionally defiling . . . legal practice involving corporations . . . stands above that involving private individuals. The corporation is the lawyer's creation. The muck of feelings and will is omitted from it *ab initio*. Where feelings are highest and clients more legally irrational— in divorce—intraprofessional status is lowest. . . . For the professional, the invention of tax loopholes within the exclusively legal world of corporate law is a much cleaner business.

Quite different are the factors which determine the status of professionals in the eyes of the general public. Abbott goes on,

It is this effective contact with the disorderly that is the basis of [their] professional status in society. I have already discussed the charisma of disorder itself. The impure or polluting holds the possibility of change, of renewal, or reconciliation. . . . While these properties make the various disorders and non orders confronted by professionals charismatic, they are nonetheless still impure. To see a crime, to converse with an insane person, to nurse a sick relative—these are defiling acts for an everyday conscience, mind, or body. Only if he can control them can their charisma be transferred to one who undertakes them. . . . He touches the problems and difficulties of our world without personal defilement.*

I think this analysis is plausible. If so, its application to academic professionalism is likewise. Although Abbott does not apply it at any length to academia, he does say that the academic profes-

---

*Andrew Abbott, "Status and Status Strain in the Professions," *American Journal of Sociology*, Vol. 86, No. 4, 1981, pp. 823–5.

sional's high status reflects his exclusively intraprofessional work. We can agree with this and go on to point out that usually, however, professors must also spend some time teaching, dealing with the unclean and disorderly, the students. Couldn't they derive prestige by effectively handling this potentially polluting material and tapping its charisma, its power for change? Indeed, some do strive to do this (can we speak of them as priests or shamans of a certain sort?)—they tell a different story about themselves—but where such are found, in the more prestigious and highly bureaucratized universities, they usually stand out as mavericks and eke out a subsistence status on peripheries of departments. There is a battle between orders of priests, so to speak, a struggle to purge impure fellows, those who traffic in unclean material.

It is those of the intraprofessional order of higher purity—or so they think—who typically have the upper hand in the larger, "better" universities. This is a bit curious, but the reason is evident. Nearly all professors are dependent upon clients, the students, but professors committed to the search for prestige and power through exclusively professional contacts do not wish to acknowledge the dependency. Students are impediments in the productive process and should be excreted. Accordingly, these professors tend to suppress everything that reminds them of students, which includes their student-oriented fellows.

A presumptive connection between contemporary professionalism and archaic purification ritual runs across the entire face of the university. I must not leave the impression that the connection applies only in some fields, such as the sciences, or in medicine (a science?), or in that discipline which is most caught up in verbalism, abstraction, detachment from the body, philosophy. The fourth and final example is the recent work of a professional scholar in the humanities, Allan Bloom's *The Closing of the American Mind.** Without the pollution hypothesis we would not expect such a wide-ranging scholar blatantly to exclude crucial facts of the human condition; but he does do so.

---

*Allan Bloom, *The Closing of the American Mind: How Higher Education Has Failed Democracy and Impoverished the Souls of Today's Students* (New York: 1987).

While it is dangerous to generalize from one instance, I believe that this book is fairly typical of certain fundamental tendencies in the humanities. True, it is also atypical in other ways, but showing the underlying agreement of view where it does exist only underlines how fundamental the agreement is: a common assumption that mind can be examined in isolation from body, and a common tendency for the thinker's body-self to insinuate all kinds of prejudices and limitations into thought that is supposedly disinterested, impersonal. We see tacit purification ritual and rites of exclusion in the service of definition of thought and definition of thinker.

Bloom's book is marvelous in some ways. It is an eloquent and forceful rejoinder to those many scholars in the humanities who fall into step with what Albert Camus called the tradition of humiliated thought—those who walk abashed in the shadow of the natural scientists' claims to exclusive access to truth. For the humanities merely express personal or collective sentiment, it is thought. Despite the professors' humiliation, they hope to coax some to pay attention anyway.

Bloom argues well that in losing the universal, what we all have in common as humans—our capacity to search for truth and to submit to it if we find it—the vitality of each of our lives gutters low. "The real community of man, in the midst of all the self-contradictory simulacra of community, is the community of those who seek the truth, of the potential knowers . . . of all men to the extent they desire to know."*

Bloom's exposure of the flabbiness and drowsiness of those who accept the cheap relativism and nihilism of our culture is merciless and brilliant: when "life style" is thought to justify any way of life, and the sincere expression of something as "one's value" is thought to justify the belief that it is in fact valuable.** Quite a few college students have given this book to their parents. The most plausible explanation is that they wish to prod them into serious thought about what our moral direction should be. Such students hunger for this.

But after a certain point in the book, something goes very wrong, and I think it can be laid to pervasive features of the

---

*Ibid., p. 381.
**Ibid., p. 235.

alienated culture of professionalism, the urge to define oneself by contracting within one's group, and purifying it from outside influences. Refreshingly, Bloom had retrieved the Greek philosophers' claim that there is a universal human nature, that it determines what is in fact valuable for us, and that if we would fulfill ourselves as creatures with the capacity for rationality we must submit ourselves to the truth. He is right: such fundamental issues are seldom discussed in the university. But in proclaiming essential truths about the universal human condition, Bloom brutally excludes relevant evidence concerning that condition.

Through the millennia since the ancient Greek philosophers, various versions of universalism and egalitarianism have been advanced concerning the nature of "man *qua* man," the universal essence of mankind and the rights, glories, and obligations inherent in that essence. It should be perfectly clear to us by now, however, that these theories defined this essence in the most restrictive and arbitrary ways. In Athens the essence was thought to be adequately instantiated only in male citizens, those who were properly inscribed in the legal records of the city. Accordingly, only they were accorded the rights and perquisites of the human essence, and women, slaves, barbarians, and children were left out. It was not much different two millennia later for the framers of the founding documents of the United States, those who were inspired by doctrines of "universal human rights" and "self-evident truths" graspable by unaided reason. Thomas Jefferson excludes women, for they are not to be sullied by having a public identity:

Were our state a pure democracy, there would still be excluded from our deliberations . . . women who, to prevent deprivation of morals and ambiguity of issues, should not mix promiscuously in gatherings of men.*

It cannot be my point here to get into all the issues. I must insist on a single one: how can a thinker such as Bloom fail to discuss how self-proclaimedly universalist views of human nature nevertheless manage to exclude the vast majority of the human

---

*Quoted in Gloria Steinem, "If Moral Decay is the Question, Is a Feminist Ethic the Answer?" *Ms.*, Sept. 1987, p. 57.

race? Bloom does not face this issue, and I think I know why. He must sense that it would be disastrous, for his prejudice and aversion would be so obvious that it would be impossible to conceal it.

Not that it is any too well hidden as it is. It appears clearly in his sections on race and sex, in which his archaic, unexamined attitudes are easily noticeable at the end of our century. He fails to empathize with women and blacks, hence his thought about them is superficial. Claiming to regard history as one of his (and any educated person's) passions, he nevertheless examines the problems of women and blacks in a practically depthless historical perspective. Suddenly they find themselves with apparently equal rights in the university, but Bloom fails to point out that it is an institution fashioned over the decades and centuries almost solely by men, indeed privileged white men. He himself acknowledges this tacitly by his repeated use of sexist language, for example, "The tiny band of men who participate fully in this way of life are the soul of the university."* This is not "man," as in "man *qua* man," which might be made to seem generic for "human-kind," but it plainly means *male*.

Now, in this male-constructed university, women are prepared to enter the professions, which they increasingly do. But Bloom only notices some of the tensions they endure: for instance, the conflict between their professional careers and their possibilities for motherhood, and the danger of wrecking the family. This seems grave to Bloom, in part because he supposes that husbands, with their male nature, cannot change. Or is it only in an "age of individualism" that, supposedly, most men cannot be taught to care deeply for children and family?** At bottom, Bloom has no coherent view of the historical situation in which we all grope for answers amidst possibilities not fully tried, and he prefers berating "historically rootless" fellow humans to seeking and finding truth about us which helps us.

If possible, his lack of empathy with, and understanding of, blacks is even more abysmal than his failure to comprehend

---

*Bloom, op. cit., p. 271.
**Ibid., p. 129.

women.* He notes that most of them fail to integrate into the university, even after being invited in through blandishments, and clearly implies that they segregate themselves in separate living quarters and in Black Studies programs because they cannot compete on an equal footing with whites and orientals. No historical sense of these human beings' reality is evidenced. Anyone with any desire to seek the most cursory knowledge of "human nature," and any desire to apply this knowledge, would see that the most pressing of all problems for blacks, as it is for women, is to band together in support groups to learn to value and respect each other (perhaps in future this will no longer be necessary). Bloom refuses to see that hatred and belittlement by oppressors through the years is incorporated in the souls of the oppressed as their own inner attitude toward themselves. This is the man who speaks so confidently in his subtitle of the soul: *How Higher Education Has Failed Democracy and Impoverished the Souls of Today's Students.*

Bloom is particularly obtuse when early in his section on race he writes, "Thus, just at the moment when everyone else has become a 'person,' blacks have become blacks." Blacks can be pardoned for being skeptical about the range of "person"—or "man" in "man *qua* man"—in the light of thousands of years of the most arbitrary restriction of the terms' reference. And even if they are sincerely and intelligently applied to them, they can be pardoned for wondering what lies behind the pretty words. They sense a slippery, archaic background of behavior, vicious prejudice.

But it is not the details of one man's prejudice that should most concern us here. I have chosen Allan Bloom's book for attention because it is a vivid instance of profound failings in the humanities. For a very long time classicists and humanists have presented sweeping views of humankind which are distorted in one way or other, and which are so because the thinkers are blind to the role that their own reality as body-selves plays in what they will see and what they will not. For example, it is an important thought that there is a human nature, that there is an

---

*Ibid., pp. 91ff.

objective truth about what is valuable, and a truth about truth itself. It certainly should be discussed. But it is also essential to point out that such thought is so general—and it casts such a brilliant aura of apparently self-evident truth—that all kinds of influences and prejudices deriving from the thinker's habitual attitude as a body-self can smuggle themselves into the thought a priori and distort it. "The essence of humankind" amounts to "privileged male like myself." This is the occasion for insidious self-deception. As I noted earlier about myself when I fell under the spell of the very truth I was believing, "One must subordinate ego": this truth I asserted (egoistically) blinded me to the crucial fact that was most relevant: I was not achieving that subordination. So the universal truth uttered by a classicist like Bloom (let us assume it is true) blinds him to the exceptions he is making to that truth, exceptions that favor his own kind. His highly professionalized mind is blind to the furtive influences of his own body-self on his thinking; he is engaged in unacknowledged purification ritual which derives from ontological anxiety. "I am wholly and purely myself because I am wholly other than those base others. They are entangled in matter (and *mater*) and they threaten to pollute my purity as a distinct mind which has access to self-evident truths."

However skewed were traditional views of human nature generated in humanities disciplines, still they lent a certain coherence to the curriculum. Typically, this is now gone, and Bloom in this respect is a throw-back. It would be nice to think that today there is creative chaos in the humanities, but it looks more like plain chaos. Take one example: the appropriation by professors of English and literature of the so-called deconstructionist writings of Jacques Derrida and other Parisian intellectuals. These writings issue from a tradition in European philosophy nurtured by Martin Heidegger which aims at dismantling the façade and upper stories of venerable philosophical systems, but all with the purpose of discovering their hidden corners, margins, underside, and all this with the master purpose of finding what is still alive and appropriable within them, living philosophical tissue.

Doubtless some good work has been done by professors of English and literature in this area, and given that most academic philosophers in the U.S. are oblivious to anything outside the immediate past of Anglo-American analytic work—and that philosophical thinking will get done *some* way—it is understandable that these professors have stepped in. But the isolation of the relevant fields in the university—history, literature, psychology, philosophy—exacts a heavy toll; purification rituals of initiation and exclusion abound. Much "deconstructionist" thinking in English and literature departments in the U.S. has proven to be little more than a fad, for caught up in jargon it has lost touch with the very tradition which lent it sense and direction: the recuperation of vital possibilities of philosophical growth and coherence in the positions of past Continental thought. Its upshot here, I am afraid, is little short of nihilistic, and its effect on students largely baneful, reinforcing parochial self-indulgence and mindless skepticism—"who is to say?"

The atmosphere of unreality which hangs about the research university is inescapable. Professors of literature speak eloquently of philosophical matters, but when I ask them about the primitive matter of the truth of literature they typically grow silent or incoherent. Even so elementary a point as Aristotle's is unknown to most of them: that poetry of all sorts—dramatic, lyric, epic—can be true of actual existence when it illuminates the *sorts* of things and events which *may* be instantiated in actual existence. When professors of literature cannot come to grips with the question of truth, a suspicion of escapism haunts their work.

Examples of fields in the humanities which share subject matter but which are isolated professionally and bureaucratically could be multiplied. There can be orderly learning and researching without that order—and purity—which alienates, distorts, and withers. If we are to restructure the professionalized, segmented university into a viable educational institution, we must determine what that order could be.

VII

Academic Professionalism as
a Veiled Purification Ritual

> The proficiency of our finest scholars, their
> heedless industry, their heads smoking day and
> night, their very craftsmanship: how often the
> real meaning of all this lies in the desire to keep
> something hidden from oneself!
>
> —Nietzsche

It is no accident that Nietzsche's observation that scholars deceive themselves was made at the very time the modern university was taking shape both in Europe and the United States—the last decades of the nineteenth century. For all secular institutions pulled away from the archaic background of experience and divided themselves into bureaus in order to perform exhaustively the tasks they had set for themselves. In the university the bureaus are specialized fields of research which become so caught up in themselves that they forget the questions that define the existence of educational institutions: Who am I? What can I know? What shall I become? The feverish activity of specialized research pulls away from the background, conceals archaic procedures of identity formation, and abets self-deception.

Nor is it an accident that Dostoevsky's observations on bureaucracy were made at the same time. In *Notes from Underground* a character is presented who travesties the educated state. He turns in upon himself in relentless, monstrous self-reflection, endeavors to diagnose his strange sickness, but never nails it down. For his sharp insights and analyses have jumped out of the matrix of inherited social life, with its traditional ways of dialogue, meaning-making, and attunement with Nature, and have run wild. Soon the reader sees that the unhappy clerk is engaged in an effort to define his being by opposing himself to others—an unacknowledgeable, perverted purification ritual. Caught up in his bureau, the Underground Man has lost the primal disclosure of the world around him, a reliable story of his place and his nature—has lost himself.

Notice in the name he is given the loss of contact with the face of the Earth which turns toward the sky and responds intimately to the cycling sun and moon. Lost as well is any vital interaction with others in culture. He lives in "a mousehole." He is merely a civil servant, probably a petty clerk. But any clerk at any level is invested with considerable authority, for the structure is hierarchical and linear; every petitioner's request must pass every stage of appeal and every clerk. Does it go through? The clerk can say No. The apex of a bureaucratic pyramid requires the base; there can be no lustrous pinnacle of power without the minions at the bottom.

The clerks are aware that they keep their power only by keeping their lowly place within the whole. Blocking petitioners' access to higher authorities, the clerks' consciousness of power and their consciousness of lowliness and hypocrisy increase together. It is power bought at the price of loathing of self and loathing of the petitioner for being dependent upon someone so loathsome. But because the clerks can block the petitioners, they can regard them as more lowly and loathsome than themselves. They claim a perverted and self-deceived superiority and purity.

Dostoevsky gives us a clue to the Underground Man's strange sickness. "I could not become anything, not even an insect." His sickness is that he cannot fully *be*. At the end of his tortured monologue, exhausted after so long an attempt to find his way out of his underground world and its maze of egoistic self-absorption and self-deception, we are given a further clue. As the man tries to explain his boredom, restlessness, and spitefulness, he says he "sticks his tongue out at everything" because he has never found anything which he adored, which overwhelmed any possible impulse to stick his tongue out at it. He seeks for an identity within that which is adorable. Not finding it, he settles for a shrunken ego fragment that is purely itself because it is *not* some other being. When acknowledgeable purification rituals which empower through identification with a source worthy of one's reverence are unavailable, one is boxed up in perverted purification urges.

If I am right, sneaking purification rituals permeate nearly all secular institutions, from the crassest bureaucracies to ones most august, and with particularly damaging impact in universities. The eccentricities, distortions, and oversights of academic professionalism are so gross, I think, that we cannot explain them without supposing systematic self-deception, a masking and shunning of certain topics and persons. Recall the four cases of professionalism sketched in the previous chapter. In each of the first three cases—medicine, archaeology, and the relation of sociology and anthropology—we find emphatic (even strident) claims to scientific status mixed with practices which are grossly unscientific, for they wall out relevant evidence. In each of these cases claims for the scientific status of the discipline exist incongruously alongside the unvoiced but manifest pretension to be able to tell in advance of observation what will be found. This is a prejudicial stance adopted by an unvoiced claim of *pure* mind and *pure* method. The behavior is so out of keeping with the professionals' own stated methods and objectives that only their suppression of their own motives can account for it.

My fourth example was a case of highly professionalized scholarship in the humanities. While there was no claim here to scientific status, the case exhibits the same generic kind of prejudice. A claim to self-evident universal truth about human nature masked out those features and implications of the claim that were grossly inconsistent with the claim itself. We witnessed prejudice blind to its own existence and clearly in the service of the identity-needs of the theorizer. He would become purely and wholly himself by wholly excluding from his touch and concern vast groups of human beings who did not, for some unexplained reason, measure up to the essence of "man *qua* man."

I wish to characterize as a veiled purification ritual the refusal to mix a stance with other views (and evidence) which are palpably relevant to it. Mary Daly calls it methodolatry. Each field's formalism defines and guards its boundaries.

No doubt we have already exposed powerful factors in the genesis of professional hyper-specialization and parochialism: the ubiquitous role of the money economy in fashioning a social context in which "productivity" is construed and rewarded in the crassest terms, and in which effective monopoly of production can be achieved; the understandable human propensity to hang on to specialists' skills won only after the greatest effort and consumption of time and energy; the general role played by inertia and mimetic engulfment once official modes of defining the self are set into motion within sharply defined grooves; and the great progress which *has* been achieved in some highly specialized fields at some times. I do not doubt that each of these must be recognized to be necessary if we are to explain extreme parochialism in certain scientific and professional-academic endeavors.

But I doubt if either singly or together they are sufficient to explain it, because it is more or less easy for the secular professional consciousness to bring these troubling factors to thematic awareness. Nevertheless, the parochialism has continued, nearly unabated. This strongly suggests that some unacknowledgeable factor is at work—a factor which, in conjunction with the acknowledgeable ones, is sufficient to keep it going.

It might be objected that concerted effort to bring the acknowledgeable factors to thematic awareness would ease the parochialism. This may be true. At best, however, it would only palliate the situation a little; it is insufficiently radical. Indeed, it would probably contribute to obscuration and self-deception in the long run: Once the acknowledgeable factors were brought to thematic awareness, it would be tempting to conclude, "Just these factors couldn't be producing that degree of parochialism" (and that's true!); *"therefore that parochialism does not happen—could not happen!"* In fact, I imagine that this shifty self-deception already does occur on some dim level of consciousness.

Finally, if it is plausible to assume the validity of my overall claim that secular and professional consciousness closes in upon itself, pulls away from its archaic matrix, and conceals it, it is also plausible to suppose that some purification rituals, which are notoriously deep and pervasive archaic practices, may still be at work in the obscured background. What exactly should we be looking for?

As we have every reason to expect, purification practices and experiences of pollution and taboo are extremely difficult to corner and understand. The secular consciousness has made so little progress in understanding them because the topic of pollution and taboo is itself sensed to be polluting and taboo—"Don't touch!" It is glimpsed—out of the corner of the eye—as "not to be faced squarely," and it is recognized just enough to avoid full recognition; self-deception occurs.

In addition to this generic reason for the neglect of phenomena of purification is the great complexity and evident difficulty of the phenomena when they are faced. This study can only touch on the salient points (in another more technical work I am attempting a lengthy analysis). But without doing this much here my critique of the university would obscure some of the roots of the malaise and contribute in the long run to the problem.

I have already referred to Mary Douglas' work, *Purity and Danger,* ground-breaking as it is with respect to professionalized higher education. It will never be as easy again to divide the world into "primitive peoples" who indulge in purification rituals and we "advanced" urbanites who are free, presumably, from such archaic burdens. In her remarkable analysis of ancient Hebrew practices of purification, Douglas writes,

The underlying principle of cleanness in animals is that they shall conform fully to their class. Those species are unclean which are imperfect members of their class, or whose class itself confounds the general scheme of the world. . . . *Leviticus* takes up this scheme and allots to each element its proper kind of animal life. In the firmament two legged fowls fly with wings. In the water, scaly fish swim with fins. . . . Any class of creatures which is not equipped for the right kind of locomotion in its element is contrary to holiness. Contact with them disqualifies a person from approaching the temple. Thus anything in the water which has not fins and scales is unclean. . . . Nothing is said about predatory habits or of scavenging. The only sure test for cleanness in a fish is its scales and its propulsion by means of fins.*

We modern, post-Cartesian intellectuals tend to think of classification as a cerebral matter merely. But clearly the He-

---

*Mary Douglas, *Purity and Danger: An Analysis of the Concepts of Pollution and Taboo* (London: 1966), p. 55–56.

brews' classifications had the deepest behavioral and existential significance. In determining, for example, which manners of locomotion were appropriate to creatures in each domain of the earth, they determined which of their own modes of intercourse with these things were appropriate and pure, or inappropriate and impure: from this basis spring dietary laws. Eels, for example, locomote improperly in the water and hence are unclean.

It is particularly the eating of these unclean creatures which is polluting. There is evidently a dread that a disordered reality will enter the body and disorder the self. What is disordered outside the body must be kept outside. Likewise, what is perfectly acceptable, indeed inestimably valuable, if kept inside the body—saliva or blood for example—will be polluting if ejected improperly, particularly if it is recontacted or reincorporated in the body. Pollution involves mixing what ought to be kept separate, especially when there is an untoward mixing of the materials inside and the materials outside the body. To cross the bodily boundaries improperly is a transgression which threatens the identity of the individual.

It is perfectly clear that it is not just the *body* which is experienced as disordered and polluted by improper transits of materials. It is one's *self* which is so experienced. The vast legacy of Cartesianism in modern thought and experience tempts us to think that the self is a pure consciousness connected ever so tenuously with the body. This throws us out of touch with crucial phenomena of our own lives. As we directly, pre-reflectively experience our bodies, we *are* them: any deeply disordering humiliation or pollution of the body is a disordering humiliation or pollution of ourselves. These phenomena are immensely intriguing and reopen the question of what it means for us to be "animals caught up in the life of the mind."

As we directly experience things—innocent of philosophical preconceptions—we open directly onto the world: the self is modeled mimetically on it: disordered life in the world disorders the self, and ordered life orders it. It is just because of this direct opening that the self is so vulnerable, and why extreme care must be taken in mediating the passage of materials from inside to outside the body, or the reverse. We are our bodies, yes. We are animals, yes. Nevertheless, it is only because we are creatures who *transcend* ourselves in multiple ways that we have the experiences that we do, for example, of being sullied, polluted. The self is transcending and mimetic and *also* an individual body. As such it can either flourish in the world or be invaded, discomfited, or extinguished by it. This is complicated business.

Pollution involves mixing what ought to be kept separate, especially, as I have said, when there is an unregulated and untoward mixing of materials inside and materials outside the body. Edwyn Bevan, an earlier commentator, notes trenchantly,

Probably the great majority of people . . . would feel that water into which they had washed their teeth was unclean, not for others only, but for themselves; they would much rather put their hands into water which another man had washed his hands before them than into water into which they had rinsed their mouths.*

Allowing some room for individual and cultural differences, I think Bevan's account is true, and it points to the extreme importance of the inside of the body for the structure of the self. The pre-reflective experiencing of the contents of our bodies must belong to the immediate sense of personal self, and to recontact or reincorporate one's own saliva, once ejected, must be experienced as reincorporating portions of one's person that are no longer personal—that have, as it were, died. If Bevan is right, it is even more alienating than contacting water in which *another* person has washed his *hands*. In any case it is vastly, I think surprisingly, important. Obviously, its importance cannot be reduced to terms of germ theory. What are the chances that we experience our own ejected saliva as polluting just because we think it might have become infested with germs? What if the saliva is deposited on one's own chin? It is unlikely that the main cause of one's aversion is the thought that it might contain harmful bacteria.

I am this body, but I am also the being who identifies with other humans; I transcend through identification. When my own saliva is experienced by me as being in public space it is experienced by me as *experienceable* by *other* humans. *Other* humans

---

*Edwyn Bevan, *Hellenism and Christianity* (New York: 1922), Chapter 8, "Dirt".

must not be mixed with *this* one, for that will tend to pollute and disintegrate the particularity of *this human* being. William James spoke of the inner and outer selves. My own saliva must not be recontacted or reincorporated by me, for that would be to mix a part of me that is no longer intimate and inner with what remains such.

Nevertheless, this "outer me," this social nexus of reciprocating recognitions, is not simply *not* me, either. It is the corporate body of humanity with which I deeply identify. That is why it affects me so profoundly and holds both immense promise and immense threat. Engulfment can be ecstatic joy or terrifying pollution and possession. Engulfment in compatible others in appropriate circumstances is consummating intimacy and ecstasy. Engulfment in incompatible others is self-alienation, disruption, or demonic possession. (Even in joyous erotic relationships, when lovers probe each other's mouths with their tongues, it is not clear that they would happily accept each other's saliva if it passed through space in the form of drool. It would be too public, too experienceable by *others*—even by *them themselves* when separated in space and capable of objectifying themselves. The crudeness of the example is, of course, the point).

We are expanding on Douglas' idea of pollution as a mixing of what ought to be kept separate. The disorder of experienced reality is the deepest threat to our being, and the threat is not confined to the ingestion of food; it includes the various forms of mimetic ingestion of persons.

Note that it is fellow humans, not lampposts or dogs or cats, whose judgment of us is decisive. James speaks of the "outer me" as "the social self." Paradoxically, I am most deeply threatened by others because, in a sense, I—as social self—am in a position to threaten myself. This is what is so difficult to understand. The mind must wrench itself and pick out of the murk an unaccustomed topic, an unaccustomed *individual*. I *identify* with a *corporate* individual which is divided into sectors, levels, organs, each with its valence and value. To identify myself as a certain sort is to identify myself as belonging in a certain organ of the *social* body, and others already there can either reject or accept me. Because I identify with them, their judgment of me is utterly decisive; in the sense of myself as social self I can reject myself.

But what does this mean, really, "the corporate individual" with its various "sectors, levels, organs"? The arch-foe of Descartes, Giambatista Vico, made a penetrating observation in his *Scienza Nuova* (1725): "Words are carried over from bodies and from properties of bodies to signify the institutions of mind and spirit," and this is no merely verbal matter. In fact, so overwhelming is the ubiquitous human body as it exists in shadowy and slippery mimetic interchange with others in the surround, that the image of a single, huge, social or group body pervades all that we do.* I am trying to expose the basis of Vico's insight that the sense and meaning of the particular body gets fused with the sense and meaning of "institutions of mind and spirit"—the corporate individual, the group, *that* body with its various corporate levels and organs. Science, particularly mechanistic science, fixes and objectifies a particular human physiology at a unique point in space and time before the "omniscient" observer, and analyzes this body into causal conditions, elements, and functions. But archaic consciousness—consciousness as we directly live it—is enveloped and dominated by whole bodies, *both* the body which is our particular one *and,* in the most colluding mimetic intimacy (which at times is a great threat) the bodies of others around us which comprise *our corporate body,* the outer self, the group. (Even when we are threatened by others we may covertly mime their mode of attack even as we overtly shrink from them. There is no assurance that we will be thrown back upon "our own resources" and find our individual "center" even when attacked by others; hence occurrences of masochism.)

---

*Cf. *1 Corinthians,* chapt. 12, "For just as the body is one and has many members, and all the members of the body, though many, are one body, so it is with Christ. For by one spirit were we all baptized into one body." The idea of group body and group mind has been attacked by positivists as "metaphysical" (e.g., Hans Kelsen). They argue that beliefs are caused by events inside the individual organism, hence only individuals have minds, not groups. The latter are mere aggregates. But the cause of a belief does not adequately characterize it; only what it is *of* does so. When the believer belongs to a group, and the beliefs are *of* what the others' beliefs are *of,* he or she participates in the group's beliefs, the group's mind. To speak of a group's body and mind *is metaphorical.* But I don't think there is a literal truth which captures the reality as well. So it is an essential metaphor.

Although each of us remains a particular entity, which can be fixed in abstraction and studied physiologically, as we live pre-reflectively and immediately we are also caught up through our bodies in the encompassing image of the social body, the corporate individual. We are—particularly evident at some moments—absorbed in it, and posted at various parts and levels of it. Intellectuals, for example, tend to identify with other intellectuals, and the intellectuality of all tends to be associated automatically with the head, the capital, the directive agency of both the corporate and the individual body. Heads associate with heads—and with their typical functions in the group—arms with arms, feet with feet, etc. As we actually live the personal body, it is the mirror image, the microcosm, of the corporate body, the social group and its values and valences. Those who do the *lowest* work in the society do that which pertains to the lowest functions of the body, its pedal and eliminative functions— janitors, sewer workers, etc. Those who are in *middle* management execute others' directives, and are the "right arms" of the *top* or *head*.

Now, how are we related to others in other zones of the corporate body? Our membranes are permeable to psychical pollution from untowardly adjacent parts and "organs" of the social "organism." Ernst Cassirer recounts the ancient Hindu myth of Purusha who is sacrificed to the gods, cut up, and his various bodily parts become the essence of various castes of person. Presumably we academic intellectuals occupy the region of the head. But what if we get too close to lower parts of the social organism—the untouchables? Like Cassirer, most of us are appalled by this archaism, and would like to believe that it belongs in the past. Yet if Mary Douglas is correct, we still live at this archaic level, along with other levels we have achieved. For example: The inorganic, linear, and external relations of the bureaucratized university have driven out the *manifestly* organic relations of a community of scholars, artists, and scientists, but they have simply paved over and obscured the *background-remnants* of the still active archaic-organic relationships we are now detailing.

So we are subject to the threat of pollution not only by untoward transits of matter across the boundaries of the personal body. This occurs of course, but we must amplify and enrich the context. We are polluted by untoward contacts between ourselves and others who embody different functions within the *social* organism. I have argued that we dread to recontact or reincorporate our own saliva, for example, because we experience it as experienceable by others in public space—whether actually experienced by them or not. We dread having our most intimate "mineness" mixed with the others' "otherness" because we dread being disrupted at the heart of our private and personal selves. We particularly dread the most significant others, significant *either* because they must authorize one's inclusion within a particular social caste, *or* because they are clearly beneath one. It seems to be the former who are most threatening, however, at least on occasion. If I, who identify myself as an intellectual, am excluded by other intellectuals, I cannot place myself in a segment of corporate identity, and my identity is imperiled.

Typically nobody is in a good position to see the archaic correlations linking the personal-bodily self and its authorizing group, the corporate body—least suited of all, perhaps, are professional academics, caught up as we are in our intellectual principles and mental interests which systematically eclipse the body. The purity and identity of the individual body-self is tied to the purity and identity of the individual group of which it is an intimate member, and the group forms a region of the corporate body of the society. It is particularly one's professional academic peers who are not to see one's matter out of place—one's spittle or urine—or any *position* (intellectual or otherwise) which is *mistaken, off, maladroit*. It is particularly those who *head* the group whose opinions of one are crucially important.

But, as I said, we can also be disrupted by untowardly adjacent parts of the social organism, particularly lower parts. One unusually perceptive professor writes,

Sometimes even success in sharing can be a problem. We manage to share with students what we know and appreciate, and they love it and eagerly grasp it. But their hands are dirty or their fingers rough. We overhear them saying, "Listen to this neat thing I learned," yet we cringe because they got it all wrong. Best not to share.*

This is extraordinarily subtle and perceptive. Notice the power of the physiognomic metaphor which we live: It is the students' *hands* which are *dirty*. The hands, the instruments, which accept the beautiful gifts from the professional *heads* and minds, are dirty, unworthy, polluting. Best not to share, to get too close, to be contaminated. Beneath the shiny surface of contemporary secular sophistication and precision lies archaic human reality, I believe, and only such an hypothesis can explain the strangely exclusionary behavior of many highly professionalized professors.

Combined with the need to achieve professional competence in order to *be* something definite—but typically hidden by this professional behavior—are archaic identity needs. These tend to go unrecognized. When they threaten to become thematic their shocking nature usually prompts their repression—self-deception occurs ("Your dogs are barking in the cellars," says Nietzsche). The result is that the ability of professional competence alone to form the self is overloaded, freighted with hidden baggage. The academic person all too easily pursues professional objectives compulsively—frantically, numbly, fearfully. He or she is in no position to see the "irrational" side of the pursuit—particularly that the need for recognition from the professional peer group is so immense that the group acquires the numinous authority of a tribe. One's identity is engulfed in the identity of the group; those who fall outside it are *other*, and their presence within it contaminates both it and its members. Students are *other*.**

---

*Peter Elbow, "Embracing Contraries in the Teaching Process," *College English*, Vol. 45, No. 4, April 1983. I am indebted to Rachel Hadas for this quotation.

**With respect to this whole matter of archaic consciousness, see Ernst Cassirer, *The Philosophy of Symbolic Forms*, Vol. II, *Mythical Thought* (New Haven and London: 1955), particularly pp. 54–56. Further evidence of the unity of the group, its individuality: its ability to deceive itself. As is the case with a member, the group can see something out of the corner of its corporate eye, and acknowledge it as "not to be acknowledged further." In an unacknowledgeable and immediate consensus, each member knows that something sordid, say, is going on, and each knows that every other will say nothing. A classic

This is very unattractive territory to begin to explore, particularly unattractive for professionalized academic intellectuals. If the ideas we have just discussed are true, intellectual advance in our civilization has not been able to get beyond an archaic subsoil. At some level of behavior which is rife with self-deception, we are still possessed by various forms of "body magic." But how can this be? It is a repulsive possibility. It seems to threaten the very basis of intellectual life—and, unless it is understood, it certainly does threaten it. The university is not a gleaming ivory tower (I think of the campanile at Berkeley), but more like a beleaguered outpost in a jungle. We are exploring a territory in which the ground slides out from under our feet. This is the territory in which the neat cut-outs and individuations we make conceptually every day—and which are adequate for some of the low-pressure tasks of our lives—dissolve and merge like slime. This is the territory in which "scapegoating" occurs, and thinking that only "primitive" societies, technologically backward ones, do such things is no longer acceptable after the mechanized and electrified atrocities of our century, which have aimed at the extermination of whole peoples.

I don't think it far-fetched to hypothesize that some of the neglect of undergraduate students can be laid to their living in unwelcome intimacy with professors and polluting our pure intellects; that we load them unwittingly with our "projected" aversion to the messy, unruly, backward, and dirty body—particularly the underside of it; that they become scapegoats and are shunned. I think it is probably a case of veiled, self-deceived, passive aggression—along with whatever else it is.

Let us dwell for a moment on René Girard's noteworthy work, *Violence and the Sacred.* Pollution taboos proscribe mixing what ought to be kept separate, and since mixing (on either the more obviously individual or the more obviously communal levels) threatens one's very survival as a determinate being, it

example is the "good Germans" of the Nazi era who sensed that terrible things were going on, but who tacitly agreed that none would acknowledge them—thus "erasing" them. Another example is an academic department that coddles and screens in silence the members who do what the group wills but does not admit.
*René Girard, *Violence and the Sacred* (Baltimore: 1977).

excites both anxiety and aggression against that which threatens the mixing—and, of course, the mixing is itself aggression. According to Girard, the central task in the maintenance of cultural and individual identity is the control of the aggression, anxiety, and violence endemic to identity itself. To define ourselves we draw a line between ourselves and what we are not. Then we feel threatened by pollution! Anxiety, violence, aggression, and guilt, simmering within the nesting reality of individual and corporate body, are projected self-deceivingly onto a scapegoat victim— disposed of safely by being shunted out of the immediate social system.

This is the bottom line for Girard: if a person can be picked out as special, yet also as everybody's double, then that one can bear everybody's guilt and punishment. Violence is shunted off to the sacrificial victim, and the structure of society, and of the selves which compose it, is saved. Any misfit can, at different times, play the role of scapegoat: old, unmarried women judged to be witches, or persons of strange coloring (or lack of it—albinos), or beings who are special because of some special virtue, such as peculiar favor with the gods. And, of course, I am thinking that the list includes students: beings who, simply because they are with us, are intellectuals like us, our doubles to some extent, but who are grossly imperfect, unauthorized, polluting: beings upon whom can be "projected" furtively our aversion to our own vulnerable, easily humiliated bodies. Girard:

The sacred consists of all those forces whose dominance over man increases . . . in proportion to man's effort to master them. Tempests, forest fires, and plagues . . . may be classified as sacred. Far outranking these, however, though in a far less obvious way, stands human violence—violence seen as something exterior to man and henceforth as a part of all the other outside forces that threaten mankind. Violence is the heart and secret soul of the sacred . . . man succeeds in positing his violence as an independent being.*

We need others and cannot be without them, but we fear them precisely because of our need. They may fail to recognize us,

---

*Ibid., p. 31.

may let us down, or they may invade our body-selves in one way or another and lay waste to us. We face the menace of expulsion from a recognized place within the corporate body, so identity itself entails anxiety and violence. The energies of identity formation are sacred and dangerous: we are engulfed in what can exclude us, and we seek a sacrificial victim to exclude before we ourselves are excluded. Those who fail to be recognized (foreigners of all sorts, for example) are regarded as base or less than human, for they do not measure up to the standards within our experience which define the very reality of humanness for us.

The false projection of guilt and violence onto another is not mere error. In limiting violence by shunting it out of the particular organ or level of the social system—however brutally, cruelly, and self-deceivingly—the corporate structure of society has been saved from chaos and preserved. The pretension of scientific and technological societies to purity and exclusiveness, and the violence toward what is excluded, is—if anything—greater than what is found in "primitive" religion. For the sacred, as described by Girard, is that which dominates us in direct proportion to our efforts to master it. The sacred does not exist as a category which is acknowledgeable by science or rational management. It is ignored or treated with disdain, shouldered aside. Thus, in spite of the primitives' move to totalize through belief in a supernatural domain, there is always deference paid to the sacred, and the humble admission that something can always go wrong at some minutely complicated step in the efforts to control it. True, primitive procedures and beliefs are usually set up in a way that prevents them from being falsified by any possible outcome. Yet humility remains. This contrasts to the arrogance of "rational management" and the bureaucratic mind.

Girard's notion of the sacred as a violence which cannot be directly mastered helps us understand the ambiguous and slippery energy of identity formation: we are engulfed in what must be capable of excluding us, so we are both attracted and frightened. Our ambiguous attitude toward the other fills us with anxiety and guilt, and we project this onto some hapless other whom we believe cannot hurt us, the sacrificial victim.

Later in this book we will try to see if there is some other way to achieve individuation of self.

My thesis, you see, has become quite radical. I am seriously considering an hypothesis which places within the putative citadel of rationality itself, the university, what the secular mind can only construe as irrational. If the hypothesis is true, the difficulties of conducting undergraduate education in the university are immense, perhaps intractable, and the frustrations of teachers boundless. If true, there is a deeply seated tendency not to recognize whatever would pollute the purity of one's method and way of life—one's particular science or professional specialty—even though science and scholarship themselves prescribe its recognition. High on the list of "invisible" factors seem to be undergraduate students. I think I detect both in myself and many others an habitual tendency to erase them. Some powerful prejudice must be operating. Moreover it must be hidden—or only half-way recognized—otherwise it would be acknowledged, and steps taken, perhaps, to remedy it. I am hypothesizing that it is purification ritual that excludes others in order to define oneself.

A critical approach which is tacitly or manifestly Cartesian will subscribe to psycho-physical dualism, and it automatically begs the question and dismisses the hypothesis out of hand. Self is a consciousness; whatever is in its consciousness the self is conscious of; the self has no consciousness of doing X; so the self could not be doing X. Probably the deepest psychical function of psycho/physical dualism is to deny the reality of what we are doing as selves which are bodies; to rationalize and facilitate self-deception.

In declaring that the twentieth-century university is composed according to principles of seventeenth-century thought, Whitehead was putting his finger on something profound.

VIII

Pollution Phenomena: John Dewey's Encounter with Body-Self

> The world seems mad in preoccupation with
> what is specific, particular, disconnected.
> —John Dewey

Although John Dewey has proved to be highly controversial, many consider him to be the greatest philosopher of education since Plato. It is no accident that both thinkers appear at comparable times in the evolution of their cultures: when mythological consciousness has begun to give way to rationalistic and scientific currents. Both recognized that a balance must be achieved between the old and the new or the formation of human beings will be disrupted. New connections will have to be discovered or science and technology, with all their benefits, will so abruptly displace us from traditional adjustments to others and to Nature that we will be infatuated with power but unable to direct it intelligently—we will be disoriented.

When Dewey published *Democracy and Education* in 1916 he was already fifty-seven years old. He had no way of knowing, of course, that he would live for thirty-six more years. It is a gleaming, replete, beautifully organized, and, apparently, fully realized work; perhaps he thought of it as the culmination of his life, his magnum opus. In response to the chief educational question, "What shall I make of myself?" Dewey provides a new vision in which self is to be reoriented in the world through developing in such a way that discontinuities between mind and body, self and other, culture and Nature are overcome. A new story, a new myth of wholeness is detailed. When he writes toward its close that "philosophy is the general theory of education" we have some reason to say, yes, this belongs on the shelf next to Plato.

But Dewey entered a period of personal crisis. All his efforts to achieve a theory of integrity of body-self and of continuity of experience—it must have seemed a life-time's efforts—hit a stone wall. He detected blockage, a rude discontinuity between his own powers of inquiry and perception, and the very conditions of these powers in his functioning organism. These conditions hid themselves from him. For decades he had brilliantly criticized psycho/physical dualism, but, ironically, his own consciousness seemed to split off from its conditions in his organism. This insidious turn imperiled his vision of goodness as vitality, as integrated, dynamically interactive living. Threatened was his whole philosophy of education. In a real sense, his life was threatened.

Why is consciousness so limited when it tries to perceive its limits and its conditions in the body? Dewey struggled with this question in a personal urgency he had never experienced before. He began to suppose that there are factors at work in our bodily selves which condition and limit consciousness to such as extent that consciousness cannot grasp that it is limited by them. How ironical if intellectuals called naturalists or materialists fail to grasp the matter of their own bodies! Consciousness is a closet lined with mirrors which cannot dream that it is only a closet.

Dewey began to suspect that the range of his own options as a person and thinker was limited unnecessarily and that his freedom was undermined. Life was stale, flat, pointless, something was missing. Not long after completing *Democracy and Education* in 1916, in a kind of desperation both personal and professional, Dewey consulted F. M. Alexander, who was a pioneering psycho-bio-therapist.* That is, Alexander had discovered means for altering consciousness through altering bodily movements and postures. Judging from the way Dewey talked and held his head and neck, Alexander said "he was drugged with thought"— almost as if his mind were dissociated from his body.

---

*Frank P. Jones, *The Alexander Technique: Body Awareness in Action* (New York: 1976), particularly pp. 94–105.

Does Cartesian psycho/physical dualism return? No, Dewey thought, but he recognized that he faced immense personal and theoretical difficulties. He described himself as awkward, a slow learner of everyday comportment. He lauded Alexander for discovering how to apply scientific method to everyday life. Alexander could generate sensations within his own body which both formed and tested hypotheses about himself, his bodily self. What lies too close for most of us to see, Alexander had seen.

Dewey discovered something fundamental about the limits and conditions of his own consciousness. It was only *after* Alexander manipulated Dewey's body into unaccustomed positions and postures that Dewey could imagine the *possibility* of them.

Somehow the body must take the lead if consciousness is to become aware of its closet; it must be jolted by the body. But how can the body do this without being conscious, and how can it imagine new ways of living if it must do so with the old consciousness? Indeed, it may require intervention from another conscious body, another body-self. Only this way, perhaps, can sensations be generated which both *form* revealing hypotheses about one's bodily self and test these. It is self-deceivingly abstract to limit truth to propositions writable on a blackboard. Nor can self-knowledge and truth be limited to a set of "facts" which a consciousness spies in the "outer world." Self-knowledge and truth demand that a body-self intimately and courageously interact with itself to lead to consummations revealing of itself. Pragmatism is no mere accoutrement of technology, but the humane attempt to formulate a theory of truth that acknowledges the reality of body, relativity, reciprocity, and change.

Alexander concentrated on altering the way in which Dewey's head rested on his neck. This habitual positioning was so integral to his identity as a self that he could not imagine the new positionings until Alexander effected them manually. The therapist concentrated on the zone of the body's inwardness that so habitually escapes objectification that it counts as subjectivity. But now we begin to understand subjectivity as we actually live it, not as a ruse or a slogan (or as an alleged reference to a separate mental substance), not something which distracts our attention from our own vulnerable, strange bodily being, and the manner in which its consciousness conceals its limitations and organic conditions from itself—conceals them behind a screen of logic and verbalisms.

We learn the real meaning of the phrase "mind cut off from body." Caught up in the foci of its attention, and the tacit belief that consciousness floats free from the body, the body-self does not stand open to its own impulses to integrate itself—both with its own past and with the surrounding environment. This may appear when the head is not balanced atop the backbone, a dynamically integral part of the body. One's senses are constrained by fixed ideas, and cannot open to present possibilities of integration and growth. Instead of freely acknowledging one's origins, and building solidly upon them, one is captured by some of them. Head tilted up perhaps, cramped, gritting teeth, holding back tears, the little child's tensions and fears still held in the muscles and the joints of the middle-aged man's jaw. Lacking a strong body and a secure position in the world, the child as head has tried to go it alone. Properly to connect and adjust the head and neck may be sufficient to release this archaic fixation and to free the self for adult behavior. It may be sufficient to liberate consciousness by opening it to some of its own conditions in the body.

One had to grope and intuit trustingly if one were to open one's consciousness and know one's own bodily being. For example, one may see that one's posture should be improved, but have no idea of the bodily conditions which must be altered to bring this about. Nevertheless, one changes something and thinks that one has achieved the goal, whereas really one has only reached a "another way of standing badly." That is, one is so out of touch with both extrinsic values (means) and intrinsic values—so out of touch with oneself—that one deceives oneself about what one has done with one's "own" self. It is a kind of magical thinking in which we are deluded to believe that the wishing for success and the strenuous effort to achieve it will bring it about: a mode of thinking we would easily spot as fallacious if it were applied to something other than ourselves, to a disabled machine, say, which could be fixed only if the actual means of repair were discovered.

At least as early as 1899 Dewey had seen that education must develop intuitive and perceptive powers of minding, particularly the ability to perceive or intuit intrinsically valuable states of vital being and the means which actually bring them about. The capacity to calculate which ends—in theory—are valuable, and which means—in theory—are effective is insufficient. But he was only beginning to intuit how difficult perception can be. The minding body is too close to itself to see itself clearly and easily. Indeed, it generates a nightmare in which it is closeted by mirrored walls which it cannot see to be walls.

Know thyself! The words inscribed on the temple of Apollo at Delphi which haunted Socrates haunted Dewey thousands of years later and, in conjunction with continuing lessons from Alexander, prompted him to deepen his thought in the next three decades of his life. Science which becomes intelligence cannot be divorced from moral virtues of patience and courage and aesthetic virtues of composition of body and of perception—greatness of person. These virtues are not merely "values" inside some subjective Cartesian consciousness, but structures of the body and the world which must be mastered if we are to live sanely and vitally.

There is no doubt that Dewey's thought grows deeper, darker, and more difficult after his contact with Alexander, and in part because of it. In his great work, *Experience and Nature*, 1925, Dewey develops an account of consciousness embedded in its bodily conditions, and of how these can be perceived and changed. This is education on the deepest level, and it points toward a deeper understanding of pollution phenomena, our most pressing immediate goal in this study. If science is to become intelligence, we must learn to authorize ourselves in new patterns of behavior which move us toward fulfillment. Ironically, the rapid ingestion of our "liberating" science has brought "casual, desultory, and disintegrated incorporation of meanings" in the bodily self. We have lost "rectitude of organic action" and the subconscious is "corrupted and perverted."* To achieve this rectitude, he writes, we must get in touch with "our immediate organic selections, rejections, welcomings, expulsions . . . of the most minute, vibratingly delicate nature. We are not aware of the qualities of most of these acts. . . . Yet they exist as feel-

---

*John Dewey, *Experience and Nature* (New York: 1958 [1925, 1929]). All the quotations in this paragraph are found in pp. 295–302.

ings qualities and have an enormous directive effect on our behavior."

These lines, written after a decade of more or less sustained contact with Alexander, reveal the unpopular Dewey: few educators have followed him to this point in his thought. We should also speak of the tragic Dewey. "We are not aware of the qualities of most of the acts" which constitute our very being and which condition and limit our consciousness.

Now, one might think naively that since philosophers are professional cerebrators, and enjoy testing their teeth on intellectual difficulties, that they would have followed Dewey into these harder strata of his thought. Almost without exception they have not. This reminds us of the earlier failure of philosophers to understand the human significance of Kant's work. But now the significance of what Dewey is disclosing is more obviously disturbing, even repulsive. Although he does not explicitly identify the "immediate organic selections, rejections, welcomings, expulsions . . . of the most minute, vibratingly delicate nature" as including sickening recoilings of pollution experience, or ecstatic welcomings of purification experience, still he is standing right on the threshold of this recognition. He is disturbingly close. The openness of the body-self to the world, its vulnerability, and its "irrational" engulfments and aversions are all clear enough.

I think it is no accident that professional philosophers, almost without exception, have avoided this side of Dewey's mature thought as if it were the plague. This is not an accidental or merely personal response, but one which is typical and essential for academic professionals, particularly philosophers—the most mentalistic and verbalistic of the assembled professional tribes. The best explanation for their neglect, I think, is that the topics of the lived body and pollution phenomena are themselves experienced as polluting; particular sensuous events will not be singled out and individuated as topics. There is too much stress and dread for these "thisses" to emerge.

The failure of professional philosophers to follow Dewey into this area is recounted by Frank P. Jones, for years professor of classics at Tufts University, and a close student of psychology and the therapeutic methods of F. M. Alexander. I quote Jones's account at length, because it has great significance for our study.

Whatever else Cartesian consciousness—and its latter day ava-tars—may be, it is a recoiling flight from the body-self which attempts to spin away from it, to lose itself within itself, and to fabricate the belief that it is something distinct and separate from the body. Jones writes,

In the face of Dewey's positive statements about the moral and intel-lectual value of the [Alexander] technique, I have always found it diffi-cult to understand the insistence by his disciples that its application was purely physical—as if the technique were a kind of Australian folk rem-edy which Dewey in the kindness of his heart had endorsed in order to help Alexander sell his books. I ran into this attitude long before I met Dewey. Sidney Hook had given a lecture at Brown on some aspect of Dewey's philosophy. I had just discovered Alexander's books and had been impressed by Dewey's introductions to them. At the end of the lecture I went up . . . to ask Hook about Alexander's influence on Dewey. He looked at me uncomprehendingly at first and then said with obvious embarrassment: "Oh yes! Alexander was an Australian doctor who helped Dewey once when he had a stiff neck." A little later in an article on Dewey in the *Atlantic Monthly*, Max Eastman described Al-exander as "A very unconventional physician . . . an Australian of orig-inal but uncultivated mind." "Dewey was smiled at in some circles," Eastman wrote, "for his adherence to this amateur art of healing but it undoubtedly worked in his case." In Corliss Lamont's *Dialogue on John Dewey*, Alexander again appears as a quaint character who was "concerned with your posture and that sort of thing." The speakers agreed that "Dewey thought Alexander had done him a lot of good," but none of them gave Dewey credit for intelligent judgment, and Er-nest Nagel (according to Horace Kallen) attributed the whole episode to superstition on the part of Dewey. This picture of Dewey as the na-ive supporter of an ignorant Australian doctor has unfortunately been given increased currency in . . . *The Life and Mind of John Dewey*, by George Dykhuizen (1973).*

Jones's words speak for themselves—they mesh perfectly with my experience of most professional philosophers. We have here significant evidence for the pollution hypothesis. The very think-ers—many of them of considerable stature—who know most about Dewey's life and thought cannot see the immense rele-

---

*Jones, already cited. With respect to Sidney Hook I should add that his stim-ulating lectures on Dewey first lured me into *Experience and Nature*.

vance of Dewey's encounter with himself as body-self (or as he sometimes writes, body-mind). Their squeamishness and fastidiousness is revealing. The most plausible hypothesis is that they identify themselves as minds, and are in the grip of unacknowledgeable fears of pollution by the body.

Dewey's lesson is disturbing. It adds a new dimension to Faust's observation that knowledge tricks us beyond measure. For decades he had brilliantly criticized the Cartesian tendency to conceive mind separate from body, self from environment, culture from Nature. I believe he discovers great truths. Moreover, he roots truths in experience. It is too easy, he says, to think of truth as a property of a statement or proposition; this can mire us in the limitations of verbalism and a subjectivistic notion of mind. Dewey defines truth concretely as "processes of change so directed that they achieve intended consummations."*

But despite this concrete and existential definition of truth, and the key particular truth that we are not minds with bodies somehow attached, but body-minds, as he says, he had not in all those decades discovered the truth of his own body-self. This proves in the most vivid possible way that if we do not deeply and directly experience what our truths are true *of*, we deceive ourselves—even though they are truths about ourselves—and defeat the purposes of education and self-reflexiveness. Recall my deceiving myself in the very act of asserting the truth that ego must be in abeyance (for I asserted this egoistically), and Allan Bloom's asserting truths about all humans which allowed his exclusions of whole classes of persons without his noticing it.

But Dewey's case is particularly ironical. His asserting of general truths about the conditions of consciousness in the body prevented him from dilating his own consciousness and allowing his own body to take the lead in disclosing itself. Without this dilation, his "immediate selections and rejections" will go unnoticed, for they cannot initiate the processes in which they develop, test, and disclose themselves. They themselves must be allowed to develop hypotheses about themselves, and this can happen only if we are sufficiently confident and relaxed to undergo the consequences of allowing them to be tested, developed.

---

*John Dewey, *Experience and Nature*, p. 161.

Anything else is what Freud called the defense mechanism of intellectualization.

The archaic background of experience is painfully difficult to reveal. But if it is not revealed all the talk about the unexamined life being not worth living is mere twaddle, and what passes for education a sham. Dewey contributes to what the Greeks meant by chest-knowledge, humane and ethical knowledge, the union of intellectual freedom and ethical responsibility, and he points to regenerative possibilities of experience.

But it would be a mistake to infer from this that all of Dewey's thought about education prior to 1916 was a mistake. Indeed, it is because it is so brilliant that what it still leaves out—courageous self-engagement—is so evident. The culminating element of Dewey's epistemology is raw courage: chest and guts.

Well then, should the university be a large psychoanalytic institute? No. I suppose that private demons must, in the last resort, be a private matter.

Nevertheless, it is too easy to draw fallacious inferences from this admission. The simplistic distinction we make between private and public is yet another reflection of the seventeenth-century psycho/physical distinction between private mind and public body. It may prevent us from seeing what relevance these personal facts do have to the structure of the university. First, and most obviously, these ideas *about* self as body-self, and whatever truth they possess, are basic to most fields and should be incorporated in the curriculum (I here distinguish truths about self from personally experienced—but not professionally irrelevant—truths *of* self). That they are left out—even from many courses on Dewey—is appalling. Both truths *about* body-self and truths *of* body-self are relevant to our conduct as teachers. Second, the failure to grasp the concept of body-self means the failure to grasp the utter inability of seventeenth-century psycho/physical dualism to grasp the nature of knowledge and the knower, the reality of the human situation. And this means the inability to grasp how the contemporary university is structured according to the principles of seventeenth-century thought. In other words, any hope of basically reforming the university is forfeited.

The research university purports to be also an educational institution. Not to grasp the significance of self as body-self undermines every essential feature of the educating act. Self-reflexivity and self-knowledge become impaired, or impossible. Thus one's ultimate responsibility as a free knower becomes impaired or impossible: to discover and accept the truth about oneself—and to exemplify this self-awareness wherever appropriate. But also knowledge of one's most intimate relations to others in community becomes impossible, e.g., relations to the young, to students. And again, all this means that the responsibility to pass on meaning and truth from the past is blocked, for this can be accomplished only if we grasp the archaic background of shared experience inherited on several levels of experience from the past.

It is still another destructive dualism to divide in any wholesale way the personal growth of the professor from the education of the young placed in his or her care.

The assumption that teachers can create and maintain those conditions which make school learning and school living stimulating for [the young], without those same conditions existing for teachers, has no warrant in the history of man. . . . Dewey knew all this well. . . . [He] created the conditions for his teachers which he wanted them to create for their students.*

I take these points to be basic to any intelligent attempt to restructure the university. Let us now turn to further complexities of the problem, and how the belated integration of twentieth-century thought into university structure can modify that structure.**

---

*Seymour Sarason, *The Creation of Settings and the Future Societies* (San Francisco: 1978), pp. 123–124. I am indebted to Dr. Mary Faeth Chenery for this reference.
**I thank Steven C. Rockefellar for sharing chap. 8—"Poems, Letters, and Lessons"—of his book-length ms. on Dewey's life and thought. Dewey's poetry is far from incidental to the main body of his work.

PART THREE

Reorganizing the University

IX

Revolutionary Thought of the Early Twentieth Century: Reintegrating Self and World and a New Foundation for Humane Knowledge

> Relation is reciprocity . . . Inscrutibly involved,
> we live in the currents of universal reciprocity.
> —Martin Buber

No stronger case of culture-lag and the inertia of institutions can be imagined, I believe, than this: At the close of the last century and the beginning of ours, at the very time when revolutionary thinkers were reconceiving the nature of reality—the knowable—and the nature of knowledge and the knower—thus reconceiving what a university might be—the university as we know it today was being built along the lines of *seventeenth-century* thought.

In *Science and the Modern World* Whitehead wrote that what Descartes was to the revolutionary seventeenth century, William James was to the revolutionary twentieth. As early as 1892—in the last chapter of the abridgement of *The Principles of Psychology*—James had sketched the basis for the complete overturning of seventeenth-century psycho/physical dualism, the neat division of individual selves as private centers of ego-consciousness from everything else. This division seals our eyes to mimetic engulfment and pollution phenomena, deep realities of the human condition.

Roughly put, James formulated a notion of experience as neutral between subject and object, mind and matter. Some configurations of neutral experience "tell a story" of the world as it unfolds in world-historical time—something there for us all to see—and other configurations "tell a story" of a personal history, some aspects of which only the person himself can directly experience. The numerically identical bit of neutral experience figures in both contexts. Take the blueness of the sky. Caught in the relentless grip of psycho/physical assumptions we commonly say, "I look up at the blue sky." The blue is "out there" and I and my will are "in here." But on James's analysis the blue is primally neutral; it is, as such, not located, but permeates the world as it engages and engulfs me prereflexively. Using James' assumptions we contact the reality of many of our moments of mimetic engulfment in the world, which might be put this way: "Sky-i-fied I am turned upwards." We can begin to understand phenomena of engulfment and possession, and because of this to understand also those sickening recoilings of aversion when the other-incorporated is incompatible.

As James sketches it, the self is a *field phenomenon*, and we can begin to understand how we can identify with, and incorporate within our bodily selves, the corporate individual, at one or another of its levels or "organs"; and we can see how the attitude of the social surround toward us becomes our own attitude toward ourselves. Coordinately, one's own organism can be understood both as it figures in one's immediate experience of bodily processes and fluids, one's inner self, and in one's experience of it *for others* within one's corporate organism, one's social self. And one can also experience it in that sharply focused way in which it is limited to being experienced in merely physiological terms accessible to natural scientists. The body is "the palmary instance of the ambiguous." It is labile, potent, dangerous, and we can better understand its connection to the sacred.

The self is a *field phenomenon*. With this the humanities and social sciences begin to join hands with the field and relativity theories of twentieth-century physics, and the old disciplinary partitions in the university can begin to come down, since a theoretical basis for razing them appears. These are the departmentalized divisions which have paralyzed the university in unacknowledged purification rituals—the organs of the social body must be kept separate, at the risk of chaos!—and reduced it to a bureaucratic morass in which the pursuit of truth and knowledge does not inform the self-governance of the knowers and learners.

Since to be educated is to be self-reflective, and this is to be oriented in the world, twentieth-century relativity theory has great educational significance, because it conceives us as in the world, as field beings. It is not a flight into abstractions which abandons concrete reality, although it is true that many still think of "concrete reality" in terms of seventeenth-century mechanistic physics. The physics of our century is, among other things, a criticism of this earlier physics for being too abstract. The boxes of polarized abstractions which forgot they were abstractions are abandoned: self/other, mind/matter, subject/object. Not only is the distinction between matter and energy shown to be non-fundamental, but also undermined is that between mind and body. Selves are no longer imagined to be isolated existences. In reorganizing our vision of the nature of knowledge and the knower, twentieth-century physics provides powerful clues for reorganizing the university along interdisciplinary lines. However, this is highly threatening to those who conceive themselves mentalistically and atomistically, and who try to build an identity through tacit purification rituals and esoteric verbalisms.

The earlier physics had envisaged a universe of absolute spatial and temporal dimensions—space an infinitely large three-dimensional container, conforming to Euclidian geometry, which rolled on an indefinitely extended linear track of time. Part of what is meant by calling these spatial and temporal structures absolute is that they were conceived to be real independent of whatever material entities happened to reside within them—and independent also of the observers who formulated ideas about them and perceived them.

Twentieth-century relativity and field theory attacks the earlier physics at its root. The notions of absolute space and time are regarded as abstractions which seemed so "natural" that their formulaters forgot their abstractness. The very notion of objectivity itself, so prized by seventeenth-century physics, is an immense impediment for understanding even physical reality, as the physicist, Werner Heisenberg, pointed out. The notion of atomic individuals discreetly divided from each other is a product of the *group* myth and story, the *corporate* individual, of seventeenth-century culture.

Twentieth-century relativity and field theory holds that there is no pure objectivity, because "objectivity" is no more than an abstraction polarized against an equally artificial notion of "subjectivity." The drawbacks of seventeenth-century thought for understanding human beings are clearly evident. The earlier mathematical physics can only know the forceful, not the valuable or the purposeful. Set over against the "objective" world, boxed into our subjective reality as centers of consciousness, egoselves, we are deprived of knowledge which could guide us reliably through the world to the sane, vital, and valuable. We have only the language and tools of force: force for more force, power for more power. Cut off in our own minds from ourselves as bodies, and malcoordinated in the archaic, sensuously given environment, we rattle around in "a crisis of values," in rampant insecurity and nihilism.

The boxes of seventeenth-century abstractions passed as reality. For example, it seemed perfectly sensible to speak of very distant events as occurring simultaneously, because a single instant, a "now" on an absolute track of "nows," was thought to characterize every event at that instant within the huge rolling box of space. But in 1905 Albert Einstein (and a short time later, Whitehead) reconceived the universe in a way which undercut all the "obviously true" compartmentalizations of seventeenth-century physics, and found space, time, energy, and matter to be connected in a kind of organic way: none could exist without the others within the field, and the field feeds back into its parts.

Einstein, Whitehead, James, and Dewey all agreed that reality is the field of concrete interactivity. The notion of a detached, nearly passive, "value-free" consciousness or observer must be abandoned. Objectivity as the polar opposite of subjectivity must be also, or if retained, reconceived as an all-inclusive field of interactivity. For Einstein, simultaneity of events in *time* is objectively real only at that point in *space* where the events' "ripples," their field effects, occur together—for the ripples coincide and occur together *for* an observer. Even light, carrying its "messages" of events, takes time to travel. Simultaneity is relative to the situation of the observer, and will be different for different ones. Space and time cannot be divorced. Space-time is not merely an "appearance in the mind," over against an "objective reality," but is real. Also the orientation and goals of the physicist are real. Time, space, energy, matter, and observer are all real only by being relative to each other within the field. As Whitehead observed, it is this new unity and interpenetration that the departmentalized university has not been able to follow or allow.

Intelligence requires a new unity of calculation and intuition, poetry and science, perception and abstraction. Einstein exhibited an imagination which was simultaneously mathematical and scientific, and sensuously engaged and artistic. For example, he looked at a clock tower in Zurich and asked himself what it would be like to ride on a beam of light reflected off the clock face. The answer was clear once the question was asked: as one looked back at the clock tower one would experience a clock's hands which did not move. Relative to the earth one was leaving, one would be living in a different time—really, and not merely "in appearance." There is no one, absolute time.

I have already alluded to Whitehead's critique of Descartes: we do not live in a limited doll's house of clear and distinct ideas or entities, but always in the background we register, if vaguely, the infinite universe giving birth to us, and it gives birth differently in different spatio-temporal frames of reference. Whitehead's version of relativity theory is more organismic than is Einstein's. For the latter the speed of light is a new absolute or constant. Whitehead is prepared to question even this. Moreover, he dips back into the early nineteenth-century critics of mechanism, the romantic poets. Lord Byron's radical metaphor, "High mountains are a feeling," holds riches. We are no longer to think that mountains are merely "out there," while feelings are merely "in here." Mountains experienceable, so mountains really, are mountains only because the earth does—among other things—emerge through us, pour through us, in a mountainly way. They are as much a typical feeling of ours as they are anything. All particulars are particulated out of a field which engenders and extrudes them. To be educated is to be attuned, and thus to be engaged emotionally, alive to the possibilities of metaphor.

It is because James undermined the conception of mind and consciousness as a substance which can be defined in opposition to matter that Whitehead maintains that he is to the twentieth century what Descartes was to the seventeenth. James opens up radically different views on knower and known, and on everything else, including ethical and existential relationships to oneself and others. For Descartes there are acts of "pure understanding" and "pure intellection." Since the imagination deals with images, and images bear traces of matter and can be said to be extended, Descartes rules that imagination is not essential to mind and self.*

As Dewey pointed out in *The Quest for Certainty,* the creation of a pure realm, untouched by body, uncertainty and risk, always necessitates the designation of a contrastingly impure realm to absorb and take responsibility for the messy aspects of experience (as Susan Bordo shows in her important recent study—see previous footnote). And as James argues, the construal of evil as a "problem" for which a transcendent and supernatural Deity must be absolved of responsibility necessitates transforming "an essential part of our being" into "a waste element, to be sloughed off . . . diseased, inferior, excrementitious stuff."** Whatever else Descartes' geometrical method of inquiry was designed to accomplish, it does in fact function as a disguised purification ritual, the hope of which is to shore up a self beleaguered by doubt and anxiety. As the medieval way of life collapses around him, Descartes strives to find an absolute center and foundation within an individual self conceived to be a pure mind or consciousness reflecting itself within itself immaculately. But this conceals our reality from ourselves, and excites both arrogance and anxiety. For we are bodies engulfed mimetically in a world which eludes our ability to articulate the extent of our involvement. We are subjects, but de-centered ones, body-subjects.***

The Philosophical Works of Descartes, translated by Haldane and Ross, Vol. I, p. 212. Descartes writes, "I have often also shown distinctly that mind can act independently of the brain; for certainly the brain can be of no use in pure thought: its only use is for imagining and perceiving." Cited in Susan Bordo's *The Flight to Objectivity* (Albany, N.Y.: 1987), p. 90. See chapter 5, "Purification and Transcendence in Descartes' *Meditations.*"
**From *The Varieties of Religious Experience,* quoted in Bordo, p. 81.
***For a recent development of this fundamental idea, see Calvin O. Schrag, *Communicative Praxis and the Space of Subjectivity* (Bloomington, Ind.: 1986).

The gist of all this is that the knower is a participant in a world that forever eludes final capture by any set of abstractions. The knower cannot be a detached observer centered in himself (we could also say "herself," except very few women have ever conceived themselves as so detached, and we will remark on this later). The self thus "centered" within itself is deceiving itself (however important it is that we be morally "centered"—a point to be elaborated later). In the attempt to locate itself in a threatening world, the self disorients itself. As bewildering as twentieth-century physics can be on certain levels of analysis, still it relocates and reintegrates us as interacting beings in a vast world. That this escapes our ability completely to focus and thematize it does not invalidate this point. Engulfed though we be, still we have the assurance that our purposes, satisfactions, coordinations—and malcoordinations—are as real as anything else.

What constitutes humanly valuable activities and states must be decided by an experimental inquiry; it will fail to give certainly true decisions on all questions, but these are, in principle, no more difficult to solve than many others in the new world of relativity and field theory. What Dewey would call the desirable, as contrasted with what is merely immediately desired—what he would call long-range vitality, or growth for ever more growth— is difficult to decide, perhaps, but it is open to inquiry. Required is radical interdisciplinary cooperation within a broad spectrum of inquirers into goodness: the use of aesthetic imagination to re-image the earth and our place as body-selves within it—new orientations—and to combine these with ever-new analyses into novel topics and individuations.

If we are fully alert and alive we will be ready both to make new distinctions and to erase them. It was important for the earlier mechanistic physics to make a hard and fast distinction between space and time, and also, I suppose, between observer and observed. It was equally important for contemporary physics to blur or erase these. Such flexibility is even more evident on the level of quantum physics. The earlier science drew a sharp line between particles of matter and waves of energy. Contemporary physics found this to be detrimental to understanding experimental results. So a patchwork of the two was devised—"wavicle." When "an" electron "jumps" to another orbit within an atom, "it" seems to take no time at all to make the transition. So how could it be *one* tiny discrete substance or entity "traveling through" space? There seems to be only a field of dynamically reciprocating and dancing energies, interlacing "nodes" within a "field." But these are all metaphors and images: "nodes," "dancing," "fields."

Concreteness is interactivity, the "between." We no longer speak of observer over against observed, but begin with the observing and infer from this to the nature of observed and observer, insofar as we are able. And observing cannot be divorced from feeling, intending, purposing, sensing. This fact is brought home with disturbing emphasis in the quantum physics of atomic and subatomic reality. Observing cannot be divorced from either the observed or the observer, and the ramifications become exceedingly strange. In the end, however, we are better able to understand ourselves as involved, vulnerable beings who engage in practices such as tacit purification rituals.

Seventeenth-century mechanistic physics has been decisively displaced from its perch by twentieth-century thought, and the human ramifications are momentous. As quantum physics threatens to take over the foundations of physics itself, this momentousness only increases. Quanta of energy (energy in some sense—quantum wave functions) must be understood as occurring within ever more complex quanta. The whole becomes essential to locating and specifying any member or part. Since these wholes include consciousness, and since this involves spontaneities and unpredictabilities of the greatest human moment, the whole mechanistic conception of human individuals as atomic bits forced to move on a track of time must be critically reexamined or discarded. Human freedom, meaning, identity, realization and goodness open abruptly.

As Niels Bohr is reported to have said, if one is not disturbed by quantum physics, one has not understood it. We cannot further explore this pregnant topic here. But it is important at least to allude to it, and to recall Bohr's words about physics "proceeding by image, parable, and metaphor," and to emphasize that the division between inert matter "out there" and mere thought and feelings "in here" is radically misleading. We are vulnerable, transcending, and ecstatic beings caught up in a field of energy which seems to be neutral with respect to the dichotomies of mind and matter, subject and object, or even personal and social. William James's insight into neutral experience springs to portentous size. The centuries-old model of comprehension—that a whole is to be understood in terms of the ultimate individuals that compose it—is thrown into question.

We do not know yet how to describe the range of fields thoroughly and consistently, but it is clear that we had better move quickly. Bristling with armaments, some have run berserk in their fears of violation and interfusion, in their pollution anxieties, purification manias, and aggressive projections, in their scapegoating use of unwashed "subhuman" human beings. A vulnerable self makes more or less hysterical attempts to defend a precarious individuality which it does not understand and cannot face. How do we single out "a self" without masking out or butchering our complex and delicate involvements in the reciprocating field? The old facile divisions of subject matter—between individual and community, for example—no longer apply in this quest for minimal definition, clarity, goodness, survival.

It is significant, I think, that the philosophies of Dewey, Whitehead, and Heidegger all came to fruition practically simultaneously in the late 1920s, and all on the heels of Einstein's formulation of general relativity theory in the late teens. It was a crescendo of creativity. For decades Dewey had developed an experimental logic of inquiry which construed Nature as relative to experiencing, and experiencing as an arm of Nature itself—that arm of its processes which reworks itself through ends in view, and which we call "our inquiry." Experiencing is not an event occurring within a mental container. Whitehead offered a theory of perception as prehension in which things prehended mold us perceivers in our very act of experimentally aligning ourselves with them and manipulating them. Things' perspectives "irradiate" perceivers, and the basic reality is reciprocity. Heidegger described a world which is meaningful only within the horizon of our temporality, our projecting "forestructure," but we have our meaning and exist only within the pressure of a "facticity" we can never fully comprehend and control.

It is very significant, I think, that all three of these thinkers, practically simultaneously, concluded that any theory of inquiry which is not to stay mired in some implicit assumptions of the old subject/object dualisms or of absolutist physics must be guided in its initial marshalling of its subject matter by the methods and findings of the fine arts. Old divisions and inventories can be broken down only when situations are perceived newly whole, and artists help greatly here. As we saw, Whitehead claimed that the Romantic poets had anticipated aspects of relativity theory (as the Neolithic mound builders in England and Ireland seem to have done). Dewey maintained that only in art are our everyday experiences—and their conditions in the body and the environment—written largely, clearly, and intensely enough to be grasped as they are. And only then can we articulate a field sufficiently broad, open, and free of old assumptions to allow cross-fertilization between processes. The culminating event of Nature, Dewey says in *Experience and Nature,* is art. And simultaneous with but independent of Dewey's *Art as Experience,* Heidegger criticized his own early work because it contained vestiges of subjectivism and atomism. Art illuminates the earth, he says now, because the dark and preserving earth lends its materials to the artist and allows the artwork to be set back into its protective bulk; as the art contrasts with the earth it illuminates it. There are no independent existences. *If* we can use a term badly tainted by Cartesianism, we see emerge an *objective* relativism that need not entail cynicism, boredom, or despair. I do not mean nihilistic relativism: the belief that since all meanings and verifications require our activity, and in this sense are relative to us, that therefore one theory or belief is as good as any other—the relativism that undermines all truth.

Needless to say, the professionalized university, the "knowledge factory," divides the sciences from the fine arts and resists the very connections that the most creative knowers have discerned as essential to inquiry and perception.

Our civilization has yet to sort out the explosion of creativity which is twentieth-century relativity and field theory. It is ongoing revolution and the results are not clear. So thoroughly have traditional objectivism, materialism, and the psycho/physical split been overcome that it is not surprising to see studies linking physics and Eastern mysticism: the notion of one all-encompassing field of reciprocating realities is shared by East and some sectors of the (new) West.* It is not surprising in a world hungry for meaning and value to see ethical and religious inferences drawn from this new thought. Take Whitehead again. He conceives the world in participatory and communal terms, and also as an efflux of a fundamental creativity, so an idea of goodness as empathy and creativity springs up naturally.** Dualism implied that we can surely know only what science tells us, and science tells us only about the bare facts of the world-machine. In a well worn saw, we were said to know only what *is* the case, not what *ought* to be. Nothing can be known, supposedly, about values, purposes, fulfillments. But once this dogmatic notion of objectivity is destroyed, there is no reason any longer to believe that we must remain ignorant of tendencies of self-world interaction which lead to vital and meaningful life, hence are really good and ought to be pursued—tendencies as "natural oughts."

The explosion of creative thought in the early decades of this century carried thinking in many directions. Along with Whitehead, Martin Buber explored ethical and religious possibilities, developing his own version of truth lying in "the between." Very creatively he cuts out new "thisses." The primary terms, he says, are not "I" as a subject over against "you" as an object, but I-thou, a term for the bonding of participation and caring, the fundamental reality of the relationship. Buber also speaks of the divine subject, hence an I-Thou reality. Each of these fundamental terms is sharply contrasted with the I-it term, the objectifying relationship appropriate to some of our relationships with things. Twentieth-century thought opens the possibility of a new vision of ethical purpose and sacral unity.

---

*For example, see Fritjof Capra, *The Tao of Physics* (London: 1975), and Renée Weber, *Dialogues with Scientists and Sages: The Search for Unity* (London and New York: 1986).
**See Lynne Belaief, *Toward a Whiteheadian Ethics* (Lanham, MD. and New York: 1984).

In chapter 12 I will explore attempts by scholars in Women's Studies to reconceive the nature of reality and divinity, attempts which extend, in effect, the field theory of reciprocating and interdependent beings. What if the ultimate creative principle is no longer conceived as a transcendent God who intervenes in history, but as the self-generating and regenerating Earth herself, and we are invited to global empathic involvement? Being open to others' joy and pain, is that to be party to their resources, and thus to be empowered, expanded, rendered more substantial ourselves? This is not mindless mimetic engulfment, but intelligent empathy and sympathy. Beyond all engulfment in particular corporate and social organisms, does there lie the possibility, perhaps, of loving identification with Earth, and with its whole brood of Earthlings?

As is all too obvious, the professionalized, segmented university impedes this cross-fertilization between fields.

At the close of the 1920s a new conception of knowledge and the knower had almost completely supplanted the heavy legacy of seventeenth-century thought. So a theoretical basis existed for reorganizing the university. New ways of linking intellectual freedom and ethical responsibility were opened—new ways of orienting within the world and enlisting thinkers of all sorts in a cooperative effort to educate themselves. It was seen that the secular had become joined with a detached, abstracting, alienated intellect defined in opposition to the sacred, the underside, the bodily—the to-be-shunned. Ways out of this impasse had opened.

In construing self as body-self James and Dewey had linked philosophical issues of identity of self with biology, sociology, anthropology, psychology, religion, physics, education, and history ancient and modern. They had paved the way for interdisciplinary work which was to appear decades later. Glance for a moment at this horizon of possibilities before noting how it was abruptly closed.

For instance, Konrad Lorenz, the ethologist, writes of the instinct of "militant enthusiasm" exhibited by male chimpanzees in defense of their group. The similarities in behavior and physiognomy to comparable human behavior are striking; we think of mimetic engulfment, and there may be a shared instinctual component. In *On Aggression*, 1963, he writes that the "holy shiver" of heroism is a "vestige of a pre-human response of making the fur bristle." The chimpanzee may lay down his life to defend his fellows. Following Dewey and James we can see this "holy shiver" as the labile, slippery and sacred potency of the body-self engulfed in the corporate body.

Engulfed pre-reflexively on the "neutral" level, the body is ambiguous, on a knife-edge, can go either way: it can be objectified or it can be caught up in subjectivity on the individual or the corporate level (and a study should connect this to religious conversions, "swallowed up in God"). The body-self moves and tips in the archaic background and its archaic sacredness; it possesses *mana*, is powerful, dangerous. It is not to be forever objectified and distinguished from mind or soul—objectified as object of physiological study, or as "dirty," or as vacuous (e.g., the Playboy "bunny"). It is not to be denatured; it is body-self. Our biological roots can have the greatest "psychical" involvements, for dualism is left behind.

Moreover, this synthesis of biology, psychology, and religion invites a contribution from ethical theory. Can the response of militant enthusiasm, so often wantonly destructive, be reconditioned to rational and true values? This is what James desired to find, and so wrote his famous "The Moral Equivalent of War." And Dewey, introducing Alexander's *The Use of the Self,* alludes to Pavlov's work on conditioned reflexes and how Alexander's work extends and corrects the idea. Since there are central organic habits which condition every act we perform, we can hope to locate these, bring them under conscious direction, and convert "the fact of conditioned reflexes from a principle of external enslavement into a means of vital freedom." With this idea of freely reconditioned reflexes Dewey connects scientific thought to the ultimate principles of all education—intellectual freedom and ethical responsibility. In so doing he responds to Dostoevsky's fear that freedom which finds no reason to believe in itself, and no faith in truth, will turn into acts of destruction, their gratuitousness a desperate attempt to prove freedom's own existence.

But though countless interdisciplinary possibilities—ways of breaking out of the parochialisms and prejudices of professionalized academic departments—were opened by the end of the

1920s, they excited such anxiety that they were resisted or ignored. The creativity of the thought threatened fundamental disorder in the apparatus in which professionals were forming an identity as "pure minds." It was polluting, a mixing of what ought to be kept separate. James and Dewey, for example, tended to be dismissed by many professional philosophers as inadequately disciplined, amateurish. We turn in the next chapter to the positivist move to block change.

I am setting out the background, as I see it, of the current malaise of the university. No minor operation will help, for the problem involves the archaic roots of our attempts to form an identity. My diagnosis will be completely unacceptable to those who enter the professoriate precisely in order not to see the existential problems involved. In them the flight from teaching and meaningful human contact is understandable. The special authority of the university educator is a humiliating burden for persons who will not or cannot accept responsibility for their own fixations and terrors as persons, failures of self-knowledge and self-control. The temptation to drop the burden is great, to simply forego some small status as special pedagogical authorities, and to be released in return from the responsibility of facing students and themselves as persons needing to be educated.

We turn to the reactionary response of positivism in the thirties. With this doctrine seventeenth-century assumptions continued into the heart of our century, and still exercise considerable influence. Not to see this is not to see the difficulties of reorganizing the university.

X

The Reactionary Response of Positivism: Cementing Purification, Professionalism, Segmentation in the University

Under the guise of being the most scientific and progressive philosophy, the movement called logical positivism sprang up in the 1930s and perpetuated key assumptions of seventeenth-century psycho/physical thought. Its intensity can only be understood as a fear of pollution, of mixing what ought to be kept separate: mind and body, self and other, science and humanities, past and present, etc. Spreading quickly through much of the intellectual culture, it blocked the revolutionary repercussions of early twentieth-century ideas and cemented the disciplinary partitions we see around us today—partitions beginning to crack only very recently. Thus the power of the university to educate was deeply compromised.

Since we are meaning-making creatures, any theory of meaning we concoct must be a tacit theory about who we are. The core of positivism was a theory that any meaning worthy of the name must take the form of statements, either ones which are mere definitional matters in which the predicate repeats the meaning of the subject, or ones with significant content, those which may enlarge our understanding of the world at large. The latter were thought to be meaningful only if a way of scientifically verifying their truth or falsity could be conceived.

If we are not caught up in a vague secularist faith that science as we know it can tell us all we need to know about every-thing, we will feel constricted by the positivist theory of mean-ing, as if caught in a vise. For surely, much else in addition to statements are meaningful—faces, bodies, silences, sounds, tones, melodies, pictures, images of all kinds, etc. And they have content, they can enlarge our grasp of the world at large.

This is a very simple and obvious rejoinder. How could it fail to be appreciated? Because to be attracted by the positivist theory of meaning is already to have lost touch—at least intel-lectual touch—with the archaic, moody background and the sen-suous reality of our bodies. In losing touch with the full range of how we make meaning in intimate intercourse with the abiding background we lose touch with ourselves.

And, of course, in losing this we lose touch with every fea-ture of the educating act. We lose self-awareness and self-knowledge. (Can we suppose that that primal, ever-immediate sense of ourselves as body-selves takes the form mainly of state-ments?!) We lose in addition our grasp of that fundamental com-munity in which we make meaning along with others, living or dead. We certainly lose our grasp on the past: that mean-ing we inherit through mimetic engulfment in the authorizing sources of our being. And if we are so blindly committed to sci-ence that we think it need not reflect on its own assumptions—most of which are shared by other modes of knowing and which are not verifiable by science itself—we will have lost touch with interdisciplinarity as well. We will have lost touch with educa-tion and with what the university might be.

This happens even before we confront the issues of exactly what is to count as statements, or of what is to count as scien-tifically testable ones. Debates centered almost exclusively on these latter issues, which reveals a primary alienation of intellec-tuals from their own reality. Not that these more detailed issues are unimportant. As we have already noted, statements asserting the possession of "value properties"—good and bad, right and wrong, beautiful and ugly—were not considered testable by sci-ence, so not meaningful as knowledge. They were merely "ex-pressive" of personal or subjective preference and sentiment. Here the alienation from the background of our lives is palpable: for we lose our bearings in the shortest time if we lose our sense of what's good and bad, beautiful or ugly, and those primal agreements without which communal life is impossible. That most of us do not become utterly lost in the course of a day— even when terribly obtuse or confused—proves that the intellect is not all-determining of behavior.

Then why did the positivists not see that their theory of meaning was so intellectualistic as to be out of touch with our everyday lives and the very world they wished to grasp? I will try to answer this in a moment.

Neither did the positivists consider metaphorical statements to be testable and meaningful. How could Byron's "High mountains are a feeling" be tested by science? But neither are much less ambitious metaphors. Earth scientists speak of the "mechanism" of plate techtonics. But how can there be a mechanism without a mechanic? It is a metaphor, and it cannot be scientifically, empirically tested, for only straightforward factual statements can be when these can be deduced from theories. Metaphors are more or less adequate, as they do or do not lead to statements that can be tested, and we can never be sure we have the very best metaphor. Indeed, most of the concepts upon which science is based are shared with other fields. They are basic just because shared, and they can be shared because they are broadly based metaphors drawn from the remotest regions of human experience. Without metaphors, far-flung connections cannot be imagined; and they must be imagined before we can know where to look in the world to make discoveries of facts. "Science proceeds by image, parable, and metaphor," said Bohr, and Dewey knew that unless students enlist personal feeling and relevant aesthetic images they can never do science in groundbreaking ways (note the metaphor).

The ultimate irony is that positivists who styled themselves as scientific were out of touch with the metaphorical-conceptual foundations of science itself—as well as ordinary human existence and the extraordinary meaning-making which constitutes it. (Also, contrary to the positivist, most thinkers then and now agree that there are scientifically inaccessible times, places, events.)

Now why? Why did they assume that meanings worthy of the name came neatly packaged as statements which could be picked out of consciousness and written down? Why did they not see that we typically *grope* in the dim and gritty *world* to make sense of *things*—and that we *squirm* and *strain* through the full range of communication as body-selves to turn the experienced world just a little so that new aspects and connections of things can come into view? Particularly, we extend metaphorically the meanings of our bodies into regions previously considered separate from body, or not considered at all. As Vico said, this is the basis of our institutions of mind and spirit.

Positivists held, in other words, to the seventeenth-century view that consciousness is separate from body and matter. And they did this, I think, out of powerful and unacknowledged needs to establish their own identity as selves who were *minds*. As the first three decades of the century witnessed an explosive bursting of traditional dualistic partitions, so positivism was a determined effort to re-erect them to prevent the mixing of what ought to be kept separate. This is the most vivid possible evidence of the force of unacknowledged purification ritual, for while positivism styled itself as a scientific philosophy, it failed to understand the disruptive implications of the very science it claimed to emulate. I can only suppose that an underlying dread of pollution prevented it from acknowledging these threats of mixing, for what else could explain the failure of perception in minds both sympathetic to science and highly knowledgeable of it? Only archaic, crude, and unacknowledged forces of identity-formation, bent on individuation through separation and opposition, can begin to explain it. These are forces of identity-formation linked to engrained commitment to psycho/physical dualism, to the self as atomistic ego-consciousness, member of an atomistic group.

The importance of this is not merely historical or theoretical. The rapid spread of positivism in the professionalized university cemented the division of departments at the very time when an opportunity for reorganizing and revitalizing the university had begun to dawn. Positivist thinkers articulated an atmosphere of reaction and fear which still permeates the university. When things and people lose their firm outlines, terror is excited, as if images of impressionist art, in which light and atmosphere control form, and objects are merely oscillating, vibrating zones of color, had become relentless nightmare figures.

Briefly put, positivism is an anti-philosophical philosophy. Aristotle defined philosophy as the study of reality *as* reality, not reality under this aspect or that, as quantifiable, for example. Dewey defined it as the search for the generic traits of existence. Philosophy, in its various forms, seeks for the conceptual connective tissue that can make sense of all our levels and moments of experience in the world; in one way or another it tries to find metaphors, images, concepts to comprehend the world-whole. For good reason the Doctor of Philosophy degree was to be awarded to any thinker in any field who penetrated in one way or another to the conceptual and thematic foundations of any or every field. When positivism reduced philosophy to being merely "an underlaborer to the sciences" it annihilated it, and in so doing contributed greatly to the moral collapse of the university. For in undermining philosophy it destroys any possible connective tissue inherent in the enterprise of knowing, and leaves the governance of the university to bureaucratic principles of management merely. Now that philosophy is just another department down the hall, and a small and politically weak one at that, we know the collapse has occurred. (Then why not eliminate this department: spread the people hitherto classified as philosophers throughout the university? Because not having any definite corporate part within the bureaucracy is to have no reality within the bureaucracy. The only possible solution is to begin to change the bureaucracy, and I will have concrete suggestions soon.)

The ultimate educational force is who I *am*, and who we *are*, and what if that cannot be faced? Without philosophy as the study of reality itself, there can be no confrontation with our own reality as beings who as much need to find their lives meaningful within the whole as they need to eat and sleep. If the need is not satisfied authentically it will be satisfied cheaply. If universities cannot confront questions of meaning—and of goodness, vitality, purpose, beauty, reality, the universe directly lived—they suffer moral collapse. This has happened.

The capacity for philosophical activity is inherent in human beings just because they are human. Not to grasp this is not to grasp ourselves, to fail ourselves, to be unethical at an utterly primitive level. Once we accept our finitude we see that inquiry is endless. Philosophical creativity—the imagination of new metaphors, syntheses, analyses, topics, hypotheses—is endless in every "field," and we cannot predict future leaps of feeling and creativity, for to suppose so is to imagine that before imagination enlarges its domain it can imagine what the enlargement will be. But that contradicts itself. Purity of heart, said Kierkegaard, is to will the boundless, the openended; any other object willed with such passion must be a purity unto death, for it is bounded, stifling.

The limits of the imagination are unimaginable—it must be said again. Ever new images and metaphors, currently unimaginable, loom as possibilities, as sheer *thats*, not-yet-knowns. So perceptions of actual things and connections in the world, to be made possible by these currently unimaginable images and metaphors, are themselves unimaginable. We live in an awesomely open, boundless world; and this open "story" we tell about ourselves *is* philosophy. Since it "dirties the hands," "mixes what ought to be kept separate," it cannot be pure in the sense of a specialty, but only in the transcendent sense of "open to the boundless."

Without that tissue of commitment in meaning-making and knowing in which we confront our own freedom and responsibility in the world, the curriculum becomes an arbitrary sequence of courses; there is no connective tissue. Engaged in a council of despair, some conscientious professors conclude that only arbitrariness can save our freedom and keep some breathing room for the humanities—since there is no *reason* we can give for their existence in the university (it could only be a philosophical one). They assume that knowledge of human beings in their humanity—humane and ethical knowledge—is impossible: knowledge of what is best and worst and of what we should try to achieve in education. A fairly prominent professor speaks disparagingly of the "Humanists' myth of the coherence of knowledge," and maintains that curricular structure can only be "an arbitrarily chosen set of priorities"; and finally we read of the "absolute arbitrariness of language" itself.*

---

*George Levine, "Notes toward a Humanist Anti-Curriculum," *Humanities in Society,* I, No. 3, (Summer 1978), 221–243.

This betrays the old assumption that mind is a subjective domain cut off from bodies, from Nature, and from the strands of humanity's cumulative interpretation of itself in myth, arts, and literature—the domain of cognitive feeling. Arbitrariness championed by professors corrupts and dispirits our freedom, turning the leaps of our transcendence into intoxicated thrashings-about; ultimately it bores us. Not only are we left with no story in which we can play a part, but no settled sense that this would be desirable (assuming it is not a false unity and a forced coherence).

That is the main point: cognitive feeling. The meaning, the sense we have of vitality, rootage, attunement, fruitful reciprocity, is the work of the body-self, the primal level of feeling-intellect, the level which antecedes all dualistic abstractions: past/present, self/other, cognitive/emotive, intellect/emotions, culture/nature, mind/body. There can be living tissue for one world known only if there is living tissue for one knower. The dualistic abstractions cut the heart out of us. We are left with nothing to connect head and stomach, head and groin, or past and present, self and others. Living thus, in no matter how sophisticated a way, we are trivialized—secretly or openly bored. Nietzsche's prophecy of nihilism comes true.

To say, as many do, that positivism no longer exercises a strong influence in the university is a self-deceiving fiction. Positivism was—and is to a great extent—"in the air," not just confined to philosophy departments, and practically no department in the university goes uninfluenced. In some cases it is gross and inescapable to any attentive eye. The constricted attention to "testable facts," and the cognitive as opposed to the emotive, cripples the imagination and unnecessarily restricts the scope of study. This occurs in many departments of history and economics, for example—also in "the better" departments of art history and music history, or musicology. Woe to the student who lets love of art intrude into the search for "testable facts" relating to the "mechanics" of the production of it, or about the demonstrable socio-economic situation of the artist's place or time. What the art *means* to us tends to get lost in the search for "causes" thought to be demonstrable by science. But what the art means to us constitutes its substance and value—and the whole reason for creating it in the first place, and studying it later, evaporates. The meaning of human productions is the light they throw on the world and our place and possibilities within it. Without this meaning there is no moral energy.

Another example: psychology was to be done "scientifically," not humanistically, and the seventeenth-century split between the sciences and the humanities reigned supreme, and science took the lion's share. Only recently has this dogma shown signs of abating, but it has left psychology as "a field" a mere name. These departments tend to subdivide into noncommunicating specialties. Chaos reigns in "the discipline" of psychology. The department which goes under that name is typically no more than a political unit of a bureaucracy, and our imaginative and cognitive grasp of ourselves is disturbed.

The revolutionary twentieth-century thought I have outlined, which could have provided the theoretical basis for loosening the rigid divisions and departments, was dropped, or never understood. As far as university structure was concerned, it was as if seventeenth-century thought had never been superceded. Most natural scientists attached to the university pulled ever deeper into their laboratories and worked on manageable problems, given their level of talent and their access to experimental apparatus. The social sciences and psychology adopted simplistic conceptions of what they thought natural scientists were doing, and "behaviorism" and "physicalism" reigned supreme. The humanities became ever more isolated in their concerns with what is "merely subjective."

By and large, both students and professors lead double lives in the university, even today. An extraordinarily emaciated version of Apollonian reason is split off from the rest of our animal-mental selves, the emotional Dionysian levels—the "cognitive" split from the "emotive." What passion I see in students is mainly in the somnambulized hum and chatter of the electronic game room in the student center, or the rapt attention paid to soap operas—incredibly two-dimensional but realistic-appearing spectacles of "real" life. Our hunger for "real, red-blooded life," is unappeasable, but as it increases is more easily led into delusion.

Faculty too frequently act like zombies. At times their heads "smoke with productivity" as they pursue their specialties, or at times they are involved in committee work, the ulterior point of which is typically to conceal that there is little or no humanly significant point to it. Their tasks are mainly procedural matters within the bureaucracy, the point of which is to guarantee pointlessness. We witness a flight from the human—in all its ambiguity, uncertainty, and vulnerability—and into the artificially clear and confined. William Irwin Thompson focuses it:

Utterly engrossed in the details of committee work, these specialists could pluck hairs from the face of terror and never have to look it in the eye. . . . And the culture will remain the same until the problem is seen as a whole. The problem . . . is that our institutions are no longer in sync with the pattern of human growth through time. We think that time is a line which moves from bad to better, poverty to progress, from ignorance to knowledge, from grades 1 to 20. The point of the line is to develop an identity through a function and then maintain that function for as "long" as possible. Any deviation from the line is deviant behavior. The sins of the fathers are passed on to the sons, and this unfortunate patrimony is our inheritance from the industrial era.*

What a far cry from the Neolithic mound builders, who seem to have existed in space-time in such a way that they could commemorate their ever present origins and experience regeneration at every transitional stage of their lives. Is our split-up linear existence really progress in any valuable sense? Or is it merely in the sense that an abandoned vessel blown by the wind describes a progress across the surface of the sea?

What is this final drift into a useless and lonely old age? What have we done to ourselves? The university should be an educational institution and should have some answers, or at least some questions. But its reaction against drift is a frenzied pace, a tunneling thrusting which walls out the questions. The lesson of this inertial "progress" is that we do not escape the forces of purity and the sacred in this anxious search for identity, but only conceal them and fall victim to obsessive, even demonic forms which finally leave us empty.

---

*William Irwin Thompson, *Passages About Earth* (New York: 1973), pp. 14–15.

Because we do not acknowledge purification ritual it does not follow that it is not present. Indeed, it may be present in particularly intense, distorted, and uncontrolled forms. How about students? They are equivocal entities. Are they academics or not? But they are peculiarly close to us! They rub elbows with us nearly every day. Improperly insulated, they are threatening to our identity as professionally certified minds. If we give them our mental gifts they too often accept them with dirty hands.

In an older, "less enlightened" age there were elaborate purification and initiation rituals to keep students in their place. Waiting for freshman entering university were convocation ceremonies in which a dean lectured them on the privilege which was theirs and on the glories which awaited those who could stand up to the challenge. And for those who did finish, an elaborate graduation ceremony awaited them, a rite of passage, with the ranks of those present emblazoned on their quasi-sacral gowns.

Nearly everyone knows that today it is next to impossible in large universities to get a sizable body of faculty to even attend graduation ceremonies.* But does it follow that purification rituals to distinguish professors from students are not in practice? It cannot follow, for they are present in overwhelming force just because they are unacknowledged—present sneakingly and dishonestly in shunning and neglect. Students are nearly invisible. If purification ritual were ever acknowledged, there would be sudden change.

---

*See "Whatever happened to 'The Faculty'?" *Academe,* May–June, 1988. The editor writes: "We like to think of ourselves—or at least in times past have thought of ourselves—as members of an entity that transcends differences of rank, field, location, compensation. We like, that is, to think of ourselves as members of 'The Faculty.' " He then summarizes the articles in the issue which undermine this wishful thinking. Undermining factors include gross salary differentials between "stars" and others, the erosion of collegiality, the proliferation of part-time instructors to teach the great mass of students and to keep the budget balanced, the lure of "specialized disciplinary associations" which overshadow "campus-wide and cross-disciplinary" groups. I especially recommend a cartoon, "The Adventures of Superprof"—"Hhmm! I'll use my SUPERREPUTATION to get up to the stratosphere . . . where the pay is higher and the teaching load lighter!!"

The only antidote to moral collapse is moral construction. Once we see through the cloud of debris left by positivism we are encouraged by the possibility that twentieth-century relativistic field theory in physics and philosophy might give us a new understanding of ancient principles of ethical life: for instance, the golden rule in the Hebrew-Christian tradition, or a similar principle of reciprocity in many cultures. When I no longer believe that I am merely an ego-self, it is more difficult to look out from a bastion, locked into a single point of view: I as agent, the other as patient. To understand best what in fact I am doing to the other I must imagine what it would be like to have the act done to me, for this counteracts the ego's blinkered awareness, caught up as it is in the instant of acting, not being acted upon. Take a mendacious and self-serving act of seduction. I will not begin to comprehend what I am doing unless I imagine the act done to me—or, differently put, unless I empathize with any other to whom this act is done.

But even if I should never grasp what I am doing to the other, and even if this specific act should never in fact be done to me, something *is* happening to me within the reciprocating field, something masked out from the pinpointing egoistic field of vision which imagines that all that is happening is something done by me to the other. Subtle and intricate reciprocations occur within the background. In subjugating and deceiving I am depriving myself of what the other could give me if he or she were treated as an ethically autonomous and respected being. I am, for example, depriving myself of the insights into myself—the constructive criticism—which only those others can give me who trust me not to deceive and coerce them. Whether or not I imagine myself seduced, in seducing the other I am in fact being seduced in a subtle but real way. I have seduced myself into thinking that I do not need the other as an autonomous and respected fellow, and I am thereby impoverished.

We are ecstatic beings. We always stand beyond ourselves in some kind of involvement with others. In a broad and unusual sense, we are always responsible, because always *responsive* in some way (we always suffer the consequences of what we do to others). We become responsible in an *ethically valuable* sense when we imagine what it would be like to have a specific act done to ourselves. Ethical facts are facts of a particular sort of reciprocity: that deliberate mimetic response and empathy with others which is compassion. This is to be morally centered as a field being.

In relieving us of the modernist dilemma of *either* subjectivism, the merely personal and arbitrary, *or* an objectivism which offers no hope of discovering any distinctly ethical facts or value-facts of human relationships, contemporary relativity and field theory returns us to a new appreciation of old ethical principles and of new curriculur possibilities. We know that persons need to be recognized *as* persons. We know that they must be identified as members of a group of persons, and that if they are not recognized at all, or not recognized as members in good standing, they suffer and are troubled (even the lonely genius wishes to be heard by the yet unborn). We know that they need to feel at home in the world, and to be respected by those whom they respect. We also know that if they cannot trust the truthfulness of others' recognitions of them, they suffer, are troubled and stunted. We know, moreover, that if they identify intensely with only a very restricted group of others, that they risk generating such fear of other groups that their very survival is threatened. We know, finally, that if they systematically deceive themselves about archaic matters of their own bodies that they will exist cut off from themselves; they will lack vitality. Vitality and the absence of crippling suffering and anxiety are as clearly valuable and good as a square is clearly composed of four sides and four right angles. Clarity and evidence are not the exclusive property of mathematics and geometry.

Even if this were all the humane knowledge we possess, it would be a lot. We need invoke no dogmas, surely not that of a fixed human nature. We can agree that human beings do not have a nature in the way that an oak table has one, or even as other animals have. I am free to take an indefinite number of views of myself, and I experience myself as open-ended and ever more than anybody could ascertain about me. Often I do not perfectly coincide with myself, and there is some truth in Jean-Paul Sartre's idea that because of consciousness of self, there is a kind of split within me, and I am what I am not, and am not what I am. This is a puzzling aspect of my transcendence. Still,

Sartre overemphasizes fully reflexive, intellectualistic conscious-ness of self, and underemphasizes times of prereflexive involve-ment and flow, in which I am in solidarity and harmony with myself and others.

Ethical knowledge is relativistic *in a sense,* because it defines goodness relative to the realities and needs of human beings: we are ecstatic, historical, interpersonal, and crave meaning. Good-ness is a fact of functioning well, and of fulfillment—no mere "emotive" matter. Even a field being can be morally centered, for I can return to myself in reflection as this body-self, I myself, as I alone who am responsible for my choices. The self springs to vigorous life only when the ethical question, "What is good for me to do and be?" is asked e-motionally—when I move, am *alive.*

Perhaps we can call this an objective relativism which counters the nihilistic relativism of the isolated ego-subject who thinks that ethical beliefs are merely arbitrary preferences. Armed with Aristotle's wise dictum that an educated person seeks no more exactitude in a subject matter than the nature of it allows, we have new hope for achieving ethical knowledge and for reorganizing the university.

Of course, the positivism taught in tiny philosophy depart-ments did not cause by itself the positivized university. Nihilism, moral despair, and the guaranteeing of pointlessness in busy work has been building for decades, and has produced a beauti-ful little crystal in this philosophical doctrine. But refracted through this crystal we better see the surrounding atmosphere. Persons are not respected and recognized *as* persons in their field-reality and sacredness, but are objectified, treated as objects to be engineered, manipulated and measured—their "productiv-ity" determined. Since education is essentially a relationship be-tween persons recognizing each other as persons—as beings capable of ethical freedom and responsibility—it battles to sur-vive in crannies of the university. The basically unethical ap-proach to persons breathes from the very language that powers the institution: "student contact hours," "full time equivalent students," and the phrase most tell-tale: "the delivery of instruc-tion to consumers of 'education.' " These words express contact between *things,* not between persons recognizing each other *as* persons. We cannot habitually speak a language and be unaffected by it.

Intellectual production in the university is understood in a way which denies the full range of human transcendence and meaning-making. The basic conception is remarkably crude: things leave A's hand or mouth and enter B's eyes or ears. The prime candidates for the entities transmitted are statements or formulae, for these can be put on the blackboard or printed page and distributed to others. If significant, the emitter of them is thought to have produced a significant result.

But the measure of this significance is stunted, physicalistic or quasi-physicalistic. For example, how many professional peers register their receipt of these transmissions in their own transmissions? And how frequently are transmissions made, what is the size of the entity transmitted, and through what organs are the transmissions made? The evaluation exhibits similarities to that made of a baker: How many carrot cakes are sold to how many buyers, and in which social strata of clientele? How frequently are they sold—and when were they delivered? Are they still fresh? I am speaking hyperbolically, but this is the point: A mode of evaluating professors which has a rightful place within a balanced view of achievement becomes grotesque distortion outside it. And it buries the fact that reminding us of what is already known can be a significant contribution in the humanities.

Listening and reading done by the professor are construed as "consumption," not "production." But this cannot be reliably quantified, so it tends to fall through the cracks and be forgotten; likewise the "production" which is teaching.

We have ferreted out the main reason for the "the publish or perish" mania. Publication can be measured, ordered, and contained within our scientistic categories; it is neat, pure, and decisively authorizes the producer within the national professional framework. Professors are pressured to box themselves in the same generic assumptions—scientistic and positivistic ones—as are bureaucrats generally in our marketing society. Actually, the self's boundaries cannot be fixed, as if it were an atom, for it ranges with its powers of empathy and identification, and these

vary. And it is vulnerable. But the positivized and professionalized self masks out this fact about itself. It objectifies itself as if
it were a non-human physical entity, limiting itself to the contents of the envelope of its skin—and what it can express, push
outside. So it must imprison itself within standards of evaluation
foreign and inimical to itself.

Bodily boundaries are fundamental, but the self cannot be
confined within them. It can only self-deceivingly conceive itself
so—a mere internal *thing,* an engine of production, the value of
which is determined by the professionally perceived value of
what it expresses and produces. And since it is "a solid, self-
contained thing," one may deceive oneself that pollution is
impossible.

Charles Peirce was probably the greatest American philosopher of science. He argued that communication need not involve
any tangible, physical transmission, at least not in every instance.
If A's belief that B will listen intently and respectfully to him is a
necessary condition for A's thought to proceed as it does, then
the two have communicated, and if A's thought is important, the
communication is important.* This is a phenomenon of interlacing fields and nothing crudely palpable need pass between them.
But it is literally inconceivable to many that a professor be given
tenure solely because of his or her ability to listen respectfully
and intently to colleagues and students in such a way that the
thought of all is enhanced. When I suggested this to an urbane
and alert colleague, much honored by the university, his jaw
went slack, as if he might lose the contents of his mouth. I imagine he experienced it as a threat of pollution.

The positivistic move to limit meaning to statements which
can be uttered or written down is a momentous decision which
reveals a tacit world-view. Yet again it is psycho/physical dualism: meaningful statements are construed mentalistically, but
since a self must utter or write them, nothing is left to do this
except the body construed as a mechanistic physicist or physiol-
ogist would conceive it—a chunk of electrically wired matter.

---

*C. S. Peirce, Letter to Lady Welby, Oct. 12, 1904, in *Values in a Universe of
Chance: Selected Writings of C. S. Peirce,* ed. P. Weiner (New York: 1958),
p. 388.

hence the crude physicalism and naivete that must always attach to mentalism. Statements—at least as expressed—are *things* that leave one organism and enter others somehow. Hence the banal forms of evaluating professors' work, the boxes in which productivity is recorded.

Deeper than the meaning of statements is the meaning of a person's presence. This trusted other need not say a word, or even be present in the same physical locale. We need only feel him or her attending respectfully, intently to us, listening. In a sense appropriate to field beings, the other is internalized. All communication by way of statements presupposes a more fundamental level which we must struggle to express in statements. Perhaps nothing in prose is even minimally adequate and we resort to poetry, music, or other forms of art and evocative expression. The meaning of persons resides on this level. Is there anything more meaningful and desperately needed than the example of a respected and caring person's life?

The way the modern world, since Descartes, has come to think of matter, as "primary qualities" of inert stuff arrayed in space and objectified before us, is inimical to our efforts to grasp our own selves as bodies, bodies lived and sacred, ever incompletely objectifiable, requesting the respect of non-objectification by others and deserving of it. If we probe into others' bodily cavities without having been responsibly invited, we are not just probing into hidden areas of skin or hidden volumes, but violating the inner sanctum of autonomy in which that person must trust to himself or herself to respond effectively to the enticements, obstacles, demands, and shocks of the world. Though the self is bodily and has internal shapes, no geometry or physics can comprehend how they are lived and how they constitute the self.* Though the self is worldly, no set of Cartesian coordinates can break it up and objectify, demarcate, and locate its elements within the world. The body-self participates in the world

---

*By geometry I mean Euclidian geometry and Descartes' translation of this into algebraic formulae. I have been impressed by Michael Thompson's use of non-Euclidian geometry in his valuable *Rubbish Theory* (Oxford: 1979). However, his attempts to grasp the barrier between private and public and to correlate this with the barrier between the inside and the outside of the body are weak.

through love, fear, anger, celebration, commemoration, and responsibility, beyond the capacity of geometry and mechanistic physics to imagine.

Positivism, and much of the later "analytic" philosophy, epitomize professionalism. Not only are the exclusions and dichotomies rigid, simplistic, and extreme, but are out of touch at many points with the professed interests of the professionals themselves. A powerful factor must be at work in the background, repressed and unrecognized, and the most plausible possibility is fear of pollution. To conceive of oneself as a mind or consciousness separate from the body and the rest of the world, conceals one's vulnerability and ambiguity as a body-self within the interactive, interdependent field.

The sickness of the university is primarily ethical. It has failed to address the real needs of persons—failed to provide the knowledge that can orient and shield us from at least some of the dangers and anxieties of living. Certain positivists extolled the virtue of kindness; and better that, of course, than other things. But within their view they could provide no *reasons* for asserting the *truth* of as simple a statement as, "Kindness, in general, is good." For them it merely expresses an emotional state or preference. So why believe it? This question must have arisen in those thousands who read A. J. Ayer's popular treatise on positivism, *Language, Truth, and Logic*—a nihilistic book summing up the age.

The high-water mark of academic purity and professionalism has been reached. Now the tide can only subside. But it is important for us to realize how high it reached, what a tremendous volume poured through for so long, and why it still continues as so powerful a force in the university. Without this realization our plans for reconstruction are wishful thinking.

At the close of the 1980s, we see "holistic" thinking beginning to take root and spread across disciplinary barriers. It is a pity that so little of this is aware of the laborious foundational work, reviewed in this book, which prepared its soil, and which was interrupted by the resurgence of purity, professionalism, and positivism in the 1930s. Understanding this revolutionary thought would deepen what is being done today. In any case, even training in some medical schools is now including some reference to holistic thinking. The inherent limitations of body/ mind dualism begins to be apparent, slowly. Simplistic individuations and puerile notions of independent existences begin to give way to an organismic view of the whole field of reciprocating and interacting reality. A few years ago it was considered progress to be able to refer to "psycho/somatic" factors such as "stress" in the etiology of illness. Now even this is seen to be simplistic and subtly atomistic. For there is no single factor (acting as an "independent variable") which causes everything else to happen, as if it were a billiard ball which collides with a rack of balls and sends them flying. A crucial factor is the dominant attitude, the sense that the person makes—in his or her freedom—of what is causing the "stress" (I will not belabor the point that this is an ancient thought). And this sense, freely made, cannot be located in any discrete entity, or at any point or point-instant, within the field. It is a whole-field phenomenon, which involves the conscious body, to be sure, but consciousness "itself"—or even the body-self *by itself*—cannot be pinned down.

If the sense we make of things could be located at discrete points we would be tempted back into the causal analyses of mechanistic and atomistic physics, and would lament that there can be no first or initiating cause which could begin the free activity. On the holistic view, freedom is simply the ability of the person, as body within the field, to initiate fruitful inquiry, cogently to assess evidence of various sorts, and to act accordingly. Freedom is the ability to take charge of one's life intelligently, regardless of which causal "chains" bring it about. It is a value-soaked matter, and only whole patterns in the field are relevant. Dewey's appropriation of Alexander's thought exemplifies freedom: auto-conditioning by the body-self in the world.*

---

*Since the surpassing of seventeenth-century physics by that of this century, the exclusive disjunction, either freedom or determinism, has also been thrown into question. For example, Ilya Prigogine's work on dissipative structures in chemistry and biology: as old structures decay and fall away, room is left for new to emerge as self-organizing systems—ones not predictable on the basis of prior knowledge of the old (I. Prigogine and I. Stengers, *Order out of Chaos: Man's*

More and more it is being seen that the endemic disease of contemporary urban populations is the abiding feeling of futility and powerlessness.** This is ironical in the light of our boasted "power over Nature." But this "power" is perverse, because the price we have paid for it is, with distressing frequency, alienation from, disruption of, and oppression by our own bodies and moods. We try to ride over the body's cycles and its sense of place and time and force it onto linear tracks. We ask of it, as if it were a machine, do its behaviors "produce," "go through"?

Ironically, our malaise as European Americans is not so very different from native Americans'—those whom our kind forced from their homelands into "more desirable" reservations. Even when these new environments were more sanitary—by certain selected measures—the "Indians" died in great numbers, because cut off from their traditional field of activity, the spatio-temporal-cultural field in which their revered ancestors were perpetually present to them. They were powerless at the heart of their being, because powerless to invoke and participate in what they most revered. They suffered from a fatal dis-ease of the soul—the field, in which sacred, labile energies of body-self had become inaccessible to intelligent formation by that self. Dewey's agricultural metaphors and Buber's insights come full circle: there is vital growth only in the field of inscrutible reciprocity.

Notice in conclusion the use of a textbook which typifies the positivism which has permeated and stifled the university so long. This is Irving Copi's *Introduction to Logic*. It has passed through seven editions since its publication in 1953, studied by many tens of thousands of students. At least as late as 1982 Copi cites the famous lines of Robert Burns,

---

Dialogue with Nature (New York: 1984). This suggests at least that the human nervous system may be such a self-organizing field at certain crucial moments, and that when the person's behavior is describable as intelligent self-direction, this is all we need mean by freedom. We need not mean "event without a cause."

**For example, see Blair Justice, Ph.D., *Who Gets Sick: Thinking and Health* (Houston: 1987). For the role of mental imagery in the etiology of cancer, see O. Carl Simonton, M.D., et. al., *Getting Well Again* (New York: 1980 [1978]).

O my luve's like a red, red rose. . .

and writes that these lines "are definitely not intended to inform us of any facts or theories about the world. The poet's concern is not with knowledge but with feelings and attitudes."* He persists in the positivistic distinction which divides the informative or cognitive from the expressive or emotive functions of language, and which divides facts from values. The lines merely express the speaker's feelings. Because no propositions are produced that purport to be about relationships or events directly testable by science, the "statement" is not informative.

Many assumptions lie buried here, and most of them positivist, or Cartesian, and dispiriting, nihilistic, tedious. Since it is one's own feelings which are expressed, it is assumed that one must already know what they are; they merely get ex-pressed, pressed outside for others to inspect. One's consciousness is inside one, somehow, and whatever is in consciousness one must be conscious of.

On the contrary, our feelings are about things and people in the world, and we may not grasp what our feelings *are* until we have grasped how they are like—or how they are about—certain events or things in the world, for example, a red rose. For then we grasp our feelings in terms of the context in which our feelings appear to others and are grasped by *them*. Our feelings consummate their very reality in being grasped by us in the terms in which they are grasped by others, and though they may exist in some form before being explicitly "expressed," I myself may not be able to grasp them in their inchoate state. In poetic "expression" one's own being is consummated concurrently. Thus good poetry is profoundly cognitive and informative, for it reveals us to ourselves as well as to others.**

Again, the engrained commitment to psycho/physical dualism. It may be impossible to neutralize it in the culture. Persons are assumed to be already individuated by the unique, self-

---

*Irving Copi, *Introduction to Logic*, 6th ed. (New York: 1982), pp. 71–72. Perhaps the 7th ed. is changed?
**Copi allows that some poetry serves a "mixed function." But in not *explaining* how poetry might be informative (or a "criticism of life") he leaves the impression that it cannot be importantly informative (p. 71).

illuminating consciousness which burns somehow within them. The key questions of how this individuation is achieved within community, and how self-knowledge is achieved, are simply begged. Students' (or professors') life-forming questions cannot be acknowledged.

I have alluded to Copi's widely-used textbook because it sums up so much. We see patent dogmatism, an ideology out of touch with the most creative thought of the twentieth-century— that which keeps the university segmented, ethically insensitive, resistant to change.

Despite the sophistication of contemporary materialism and analytical modes of thought, the dominant conception of meaning is Cartesian and mentalistic, and cannot make sense of bodily existence and pollution fears. Powerful purification and taboo practices must be tacitly at work in academic professionalism. They have seldom, if ever, been recognized. But that should not surprise us, since in "advanced" urban environments the topics of purification and taboo are themselves taboo.

Better aware of the realities, let us examine ways of reorganizing the university.

XI

Recovering from Positivism and Reorganizing the University

> But the trend towards the 'bureaucratic system' [is] irresistible.... the universities, as well as technical academies, business colleges... and other middle schools [become] dominated... by the need for the kind of "education" that produces a system of special examinations and the trained expertness that is increasingly indispensable for modern bureaucracy.... It is even now possible to see the ultimate upshot of this development: state, civil society, the economy, and the multiversity will fuse institutionally as each exercises an interlocking control over the others.... The state-multiversity-industrial complex will be the one organizing, knowledge-producing and goods-and-services-delivering entity.
>
> —Harry Redner, "The Institutionalization of Science"

But we know now that this engorging, totalizing, delivering movement, outlined by Redner, can occur only because it masks out essential features of the education of human beings. Education cannot be delivered. Instruction can be. Education requires that the person freely confront the question, "What am I going to make of myself?" At best we can stimulate somebody to ask this. But we cannot deliver it. If we think we can, we violate the other's being.

Clark Kerr in his famous *The Uses of the University* referred to the university as "a mechanism... held together by administrative rules and powered by money." As with all such mechanisms manufactured to realize limited purposes, the only question that can be addressed to them is, "Does it go through?" This will not do, for our relationship to the world is organismic and participatory, not mechanical, linear, bureaucratic; we exist within the reciprocating field. Any mechanism which presumes to totalize by abstracting and cutting up the world into a mere aggregate of discrete parts will violate us at the heart of our being and our freedom. It masks off the field, those archaic and obscure sacred energies which form us, the concrete wholeness and connectedness we live. Posing as an "educational " institution, the university become multiversity eclipses the chief question of education today for all: can we identify with fellow humans *as* fellows, interdependent and sharing many interests, or can we define ourselves only in terms of what we are not—an identity for us which is pure because it contrasts with those others who are base and polluted? Since our early experience is almost inevitably limited to a local group, do we learn to equate humanity with superficial characteristics of that group, so that groups with other characteristics are believed to be sub-human?

Our technological achievements in transportation and communication have marched across an archaic subsoil that has hardly changed. We are now able to span continents and make contact with peoples who have lived in different cultural worlds. But that may only mean that we will find more others to shun and humiliate—those abysmally *other* beings. Protesting the actions of our nation in the Philippines during the Spanish-American war, William James wrote that "little brown men" are only objects for us, not embodied subjects living forward in the light of their future. Our contact with them brings no intimacy. "They are too remote from us to be realized as they exist in their inwardness."*

The challenge of education springs up: to make some sense of our freedom, history, and common humanity if we are to be at all. It is a challenge that easily daunts. Hence the busy-work

---

*R. B. Perry, *The Thought and Character of William James* (Boston: 1935), vol. II, p. 311. See also B. Wilshire, ed., *The Essential Writings of William James* (Albany, N.Y.: 1984), my introduction.

of the academy: plucking the hairs off the face of terror without ever looking it in the eye. Unacknowledged energies of identity formation take obsessive form—production mania and tunnel vision, the refusal to listen and ruminate quietly, the refusal to be "content," in the words of Emerson, "if this day you have seen one thing truly." There are also disguised forms of purification ritual, surrogates: the drive to standardize technical methods for producing knowledge which reaches even into philosophy and is apotheosized in positivism. But standardization means homogenization and homogenization means purification. This is a sneaking, obessive form of purification, but purification nevertheless. It functions to satisfy, partially, the urge for purity and identity, and simultaneously to mask the archaic and messy sources of the urge. The mechanism of the university, neatly departmentalized, masks our sources.

What is it to be an educated human being, and not a semi-being, a miserable, bastard semi-automaton? The university drives ever faster under its own momentum, as if the apprentice's broom had slipped from our grasp and had begun to sweep away on its own. Human beings and their human concerns are swept out the door of the university.

The riots at Berkeley in the 60s deserve another look. If ever there was an example of Dionysus estranged from Apollo, this is it. Repressed energies of self, individual and communal, irrupted in nearly incredible mess and profusion. But beneath the roar of sometimes violent protest one can make out an enduring, plaintive sound, heard again in a speech that Mario Savio, leader of the revolt, gave at Berkeley twenty years after the event. He is reported to have said that "at least we established that we could *do* something." The sound emerges from the mousehole. It is the Underground Man who fears that he cannot do or be anything at all, not even an insect. Finally the problem emerges in the light of day from behind the glittering mechanism of the university as multiversity: it is the problem of human *being*. It is what the university, become huge motorized broom, tries to sweep out of sight. The same thing here as in all technologized states: Thus, in the Soviet Union, the communist government has tried at times to dismiss Dostoevsky as pre-revolutionary neurotic or freak.

I do not think that if we were just bright enough we could formulate a solution to all this—just fix it up. To think of this as another technical problem to be solved is not to understand its depth and complexity. The university proceeds with immense inertia, geared as it is into the whole secular, socio-economic system. Sweeping, wholesale "solutions" of its inhumanities can amount to no more than a wind of words blowing dust in our eyes. So I will suggest some piecemeal measures to begin to eat away at the difficulties. If they can be put into action, perhaps further opening and light will appear later.

Pessimism can be escapism. As we approach the end of the century (and of the millennium) a deep discontent moves beneath the educational establishment, indeed, beneath the society. Embedded assumptions are being questioned. Opportunities for change open around us—a simple fact.

We can take some specific steps that may begin to return the university to the human scale, and to a comprehension of our situation. What is shunted aside is personal presence within a community of truth-seeking and truthful human beings. We must reinstate this presence itself.

Now I imagine someone objecting already that this is "pie in the sky," and that we should be able to see that the university cannot be returned to the human scale, for research is inherently impersonal. The critic might concede that personal involvement of students and teachers is essential, and conclude therefore that universities should simply cease trying to educate undergraduates. This would be a good point. But we could expect much resistance to denaturing *alma mater*, since it is a rare source of identity to many nearly rootless people—a tradition to be passed on expectantly. Another reason for retaining undergraduates is that there are now multitudes of them enrolled. It seems foolish to imagine that sufficient funds could be provided to secure wholly new facilities. But what if the plan were revised so that most of the present facilities would be used, but reapportioned, and placed under a Senior Vice President with a great deal of autonomy? I think this has some possibilities, and will develop them soon.

Finally, there is the most serious reason for retaining undergraduates in the university. It is a grave mistake to regard research and the education of the young as separable activities. Students and professors need each other (at least some of the time), whether they realize this or not. I believe that if some professors are so hermetic that they never flourish in the presence of students, they should be assigned to posts in the university devoted solely to extremely advanced and arcane research, or should be required—if non-tenured—to search for employment in non-educational research institutions.

I have found that professors vary greatly in their powers of human presence and in their availability to other human beings. Often these factors vary independent of the professor's research specialty or specialties. Sometimes highly "research active" people are also deeply interested in the human beings with whom they rub elbows. It is part of the inhumanity of the multiversity that personal predilections are so often ignored. The apparent diversity of the "educational plant" partially conceals the sweeping standardizations of method and attitude—for example, the assumption that research must mean the subordination of teaching; it is another polarization presuming to exhaustiveness, subordinating one member of the pair to the other.

Sometimes this assumption is pushed to imbecilic extremes. One occasionally hears, for example, that the research university must be utterly distinct from the state college. Since, in the latter, teaching is usually stressed at the expense of research, the university should stress research at the expense of teaching.* It seems to be assumed that if two entities are to be distinct they must differ in every feature. This *is* imbecilic. It is a basic truth, I think, that two entities cannot exist in the same universe and differ in every feature. All that is needed to be essentially distinct is to differ in one essential feature. The relevant feature here should be the fraction of professors hired and tenured for paramount strength in teaching. In the state colleges the fraction should be roughly two-thirds, I think, and in the research uni-

---

*But we must proceed with caution, for increasingly the designation "research college" is applied by some to their small institutions.

versity roughly one-third. By "paramount strength" I mean a rough position on a continuum, with people at one end superb in research, but somehow only adequate in communicating its skills and joys to students, while people on the other are superb at the latter, but only adequate in communicating significant research with their peers.

It is the standing scandal of the vast majority of large universities that the fraction of professors hired and tenured for paramount strength in teaching is perhaps one-twentieth of the total. According to the public protestations of most university administrators, teaching counts as much as research in the employment and retention of professors. At Rutgers, for example, one finds boxes on promotion forms with teaching marked "of major significance," as is the box for "research" (published). But, as I say, my research indicates that teaching carries about one twentieth of the weight in determining tenure.* So it is impossible that both teaching effectiveness and research activity are "of major significance" in determining which professors are retained in the university. To affirm this equivalence is to affirm what is false. The falsity must be evident to those responsible for the system, hence they either deceive or are self-deceived. They either indulge in a mendacious public relations gimmick, or maintain a dreamy, self-deceiving state of consciousness in which certain acts are recognized only as "to be recognized no further."

My first and most important suggestion for reorganizing the university is that a certain modicum of honesty about its own operations be shown. If education of undergraduates is not really

---

*This is a rough estimate—exact figures are impossible to obtain. Of disappointed candidates who have grieved the decision at Rutgers, none has been given tenure who has been rated average or below in published research, regardless of teaching, and none has received it on the basis of outstanding teaching alone (according to the local chapter of the American Association of University Professors). Of course, this reflects only candidates who have grieved; perhaps some successful candidates do not fit this pattern. According to an opinion at the national office of the A.A.U.P., deception concerning the weight of teaching in deciding tenure is widespread in research universities. I think that one twentieth is a safe, conservative estimate of the weight of teaching relative to research in tenure decisions.

a major concern, this should be plainly stated, and a rudimentary respect for "truth in packaging" demonstrated. This is the most tangible matter imaginable for any avowedly educational institution, more palpable and substantial than the bricks and mortar of its buildings or the tonnage of its tackles on its football team. If the institution which has for its reason for being the discovery of truth, and the truthful dissemination of this to those who seek to form their lives in the light of it, is not truthful about its own operations, mustn't we say that it rots on its foundations? If this matter is not remedied, no other suggestions for reorganizing the university will amount to anything. Education is basically a moral relationship between persons devoted to truth. Without trust between them the situation is hopeless—the reality dissolves, the buildings remain standing.

Let us assume that a primitive level of honesty can be achieved, and go on to the remaining suggestions I would like to make for reorganization. On the basis of twenty-five years of experience teaching in a number of large universities with strong research missions, I estimate, very roughly, that in the natural mix of competent people in different fields available for employment, roughly one-third exhibits paramount strength as teachers, another third is about equally balanced in teaching and research skills, and the final third has paramount strength in research.*

---

*A major reason for teaching's not being recognized and rewarded has been a fairly widespread assumption that it cannot be accurately evaluated. By now, however, a good-sized literature has grown up (see, for example, *Improving College Teaching*, ed. Calvin B. T. Lee, (Washington: 1967), particularly articles by McKeachie and Arrowsmith, and *Institutional Responsibilities and Responses in the Employment and Education of Teaching Assistants: Readings from a National Conference* (Columbus: Ohio, 1987)). The many ways in which teaching can be evaluated combine to create a strong account: reports from professors who visit classrooms, from those who "inherit" a teacher's students, accounts of students' performance in later life, evaluations of teachers by students in later life as well as immediately following a course, etc. We should not expect the evaluations to be as precisely quantifiable as is typical in the sciences. To expect this is mere scientism which distracts us from important business. Of course, from an administrative point of view, long-delayed evaluative information has limited usefulness; and a student may not consciously realize the value of an educational transaction for decades. Then again, for research it might be a century. But the challenge should not deter our attack.

Once we acknowledge this more or less natural division of human talents, a horizon of possibilities opens.

My second suggestion is that in most institutions the undergraduate educational plant be divided into many colleges, with the roughly one-third of the faculty with paramount strength in teaching being assigned primary responsibility for administering and teaching within them. This should apply, I think, only to the faculty of arts and sciences. It is probably unrealistic to think that undergraduate professional schools such as business or social work could either be eliminated or brought into the college arrangement (we can hope at best for a few courses with humane content and method).

Within the faculty of arts and science, separate buildings for each college would be nice, but it is far from essential. A floor of a dormitory might adequately individuate the college, or even a block of classrooms reserved for a block of hours. I am imagining something rather informal and small, a college of about two or three hundred students and about ten teaching fellows. Most records would be kept in the office of the Dean of Arts and Science. The ideal arrangement would be a residential college with several faculty members in residence in any given year.

We need personal contact among all involved, for only through this can any of us learn what deeply moves another. There is a chasm which separates the video game room from the ordinary classroom, or nearly any social or personal situation from the classroom. The college I am imaging would supply something like a bridge between now disconnected segments upon which Apollo and Dionysus join hands, as Nietzsche suggested they did in Greek theatre.

What is desperately needed are examples of meaningful human lives, and these must be provided first and foremost in person. The best way to learn about goodness—trust, reliability, faithfulness, fairness, self-awareness, discipline, compassion—is by living in the presence of those who embody these virtues—mimetically, that is. Another way is in small, college classes in which inquiries into goodness are tied to studies of different cultures which exhibit not only cultural relativity and diversity, but those common human needs and satisfactions which cut across cultures (the widely exhibited advocacy of the golden rule, for example). Empirical research should not be irrelevant to ethical inquiry.

Finally, the arts, theatre for example, should be essential features of the colleges, with students stimulated to grasp their lived situations in artistic form. More or less spontaneous enactments of the pressing human concerns and problems of their own community exemplify perfectly the existential role that art can play. When a community enacts its perplexities and moral dilemmas for itself in a theatre, we learn to identify with others in ways that we usually do not in the everyday world; we see ourselves from these others' viewpoints, and thereby see both ourselves and them much better. Dewey's ideal synthesis of art, science, and ethics is impossibly idealistic only if we think that it is. (See his *Essays on School and Society,* 1899.) The ultimate end of this humane research would be to discover ways of living with each other which are actually valuable for human beings. Cast off would be the self-indulgent positivistic assumption that ethical judgements have only emotive, not cognitive, significance. To reclaim ethical judgments for *knowledge,* we need to reclaim what Wordsworth called the feeling intellect.

Clearly, the most important learning experience to be fostered is that of expanding the range of empathic identification, and minimizing responses of taboo-aversion to those not included in this range. The colleges should be large enough to include a wide variety of temperaments, career plans, and ethnic backgrounds, and in most instances, I imagine, would be co-educational (although some social groups would come together by gender, race, or other commonality for special support and nurturing). It should not be possible for any student to "hand pick" just who his or her associates would be. The size as well as the configuration of the group are essential features. It must be large enough not to be cliquish, but not so large that it becomes the student's "whole world." It must promote the dilation of identification and empathy without drawing, in some self-deceiving way, lines of exclusion around itself. ("Isn't our world of diversity and toleration snug and tidy?") It must both reflect itself within itself and open onto a larger, indefinitely extended world. Just what is optimal size and configuration here? Several hundred, I would imagine, but we must find out.

About a quarter of the courses required for the baccalaureate degree should be college courses, I think, most of them taken in the student's own college. The range of courses here would be determined, of course, at least in large part, by the interests and knowledge which the faculty members bring with them. But faculty will also want to learn, presumably, and they would probably use this opportunity to develop courses that cut across conventional departmental lines. Each college will develop a personality as a function of those involved. In general though, we should aim for an ideal of disciplined interdisciplinarity. By this I mean that faculty would work concertedly with each other and with students to construct a cumulative and cohesive learning experience through the four years, an experience in which civilized discourse between human beings would be at least partially restored. By this I mean the address of common problems and needs in a common language, and the search for value judgements that are true, that is, those that fix on ways of living that are in fact valuable because they contribute to the fulfillment and vitality of all of us.

The purpose of the colleges is to promote liberal, that is liberating education; that which frees from constricting prejudices and ideologies, from the prejudicial belief, for example, that the power one gains by occupying a niche in a bureaucratic hierarchy is equivalent to realization and power as a person (not just as a professional). As Jean Jaques Rousseau put it prophetically in *Emile* (1762), "Our wisdom is slavish prejudice, our customs are controls, constraints, compulsions. . . . Life is the business I would have him learn . . . manhood is the common vocation." Translating, we would say, personhood—humanity—is the common vocation, that which we should share before we specialize. To be liberally or generally well educated is to be glad to be alive, to be basically well-functioning, and to be knowledgeable concerning our common fate and eager to learn more—teachable. Then, and only then, should one specialize in a profession.

But what is to prevent the colleges themselves from becoming centers of ideological indoctrination instead of even-handed learning? There is a risk of this, yet it should not be exaggerated.

I do not think that a college should be instituted merely on the initiative of any ten faculty members and a group of students, although this should be a necessary condition. The whole faculty of Arts and Science should contribute to their formation, as well as to their overseeing, and I will presume that there are still administrators who desire to be educators, and that these should be given certain veto powers, at least. Moreover, a college that became destructively eccentric could not conceal this for long, and I do not believe that the tenure of fellows should hold within each college, but only in the overarching Faculty of Arts and Science.

Our times tend to overestimate the dangers of ideologies (even after having succumbed to one or more of them). This is due in part to the influence of positivism and its pretentious claim to scientific detachment, neutrality, pristine objectivity. This is a fiction, an ideology in disguise. All inquiry is interested, as James reminds us, and the only question is whether a tolerable balance of interests exists (we are interested in proving our theory true *and* we are interested in not being duped). We should not be upset if a college develops a distinctive point of view. There would be more reason to be upset if it did not, for this would probably indicate lack of vitality and cohesiveness.

One other point: it is a mistake to think that a group of scholars coming from classical studies, for example, would teach only classical studies. Most professors who would choose to be college fellows have long since been disabused of conventional disciplinarity and professionalism. Most would long for a chance to begin learning afresh. It is a mistake to think that only professors of English write well, or only professional philosophers philosophize well, etc. We think immediately of classicists who have been on the forefront of imaginative and humane learning—Norman O. Brown, William Arrowsmith, Frank Jones—of scientists who are masters of literary style—Sigmund Freud, Loren Eiseley, Lewis Thomas—of physicists who think philosophically and do it well—A. N. Whitehead, Albert Einstein, Werner Heisenberg, David Bohm. We could go on—and not all good interdisciplinary thinkers are famous ones.

Nor need we fear that not enough professors in the university would be willing to submit to the rigors of interdisciplinarity and of greater involvement with students. Sufficient numbers will be attracted if they are actually rewarded for such activity (rather then implicitly penalized); that is, if the hypocrisy of the university ceases. Some will be attracted even if they are not rewarded. If it is decided that the colleges should be headed by a presiding fellow for a two- or three-year term, say, we might even see some administrative talent bloom which might not do so in a strictly bureaucratic setting.

Finally, we should mark the possibility that some opposition to interdisciplinary colleges may come not only from deeply professionalized colleagues, but from students (or their parents). These are those who come to the university expecting to go directly into professional or pre-professional studies and also to be awarded a baccalaureate degree in the Faculty of Arts and Science when they finish. Such opposition must be weathered. To treat students as merely customers is to betray both them and ourselves. To give them mainly professional training but also the impression that they are being liberally educated is to fool them. To assume that they already know what they want and need in order to be educated is to assume that they are already educated, and this is to make fools of everyone.

Only the most empathic, sustained, and precise coordination between faculty, administrators, and students can begin to restructure the practice of research so that it connects with the background human condition, those mythical, instinctual, commonsensical, communal, and prescientific domains of our lives which are obscured but still active. The ultimate end of humane research and teaching in the university is to discover how we can be both field-beings *and* morally centered as free and self-responsible persons. It is a gargantuan task, but we must believe that it is possible, otherwise we will not even begin it.

Pursuant to restructuring the university I have suggested systematic truthfulness about its teaching mission and the establishment of small colleges. My third suggestion is that an interdisciplinary "think tank" at a "high" and intense intellectual level be incorporated in it. I trust that by now the dangers inherent in the call for this are apparent: that we intellectuals will slip back into a tacit psycho/physical dualism, identify ourselves as minds, and purify ourselves of the very problems we face as body-selves in history and community.

To confront common dangers is to form the nucleus of an educational community. This must be the nucleus of the interdisciplinary "think tank" I would like to see emerge. It must be a group that achieves deliverance from ego, to at least a tolerable extent, in both the individual and the communal body. It must be interdisciplinary to a degree that we perhaps cannot yet clearly imagine. A common language must be imagined (a quite uncommon one!). Physicists, writers, biologists, artists, philosophers, psychologists, engineers ... must regain the impetus of the early decades of this century, dropped by positivism, and carry it further. It must be field-theoretical and unabashedly imaginative.

The "think-tank" I am imagining must not be extracurricular, the equivalent of bedtime reading. It should draw from every sector of the university and perhaps beyond. Chemical engineers who know that their activities carry unexamined assumptions and are rife with human significance; literary scholars concerned with elucidating and extending poetic images used by scientists; etc. It would not be interdisciplinary in the narrow sense, and by this I mean something like biochemistry, a field that is sufficiently stabilized to become its own department. This group would identify and enlist novel work just as it begins to take flight and to cross disciplinary boundaries, with destination unknown. The bureaucratic obsession with prediction and control should be countered head on. I would suggest terms of membership in the group of three years, renewable on mutual agreement of the cross-disciplinary "think tank" members, and in consultation with administrators.

And what should this group do? This is no mystery. Its task is gradually to develop a shared vocabulary in which we can formulate the difficulties which threaten to terminate life on earth. What is the basis for true ethical judgements in an age of field and relativity theory? How must reason be restructured to be compatible with both physical and cultural relativity? Are there universal human needs and propensities, so that that which answers to these and satisfies them is really good? What else could we possibly mean by *good*?

In standing open to others in other fields we will be sharing each others' points of view, so gradually a more comprehensive and objective account of the world around us and of ourselves within it will be formed. The very meaning of "objective reality" must change considerably if we are to deliver ourselves from the abstraction boxes of seventeenth-century physics and psycho/physical dualism, and understand how our own subjectivity, our own points of view on things and our relativity, are as "objectively real" as anything else (just a bit more weird and intriguing!). We selves are out there in the world, but not merely as objects viewed through a Cartesian abstraction called "objectivity," as if we squinted at ourselves through an optical instrument, but as beings participating in the archaic energies of others, Earth, and the cosmos.

To give some specific examples of the interdisciplinary task of coordinating technical powers, psychological and social proclivities, and ethical needs: Bio-engineering now enables us to custom-make (or remake) living beings out of organic "spare parts," and through gene-splicing. Tempting it is to use the analogy of custom-building an automobile. But what if our product is a failure, yet its features indicate that it is a human being? Do we just junk it? Doesn't it make ethical demands upon us within the reciprocating field? Yes, we *can* do so and so, but does it conduce to our optimal development as free beings with ethical capacities to do so?

Or how do we deal with human activities which are of local origin and which traditionally have been evaluated by ancient standards fitted to that locale, but which now, abetted by technology, have serious global consequences? No single disciplinary field can hope to address these questions effectively.*

The "think tank" should be well funded—which will probably be difficult to achieve. (It will be particularly hard if the university is locked into an enrollment-driven budget; creative administering will be needed.) Fellows should be promotable

---

*Consider the burning of thousands of acres of Amazon rain-forest each day. This warms the planet and depletes our store of oxygen. Some suggest that the rest of the world must rent what remains of the rain-forest.

while in it, with primal evaluative input from both the group and the "home" department, either group able to initiate promotion. The democratically elected chair should sit on the Council of Deans. Persons from outside the university, well known for their imaginative powers and interactive abilities might be enlisted as fellows for one or more terms. Last, but emphatically not least, some administrators will have relevant research projects and must be included. The present exclusiveness of administrators in a managerial club is one of the most pernicious and destructive features of many universities.*

Substantial steps for reorganization can be taken which will not abruptly destabilize the university. To cross disciplinary lines is the life of the mind, and it can be stifled for only so long, and we have reached the limit. We should not think that this crossing, this "transgression" happens only on the rarified levels of graduate studies, and it would badly inhibit the group I am imagining if it were confined within this mind-set. The higher branches of learning interdigitate, but also there is commingling at the roots, generation of sap in the soil of pre-critical, even mythical or magical life. Here is the source of creative images which spring out of the body-self rooted in the sensuously given environment. It is often in contact with younger students, ones not yet fatally circumscribed in their interests, that researchers best share in this life and feel young themselves.

For universities to concentrate on graduate studies and to subordinate the undergraduate is very short-sighted. In this "think tank" I am imagining, a few undergraduate students—and graduate students—would play a significant part. They should be good students, perhaps those in honors programs, but by good student, I just mean the inquisitive, imaginative tenacious person. Students judged conventionally to be highly intelligent are frequently only proficient at answering other people's questions. The students I have in mind will be able to ask their

---

*See Lionel Tiger, *The Manufacture of Evil* (New York, 1988) concerning the benighted behavior of competing groups whose deliberations are systematically masked from outsiders. The dangers are greatest in a university, for its *raison d'etre* is open inquiry and discussion, and governance in the light of open discussion and self-scrutiny.

own good questions and cling to them. In any number of excellent ways, cross-disciplinary faculty fellows and these students can work together, at least some of the time. This interaction might involve formal classes tied into one of the colleges, as I have outlined them, or it might not.

Now, what long-term changes in the university can we expect from installing a substantial "think-tank" within it? Not surprisingly, it will gradually put great pressure on departmental boundaries. As more and more successful research goes on outside departmental lines, they can be expected first to tighten, and then—if the extra-mural research becomes more formidable than that occurring inside—some of the already established disciplines can be expected to collapse within themselves, to implode. Either this or departments will be merged in newly conceived overarching "areas" which are given real administrative power.

In some cases these shifts can be expected to be "catastrophic." It is highly unlikely, however, that many departments will be involved in sudden change at any one time. Conceptual shifts wrought through interdisciplinary endeavor reverberate through the conceptual foundations of many disciplines, yet they probably reach the critical tipping point at different times in different ones. This is because of the multitude of factors, many of them contingent, which create inertia and coherence in each discipline. We need not fear that the whole university might be reduced to chaos at some instant, and that some totalitarian regime will be brought in to "save" it.

But when new areas of study are formed can't we expect that they in turn will be broken down into new topics and that new lines of purity will be formed? Yes and no. It is of the essence of human transcendence and the openness of imagination that ever new configurings of the "whole" map will emerge. It is equally inevitable that they will be broken down into new units, and that practitioners within these units will probably become ego-involved in defending their zone of hard-earned expertise.

But two points should be made: (1) these will be new cuttings-up of the whole pie, new ways of looking at things which expose previously hidden features, and (2) we should not foreclose the possibility that we will some day break free to *some* extent from the bondage of anxious ego-tendance, and from that fearful definition of things in which the traits which distinguish them from others are emphasized at the expense of the traits which they share; purification rituals in which the other is debased. One of the great possibilities of Women's Studies lies in just this possibility of the redefinition of definition—and of the reformulation of ourselves as individual identities—and I turn to this possibility in the next chapter.

In sketching this reorganization of the university, it is essential that we be both concrete and visionary in a single moment of thought. Visionary proposals with no concrete footing are self-deceiving and escapist dreams. Concrete proposals with no vision remain confined within the very assumptions which should be questioned. Our tasks are mountainous, yet we do work at a propitious moment in history. After many decades of unquestioning allegiance to assumptions of academic professionalism, a new vision of what we might be doing is beginning to form. We begin to see that departmentalization into *pure* areas of research feeds that "trained expertness increasingly indispensable to modern bureaucracy," and that this bureaucracy splinters and desiccates the field of human being, ultimately dividing us from ourselves. Professional competence too frequently undermines vitality and freedom, and damages the urge to discover the truth and to hold to it regardless of which boundaries it leads us to transgress.

I feel slightly schizoid when I teach students about Socrates' protracted combat with the sophists. The latter, for the most part, taught their students how to fit into the commercial and political world they found around them, and to excel within it, "how to dress and speak for success." Socrates thought that to fit in might be worse than death, if the society into which one fitted oneself were deranged and corrupted. But I , the professor, am supported quite liberally by the very commercial and political society which I often invite my students to criticize.

Nevertheless, there may be even now the opportunity to constructively criticize the university become multiversity within the very institution itself, state-supported though it may be. Since around 1980 a decisive shift of academic consciousness appears; the world tilts slightly in another direction. Constrictions around taboo subjects begin to loosen, subjects such as Socrates might have classified under "tendance of the soul." Many academics have begun to note publicly that too much teaching is *bad,* or mediocre or slipshod, and that we all have contracted some vague but serious malaise. It begins to be seen that a chief reason for poor teaching is that the student is not addressed as an integral being, one who can care and be concerned, and a chief reason for this is that university personnel no longer speak a common language, no longer address common concerns.

Where there is a will, there is a way, and the will very much depends upon vision (the secret of will, as James put it, is the secret of the control of attention). A new vision of educational possibilities begins to form, and ways will be found to change the university. To guard against discouragement we must firmly expect that the changes will be slow. This is a reasonable expectation, for it is the academic domain in which taboos most tightly constrict and suppress key topics of the human condition: those topics which pertain to our lives as *body*-selves. It is precisely academics who most obsessively identify themselves as pure minds and intellects.

Nevertheless, we must also expect that change *may* be sudden. If tacit purification rituals and obsessions can be recognized *as* such, our whole situation will be "re-framed" within an expanded outermost circle or horizon, and everything will be altered "catastrophically" within it. Maturity consists, I expect, in being prepared for nearly anything.

Ways are beginning to be found to alter the university. What works in one will not necessarily work in another. The suggestions I have already made require some major flexibility in administration, probably more than is available in some universities.

Less ambitious measures have already been widely taken, centered particularly in a core curriculum. I have serious doubts about the efficacy of most such plans. As the name implies, the idea is to survey a body of knowledge essential to everybody's education. At its worst, it is worse than nothing at all. For, taught by a few specialist from hither and yon, it gives the impression of setting up a core, but it fails to instill the idea of what *education* is. Mere window dressing or wallpaper is pasted up, and no concepts and concerns common to all fields of learning are teased out of the students' experience, to be woven together, perhaps, by the student in a free act of making sense of his or her life and in taking responsibility for whatever truth can be found. Typically, core curricula fail to provide a community in which young and old learn about each other and the world with zest.

A major problem, of course, for the core curriculum has been to find faculty who have not been fatally narrowed and constricted themselves. As Ph.D.s they are the supreme products of an ahistorical age, split off and presumptuous. It is just the flattening of historical depth and constriction of historical width that afflicts both the "physicians" and the "patients." Nihilism runs rampant. As I detailed in the Introduction and Chapter One, students tend not to feel that they are a part of any historical movement of humankind; or that they stand at a certain station at which tasks and responsibilities (and joys) are received from elders, to be handled by one's generation for awhile, and to be passed on in turn to one's juniors in the fullness of time. The very idea of the fullness of time seems to have evaporated, leaving the field of human interactivity and reciprocity desiccated. How can there be continuity and vitality in education, how can any vital core grow up, when it is lacking in the lives of both teachers and students?

Most core curricula with which I am acquainted, these old-fashioned Chinese menus with their little of this and little of that, are patent shams. Harvard is reported to have a "Star Lecturer Series," with students expected to sit in on a few of these. I have no reliable reports on what effect these lectures have had. It is conceivable that some of the speakers are genuinely philosophical and communicative intellects, and that in a few moments can shower seeds which effect deep conceptual connections between subject matters. I hope so. It *can* be done by a few gifted and committed people, but it takes real commitment on the part of administrators and all involved to construct an environment in which such inspired interaction becomes a vital, growing thing. Only gut feelings can authorize here; no precise and official measurements of success can be forthcoming, for, as William Irwin Thompson and others have said, our institutions are out of touch with human reality, and the stages and cycles, predictable and unpredictable, of human development.

Of the universities with which I am acquainted, only a few, such as Brandeis, offer courses in a core curriculum which are genuinely interdisciplinary and educational. That is, these courses expose concepts that are fundamental to many areas of research. The professors involved seem to have broken out of the straitjacket of pollution anxieties that prevents "the mixture of what ought to be kept separate"; the kind of dread which is the same, in effect, as that which attends the mixture of meat and dairy in orthodox Judaism.

But to construct such a course is immensely difficult and time-consuming, even for those talented enough to do it. If the university is not willing to pay for it, and to honor it in one way or another, it will probably happen only rarely. All the window dressing in the world will not do the job, and by now everyone is impatient with the hypocrisy of university administrators and faculty members who broadcast to the public that teaching is of "major significance," when clearly it is not.

Where there is a will there is a way, but some universities will find it much easier than others to transform themselves into something like humane and responsible institutions. For example, the University of Minnesota has a tradition of vigorous educational efforts, and it is not surprising to see it take an important initiative in interdisciplinary work.* As I understand their new program, assistant professors with clearly interdisciplinary credentials—and there are a few—are offered berths in some "home" department on "lines" or positions specifically created and funded by the administration. These are "gifts" to the department, although part of the time these young professors

---

*I am indebted to Prof. Ellen Messer-Davidow of the University of Minnesota. See *Minnesota Daily,* May 6, 1986, and *Focus,* Spring, 1988. Notice also a conference—"Disciplinarity: Formations, Rhetorics, Histories"—held at U.M. in April, 1989. Papers such as these were given: "Disciplinary Crisis: The Case of Geography"; "Textuality and the Critique of Disciplinary Reason"; "Performance, Discipline, Subjection"; "Literary Theory and the Narrative of Professionalization"; "The Ideology of Objectivity: How French Engineers Reduced Public Utility to Numbers."

will be teaching in other departments which also, of course, are gifted with these "free" courses.

Nevertheless, a "banking system" is created to keep "credits" and "debits" straight. The department gifted with a visiting interdisciplinary colleague has the obligation to designate one of their own members (a newly hired young professor?) as a visitor to some other department.

This may not seem like much to the layman, but anyone acquainted with typical departmental—and funding—rigidity in most universities will be impressed. Departmental autonomy is slightly undermined, because more than a single department's evaluation goes into selecting interdisciplinary candidates to be looked at and retained, and a systematic effort is made to overcome pollution taboos. It is a beginning.

Other universities, more conservative and insecure, will have difficulty taking such initiatives. But even my own university, Rutgers, which suffers from a quite rigid bureaucracy, and a sometimes cliquish administrative cadre, has taken some significant interdisciplinary steps. A Council of Interdisciplinary and Crossdisciplinarity Studies was created a few years ago. Professors from nearly every area, from religious studies to mechanical engineering, were offered the chance to share ideas in a friendly setting, and extraordinarily creative world figures invited to lecture. These included George Wald, Ilya Prigogine, and David Bohm. There were fastidious demurrings from some of the more conventional faculty, but the stimulation and temporary pain can be regarded as salutary. Moreover, very recently a Center for the Critical Analysis of Contemporary Culture was instituted, the function of which is at least partly interdisciplinary. My membership in this group has contributed to writing this book.

The point is that the whole horizon has begun to open and shift—that circle presently outermost, as Emerson and Nietzsche described it—and everything within it is being thrown into flux. So encompassing is it, so altering of a whole form of life and the manner in which we tell our stories about ourselves, that we might call it a mythological shift. Positivists and their thinly disguised heirs can do no more, I believe, than try to slow it down. Even the academy, fortress of contemporary rigidity and purification ritual, is not immune now to change. This is an age of transition. Shifting the metaphor from the horizonal to the oceanic, William Thompson writes in *Passages About Earth* (and I cannot resist the urge to quote it again),

But now you can feel the waters lift and stir; new currents are coming in, but for those of us in the universities who cannot stand the flooding of our academic boundaries and definitions, there will be terror as the mythical future becomes confused with the mythical past.

It must have been this kind of current that moved my colleague and me oddly as we sat in my office with nothing to do, but with everything to do, as described in Chapter One.

Amidst all our vexations we can yet count ourselves lucky that the outer horizon has shifted just a little, and new currents flow, thus creating openings for our freedom. There are cracks in the bureaucratic apparatus, and particularly individuals in positions of power have a chance to change things, but not only those persons. Examples of change are practically numberless. For instance, U.C.L.A. is the very model of a modern multiversity—a model of professional aloofness, coolness, impersonality, deracination: it is practically historyless—and yet work of the most innovative sort in medical thought and practice, as well as in other fields, is occurring there. One need only think of the Chronic Pain Center, or the work on illness by the humanist Norman Cousins.

Also consider a new book written by a junior faculty member that has just been announced by New Society Publishers, *Getting Doctored: Critical Reflections on Becoming a Physician,* by Martin Shapiro, M.D. It "explores the process whereby young, often idealistic medical students are transformed through their education into hardened, 'alienated' professionals. Shapiro, assistant professor of medicine at U.C.L.A. Medical School, critically examines the learning experiences students confront in medical schools and how these experiences reinforce the destructive forms of power and authority which exist within the profession as a whole." He may be jeopardizing his chances for tenure.

Or consider Alex Comfort, Adjunct Professor at the Neuropsychiatric institute of U.C.L.A., who has published *Reality and Empathy: Physics, Mind, and Science in the 21st Century.* This is an imaginative and learned book, with some doses of interesting mathematics. Cousins, Shapiro, and Comfort stand at an immense distance from Descartes, and foretell radical changes in the education of physicians. No longer is the body a mere machine into which the doctor, the Great Mechanic, intervenes at will—a conception of self that divides body from mind, and explains how the very persons who deal with humans in crisis know so little of their humanity. The self begins to be seen as a field-being, a single locus of reciprocating relationships, among which attitudes (such as respect or hopefulness) of others toward the self, or self toward itself, are as fundamentally constitutive of that self as are the muscles and joints which compose its skeleton.

Other academic fields at U.C.L.A. find room for fundamental and highly imaginative scholarship through attaching professors to several departments or areas. For example, Marija Gimbutas, Professor of Archaeology—but given a long tether within the university—has employed carbon dating techniques in conjunction with decades of digs (and her studies of symbolism) to enlarge radically our conception of the antiquity and nature of human civilization. She has exposed cities built as early as 6500 B.C., which do not show any fortifications. Their architecture suggests a more egalitarian and peaceful mode of human existence. Old ideas of the human "essence" are shaken. The work to be done is basic, philosophical, and it will not wait for academic philosophers to do it. And that is a good thing too, for they tend to be the most mentalistic and verbalistic of all the academics, the ones most out of touch with themselves as body-selves in mimetic engulfment with others.

Philosophical work, basic to our society and to our personal welfare, flowed around the professional philosophical establishment at a date much earlier than the pluralist rebellion of 1978. Awareness of unreasonable exclusions and segmentations in the university continues to grow—a kind of native philosophical sense which grows.

How deep pollution fears have run throughout the university, and what an aura of sanctity still hangs furtively and uncannily about the courses of purification! The intellect floats away into the thin, pure atmosphere of empty space. It is the secret ecstasy of a subtle asceticism and egoism, and, marvel of marvels, it can be institutionalized in a university; the ascetic individual body merges with the ascetic corporate one. I recall how some of us undergraduates at U.S.C. in the early 1950s would occasionally slip across town to U.C.L.A. to hear that legendary positivist, Rudolph Carnap, begin his classes with the gracious warning that we were not to expect to be edified. The angelic calmness and remoteness with which the admonishment was delivered was thrilling and edifying beyond words to tell. I see it now as a disguised rite of purification. As if we were novice mystics in the desert, with the emptiness transformed into the medium of ecstatic flight from the flesh we actually live—a limpid horizon at dawn and a polished grape to break the fast. The calm Carnap, before us like a guru, exemplified Franz Kafka's "hunger artist," the performer who commands attention by overmastering his need for merely physical nourishment.

But much has happened since the 1950s, and in the nearly two decades which have elapsed since Abraham Kaplan excoriated professional philosophers in his "The Travesty of the Philosophers," the "analytic" establishment has developed considerable variety and drifted far indeed from the positivist background. Vast areas of even the recent history of philosophy (and civilization) still tend to be ignored, however, and many graduate departments are so deeply embedded in the bureaucratic structure of prestigious universities that their parochialism goes unchallenged. But as the university and the society change even this will too.

Not to see the university in its context and connectedness is not to see it. We have already sketched the shape of its embeddedness in the socio-economic-military complex. Large portions of the multiversity are financed by grants from private corporations or from the military or other branches of government. This is direct financial support. Indirect support accrues from the university's role as certifier of the professional competence of those who go to run the socio-economic-military complex, and who will pay large taxes to support both it and, of course, the university as a part of it.

When this occurs in the university-become-multiversity it is very dangerous. For it is difficult in the multiversity to find a center, an effective forum, in which these activities can be evaluated and coordinated with the larger educational role of the university. In such a forum one can easily imagine philosophical defenses being made of capitalism and the so-called free market. Academic freedom, as a fairly effective principle, has survived in the United States, and this is a paramount fact. So the simple equation of defense of academic freedom and defense of the United States is a tempting one. But the matter is complex, calling for intense discussions on a university-wide basis.

As unwieldly as it may be, I suggest university-wide convocations in which the whole matter of academic freedom is rethought. What are the obligations of professors to seek truth, no matter how unpleasant, and truthfully to communicate their results? Is truth to be considered solely within the narrow framework of an academic specialty, or also as it interlocks with truth in other fields, such as the humanities? Is it right to do research which can be employed eventually by a funding source for germ warfare, say, or for weapons in space? And what of the obligation to communicate truth to all who would know it? Can truth be anyone's *property,* even those who discover it? Doesn't truth partake of our transcendence, and at the point at which we are most ourselves just because we transcend the claims of mere ego? There are no easy answers here. We can only pretend there are by refusing to discuss the issues, by staying within whatever gold-lined mousehole holds us.

Problems at the other end of the scale should also be discussed in this university con-vocation (valuable term!). What about research which is not only not supported by outside financing but not supported intellectually by the current professional "mainstream"? What is the responsibility of the university as its own intellectual community to support this unpopular research? Too often we shirk this at the local level, passing it on to national or international organizations, even though it is at the local level, through contact day by day, that the possibilities of unpopular research can best be discerned. This is a vexingly difficult matter, in part because—as above—truth should not be considered anyone's private possession. We are, however, speaking here of the *meaning* (the possible consequences) of hypotheses, theories, or hunches difficult to discern at a distance, or at a single reading (as when a petition for funds is read by an anonymous referee in a funding agency).

The university still benefits immensely from academic freedom, which not only allows its explication and defense, but demands it. I am afraid, though, that we are living off the capital of previous generations of thinkers and not replenishing it. Those who make their money—some of it big money—in the university might just as well be working for International Harvester, and filing their quarterly reports with stockholders.

When we adjust our focus a little we see the interlocking directorate: professionalized university, professional academic associations, funding foundations and agencies (other than the government now), and publishing houses. The university is deeply embedded in all this. Altering the departmentalized and professionalized university means altering this interlocking directorate. As difficult as this is, it may nevertheless seem to be more difficult than it really is, and we should not be blind to the progress that has been made in recent years. As consciousness shifts, change can be expected to occur at a geometrical rate, or perhaps even abruptly. To take one instance, what appeared to be an unmovable monolith, The American Philosophical Association, was in reality hollow, ill-founded, and top-heavy, and has been altered very significantly in under a decade. There are great differences now in the program of papers at its yearly convention, and some difference in that cadre of senior professors who are able to exercise professional power and to place their graduate students in academic jobs.

Altering the policies of academic funding agencies and foundations will probably take more time. These are extraordinarily conservative institutions, on the whole, and the referees they employ are drawn from the most elite and deeply entrenched group in each academic professional association. These groups tend to stay pure, and to pass out rewards among themselves and their favored students and heirs. Administrators of foundations are even more dependent upon professional credentials as criteria of judgment than are university administrators. After all, there is some opportunity, however small, for the latter to make judgments on the basis of personal acquaintance or in response to questions of pressing and obvious human concern. In contrast, the funding agency administrator must rely upon highly formalized written data almost exclusively, and upon the judgment of elite professionals in petitioners' fields acting as judges of their research proposals.

Moreover, it is money that is disbursed. The Freudian equation of money and anality is no mere eccentricity or perversity. I will spare the reader a full rehearsal of this view, but the gist is that the ejection of money can be badly polluting, for money partakes of the inwardness and identity of both the individual and the group—as with expelled bodily matter, it epitomizes what is dearly valuable because most private, most intimately one's own—and any uncontrolled or improperly conducted ejection of it threatens the boundaries and integrity of bodily identity, in both its individual and corporate form. A primal tendency is to "hoard one's treasure," as Freud and Karl Abraham put it. But if its disbursing is unavoidable this must be entrusted to those who are impeccably discrete professionally, who will never mix what ought to be kept separate. Academic foundation and funding agency administrators tend to be highly regulated, buttoned-up types, highly anal-retentive; they must somehow hoard the treasure entrusted to them *and* disburse it.

This has the most concrete consequences. Funding for individual cross-disciplinary scholars has traditionally been very small (recall William Arrowsmith's remarks cited earlier). This has tended to persist in the face of the palpable fact that experience and knowledge grow on their edges, as James and Kaplan put it: revolutionary discovery typically occurs on the grey margins of disciplines, or between them. Seven-hundred-page tomes can be written with the aim of "exploring . . . creative processes by which a practitioner in one discipline uses the ideas . . . of another discipline."* But it makes little difference to most funding agencies. For example, as I have already mentioned, it is well known that Vesalius had dissected the heart but could not see

---

*See I. Bernard Cohen, *Revolution in Science* (Cambridge, Mass: 1985).

that it pumped the blood. Its septum had to be porous, despite the evidence of his eyes. It was only when technology, courage, and imagination had progressed to the point at which William Harvey could imagine the heart to be like a pump (the power of metaphor) that he could see that it indeed pumped blood through the body. Harvey was persecuted for his "interdisciplinary" perceptiveness. But this makes little difference to most funding agencies, for—as much as were Harvey's persecutors—they are in the grip of fear, purification rituals, ego-defense. Funding agencies have traditionally been the safe haven for the conventional and timid of mind, in both the sciences and the arts.

Nevertheless, even this segment of the interlocking directorate can change, however glacial the change typically is. Since about 1980 and ever increasing amount of aid has flowed to interdisciplinary and cross-disciplinary projects, from a trickle to a small stream. If it ever becomes "the thing to do," we can expect an abrupt incremental growth. Recall that when the outer circle of the horizon of consciousness shifts, everything shifts within it, practically simultaneously. It is a quantum phenomenon. Yesterday's revolutions are today's conventions. A new horizon has replaced the old.

Publishing houses occupy the final sector of the interlocking directorate, the inner ring of professionalism in which the university is embedded. Given the production mania which sweeps the university, the power of publishing houses, as well as of reviewing organs, is immense, nearly incredible, almost uncanny— as is clearly evident to those who live or die according to their fortunes here. In a secular, rootless age, this remaining source of authorization takes on a numinous quality, a furtive and fickle quasi-spirituality. Those who hold positions of power within these institutions hold nearly absolute power over many fellow humans. So lofty is their perch that most of them feel no need to justify their biases.

Take the *New York Times* Sunday book review section, for example. Over the years practically no books on socialism, or on non-western religions, or on theories of practice (theatre practice, say) have appeared—just to take these instances of neglected categories of publications. What is invisible within an organ can make no protest within it, and these iron lines of inclusion and exclusion have strong influence over what is advanced or passed over in university preferment. Even otherwise good publications exhibit serious biases, and when they interlock to form a "mainstream" the exclusions are grievous.

Scholarly journals are often notoriously biased in their editorial policies, and the more elite the less liable to have their biases exposed. Because they do the authorizing, who is sufficiently authorized to expose their biases? Who are the best people? The ones who publish in the best journals. Which are the best journals? The ones which publish the best people. This is an airtight argument! But, again, there are few in power to expose its circularity, for power is established within the circle, which is really a cone of hierarchy.

Nevertheless, a decisive shift in consciousness impacts even now on these relatively closed spheres of influence. There is the added favorable factor that many people in all forms of journalism are strongly drawn to "the scoop." New insights—as long as they are not too difficult to understand—are sometimes published just because they are new. Moreover, though the power of cowardice should never be underestimated, there *are* courageous editors who will publish difficult books and articles in which they believe. My impression is that this sector of the interlocking directorate of academic professionalism is changing rapidly at a few points.

Any programmatic sketch for concrete changes in the university must touch on the topic of tenure. Tenured professors are difficult to remove from the university, and when they compose the great majority in departments (as tends to be the case today), they can block change not only in their own departments, but, ganging up, may do so within the university as a whole. They can insist on the most sterile forms of purity.*

---

*An increasingly used method for breaking the grip of tenure is the employment of part-time instructors. They may be well-qualified, but they are typically paid "the wages of draymen" (recall chapter four), and are deprived retirement benefits and health-care insurance. A permanent underclass of gypsy scholars threatens to be created—an exploitation of younger academics' com-

I have been postponing the topic of tenure because the issue is extraordinarily complex and treacherous. Clearly, the right of tenure is often abused. Clearly, it stands in the way of hiring more deserving younger people who happened to appear after the job market shrank, but before large graduate departments slowed their egoistic production of Ph.D.s (another measure of the insularity of professionalism). Clearly, tenure is sometimes used to shield niggardly participation in what remains of governance open to faculty, also sluggish teaching of students and minimal scholarly endeavor. Alone and unmonitored in his or her classroom, the professor is unchallenged; perhaps the earlier drive to excel was shallowly based in the personality; growth ceases and something dies within. Too flaccid and insecure to look for other employment, the professor hangs on as "dead wood." And the guilt engendered by blocking excellent, non-tenured professors' access to university posts probably does as much to demoralize and erode community as does any other factor.

Even all this is not the worst-case scenario. It is usually maintained that tenure is indispensable because it guarantees the professor's right to speak out on controversial issues and to argue for what is believed to be true. No doubt, this is a powerful consideration; it is called academic freedom. This secure right to freedom of inquiry and expression should embolden professors, and does some. But, strangely and sadly, tenure has the opposite effect on many. The longer and more secure their period of safety, the flabbier and more faint-hearted they become, the more they fear they have to lose. Moreover, in becoming senior professors, they tend to identify with this typically more conservative, if not reactionary, group; they become unwittingly engulfed mimetically in a corporate body which adopts a perpetually defensive posture; their bleak hope is to maintain their

mitment to their fields of study (and possibly, after so many years of preparation, their inability to get a good job outside the university). This practice is particularly shameful when it is also employed to compensate for exorbitant salaries paid to a few "superstars." That market pressures should have so distorted the research university is a measure, of course, of its moral collapse.

identity by safeguarding the purity and clarity of the tradition. When tenured professors dispute their fellows they dispute the validity that these authorities gave to them. They endanger their own identity. A tradition is perpetuated which tends to stigmatize and stultify new insights and block new truth, effectively depriving others of *their* academic freedom, their ability to attain tenure, to inquire freely and effectively, and to express their findings in the same way.

But what is the alternative? Eliminate tenure? I suppose that trustees have the power to do this. But imagine what could easily happen in many universities. Administrative experts in efficiency and human engineering could eliminate professors (or whole programs) who were not meeting market demands—what students happen to want to study, corporations to encourage, and funding agencies and the government to support at the moment. Competing with other institutions for students, the temptation for universities to do this is strong. Why encourage it? Tenure gives some stability in the midst of mindless change.

In many respects, tenure is bad. Eliminating it could easily be worse. In the end I would opt for the retention of tenure. Of course, some have maintained that there is a third alternative, a kind of compromise: tenure granted for a limited time, say five or ten years, and then its possession would be subject to reevaluation and renegotiation. But this undermines the main reason for tenure in the first place: to guarantee protection from reprisal at any time.

Still, there seems to be a fourth alternative: Evaluation every five or so years but without the danger of actually losing tenure. Simple self-respect, if any exists, would prompt the professor to stay more consistently alert.

Finally, there is an alternative which is more and more being tried and which seems excellent to me. It involves the offer of early retirement to persons 55 or older, with the bonus of a full year's salary if the offer is accepted at the conclusion of the next school year. I understand that there are quite a few "takers" in some of the universities in which it is being tried, and I can only suppose that in most cases the person perceives that his or her best years in the academy are over. Perhaps the offer could be extended, on the initiative of the administration, to some in their late forties, with the bonus raised to one and a half or two years' salary.

Problems of education are problems of identity. What shall I make of myself? Since we are body-selves, this must include, What shall I make of my gender? We move within a lengthy and weighty tradition in which males' posing and answering these questions have dominated thinking. The tendency of the male body-self sharply to differentiate itself from its birthing source— indeed, from all dependency relationships—has permeated our thinking about any individual reality, any *one* of anything— which includes the meaning of this *one* world, and our place within it. Our civilization is androcentric because our hunger for meaning has been fed in an androcentric way.

Increasingly, as women speak and think for themselves, we can expect this to alter how we think of one of anything being itself and not another, in other words, to alter how definition itself is defined and individuation experienced. As Women's Studies programs are instituted, this will have the greatest impact, eventually, on the "house of intellect," as Jacques Barzun called the university. After the specific recommendations for immediate change outlined in this chapter, I turn now to long-run and more speculative possibilities in this age of transition.

XII

Reclaiming the Vision of Education: Redefining Definition, Identity, Gender

> Everything has changed but our ways of
> thinking, and if these do not change we drift
> toward unparalleled catastrophe.
> —Albert Einstein

The neglect of teaching in the university is an ominous symptom. I believe it signals a weakening of our will to live. For if we do not nurture our young and identify with them, we forfeit any hope in the regeneration and continuation of the species; we are walled up defensively within the confines of our egos and our momentary gratifications. But this means that we are not fully alive ourselves.

The sundering of vital connections of many kinds has been going on for a long time, and by now it is built into the automatic patterning of our thought. Aristotle recognized that we are a species of animal, but he placed more emphasis on the trait which distinguishes us than on the traits we share: our god-like power of reasoning. Two thousand years later this sundering reaches a limit, with Descartes. The self or soul is thought to be composed only of those traits which we share with a transcendent Deity. The self objectifies itself and splits itself off from its own body, thus aping the transcendence of God.

Ramifying from this central split between self and body, polarizing fractures spread across the field of our being in the world: self/other; culture/nature; now/then; light/darkness; totality/zero; citizen/foreigner; professor/student; male/female; etc. The dualisms are hierarchical: the first-stated member of the pair is thought to be superior to its companion, its *other*. Moreover, the dualisms totalize, that is, they are thought to exhaust the alternatives within the parameter in question. Mind over body, self over other, culture over nature, now over then, professor over student, male over female . . . in hierarchical monotonousness and dull dread of revolution from the underside and pollution by it.

The fractures spread from a presumptuous, calculative consciousness, armed with technology, which believes it can break away from its own body and from Nature and control our destiny. As unintended consequences of our calculations and actions pile up within a world which is boundless—not contained by "exhaustive" dualisms and their neat cut-outs and individuations—we begin to see that our means of control are out of control.

Reclaiming the educational vision means disengaging these automatisms of dualistic, hierarchical, and totalizing thinking. This would diminish the dread of being polluted by the subjugated members of the dualistic couples. If this can be done, the outer circle of our world will shift and expand, and basic change in the university and in our lives will occur.

I believe that one of the most stimulating injections into the sclerotic body of the university has been study of gender, some of which has found its way into some universities in Women's Studies programs. But these programs are easily isolated—as if they were being quarantined. It will be hard to contain thought about gender, however, particularly if it is seen to be a development of field-theoretical and relativistic thought, that of philosophical physicists Einstein, Heisenberg, and Bohr, and scientist-philosophers James, Dewey, and Whitehead. It will be hard to contain it because it is, perhaps, the most powerful single force breaking up disciplinary partitions.

This new thought about gender reaches way back as well, and redefines our notion of definition itself, inherited from Aristotle, and illuminates its limitation as "male bias." Traditionally, to define is to negate, for the topic to be defined is set off from everything it is not. In reconceiving what it means to be *other,* this new female-connected thought simultaneously redefines definition and reworks the very meaning of what is polluting and taboo. In attempting to raise these latter topics to thematic consciousness, it itself threatens to pollute, which is why it is difficult for it to get a fair hearing from conventional, purist disciplines.

I will develop that portion of feminist thought which is least associated with contemporary political disputes—and personality clashes—which is cross-disciplinary with a vengeance, and which is most important, I believe. For it burrows under our dualisms and purification rituals and surfaces on the other side to view a new horizon of spatio-spiritual reality. Apparently paradoxically, it does this by attempting to retrieve ancient Neolithic clues about gender relationships as a key to a new form of life. (Some evidence from archaeology will be offered below.)

Certain feminist thinkers maintain that the hierarchical dualism of male/female is the key to understanding other dualisms. This is an important new approach, an advance on the early twentieth-century thought which I see as complementing and preparing for it. I concentrate on that thinking which probes into the temporal depth of our field reality, and attempts to grasp how the body-self-thinker-as-gendered affects thinking itself, and thereby affects the university. This chapter is a thought experiment, a serious playing with ideas.

Recall my earlier discussion of the great circles and mounds of Neolithic England and Ireland, the temple-observatories of around 3000 B.C. They anticipate field and relativity theory in certain ways: time and space viewed as interdependent, and human reality sensed, apparently, as interdependent with space-time. For the mounds did not merely "gather data," but were ceremonial sites for marking and commemorating not only decisive coincidings of Earth and Heavens in space-time, those cosmic deaths and rebirths which are the seasonal cycles, but also deaths and rebirths of the human generations. The human life cycle nested within the cosmic. Inside the vast, pregnant-seeming bellies of the mounds, the people were, apparently, reawakened to their own possibilities in being reawakened to the regenerative course of Nature which brooded them. There was no idea, evidently, of a vast container of space traveling on an absolute track of time, in which each individual happened to have been dropped—dropped like an atom or a discrete bud of matter—and in which he or she rattled around for a while until each was annihilated in a final pathetic spasm of consciousness. Human beings seemed to have been more communal and connected—and perhaps not so much threatened by otherness and pollution. To reconnect contemporary field and relativity theory with this much earlier, humanly rich and pious "objective relativism" is an important task, and grasping the female component is vitally important to it. Perhaps this gathering of ancient materials will provide a model for gaining better contact with ourselves and our students.

We are witnessing, I think, a reemergence of *very* ancient mythological thinking after millennia of supression by rationalist modes which stress division and difference (irrationally) at the expense of connectedness and community. The self-advertising rationalism which culminated with Descartes can even be described as a mythology of its own. The very ancient mother-mythology and the 4500-year-old masculine overlay are different engulfed modes of bodily intercourse with the world that have their own spatio-spiritual modes for making sense of ourselves and the world.

We exist in a period of extraordinary dissonance, I believe, in which very ancient mother-mythology begins to reemerge around the edges of a rigid, patriarchal mode of experiencing, a mode which has involved our bodily reality so immediately and totally in the world-as-experienced that usually nothing has remained to contradict or chasten it. There is no assurance that the mere decision to "reflect upon oneself" will disclose this male bias, no more than self-reflection helped Dewey when he tried to capture the bodily conditions of his own consciousness. Only perhaps by empathizing with a new (and very old) way of being in the world can persons in the university break out of the grip of by now ancient patriarchal ways of experiencing and defining, an empathizing that may ultimately demand auto-conditioning, as it did for Dewey.

This masculine overlay of thinking and experiencing has its own spatio-temporal patterns, as do the cultural and corporate forms that are involved organically with these patterns. It is no accident that our psychological terms are also, typically, spatial ones. To feel happy is to feel *up,* to feel sad is to feel *down.* To be open to change is to be *open,* not *closed.* There are *big* problems and *little* ones. Not to be *in*cluded is to be left *out.* We either work *over* somebody or work *beside* that person. Often the terms are clearly spatio-temporal as well, for example, "her voice was dejected, halting, slow, " or, "he darted about nervously, then settled in exhaustion."

Recent research in Women's Studies maintains that a patriarchal period begins around 2500 B.C., and is characterized by a strong bias of the spatio-spiritual grain in favor of domination and division. The tell-tale terms are psycho/physical: mind *over* matter, men *over* women, and consciousness *over* body. The male allies himself with, and defines himself according to, consciousness, and defines consciousness as that which imposes its form on what is *other* than it—matter, matrix, mother. The male, *pater,* imposes the *pure pattern* on the mere stuff, the matter. The male feels he must impose order on the inchoate and the *base,* the *lower* matter. So powerful has been this engrained bias that even after the manufacture of the microscope, a few hundred years ago, observers were convinced that they perceived miniature humans already formed within sperm, the full human within human sperm, fully-formed horses within horse sperm. They hallucinated.* Women were mere incubators and feeders.

Other researchers trace this by now ancient masculine bias in Freud's treatment of the Oedipus complex. Freud assumed what is paradigmatically male to be paradigmatically human. The male is born of a female, of course, and identifies initially with her, with her softness and nurturance. But fairly soon the child discovers that in some apparently crucial respect he is not like the mother, and must establish and define himself as other than his maternal source. He identifies with the father, a male who has defined himself as other than *his* maternal source, and has gone out into the larger world. As the larger world dominates the smaller one of the family, so the male is other than female and dominates her.

---

*Susan Bordo, *The Flight to Objectivity,* already cited.

But what of the male child's initial identification with the mother, with her softness and nurturance? This the male child must dominate and repress *within himself*. Thus dominance and division go hand in hand with endemic, all-pervasive violence, and this Freud regarded as characteristically human, the male body as the microcosm of the macrocosm. Dominating from the head down, it correlates immediately with a world which is to be dominated from the head down. Because our materialism springs from psycho/physical dualism, it demands the subjugation of material Nature.

Clearly, Women's Studies inserts a view of gender at such a basic conceptual level that it moves vast amounts of experience and data into new configurations. It gets beneath and behind the conventional classical conception of history and throws it into new perspective. Instead of being "all there is," it begins to appear to be only a phase, however important. But if it is only a phase, a hierarchical and patriarchal one, then hitherto undreamed of possibilities of living open up, ones sufficiently powerful eventually to alter the university, I think, and maybe even the larger world which presently moves, as Einstein said, toward unparalleled catastrophe.

Let us turn to key contrasts in spatio-spiritual realties. The ingrained classical and patriarchal conception of western civilization finds our deepest roots in the Near East, in ancient Egypt, for example. A powerful example of Egyptian art and civilization is the pyramid. The ideal pervasively communicated—it saturates the body-self—is that of the unique apex as it dominates all that falls beneath it on its four sides. The pyramid is imposed upon its contents and upon the earth, and all that does not fall within its rigid determinations is excluded as base, polluting. It is a rigid and repressive structure because the higher or better must regard any movement under it or toward it as an attempt to unseat it from the only desirable position, which is near, or at, the apex. There is no tolerance or reciprocity.

Since we are body-selves and have a field-reality, the shapes in our experienced world do not characterize "mere inert matter out there," but reveal our own selves, for we are engulfed experientially in these shapes. The pyramid, as a favored shape of human contemplation and production, reproduces itself endlessly, pyramids within pyramids. The Supreme Being in patriarchal civilization is typically male—above, transcendent, isolated, bright like the sun. The ultimate human unit is the nation-state, the leader as its head sits atop it—by divine right as it used to be said—and this pyramidal structure is replicated all the way down, pyramids within pyramids, until we reach that small, intimately moulding pyramid, the family. The father agrees to his subordinate position under the higher leaders because he heads his own family. "A man's house is his castle."

The Oedipal situation, as we have outlined it, involves a family structured pyramidally. Typically, the father stands at the apex. The structure must be rigidly hierarchical to control internal tensions. Recall that the male child identifies primitively with the mother, but at some point also with the father who has defined himself as other than, and better than, the female. Thus the child is divided from the woman-identified stratum of himself. But insofar as he competes, presumably, with the father for the one female, he is divided from him also, and lives in tension with his male identity too. The child is divided from both parents and from himself. The family becomes the cradle of violence. And the picture is not far-fetched if we take seriously the role of male bias in the formation of identity: to stress atomic self, and the traits which distinguish at the expense of traits which are shared—reciprocity, beneficial engulfment, community. Exaggerated otherness, aimed at counteracting males' dread of engulfment and obliteration in the female, multiplies on every hand and fuels violence.

It is no wonder that scholars in Women's Studies—archaeologists, anthropologists, psychologists, a few philosophers—believe they have discovered something fundamentally important in their unearthing of a radical alternative to the male conception of body, self, and world. What if we install ourselves empathically and imaginatively in the female body-self? How does the world look and feel then? And we need not rely exclusively on the imagination, for within the last few decades particularly, much new evidence of civilizations earlier than 2500 B.C., and not centering in the Near East, has come to light. They comprise what Marija Gimbutas calls Old Europe, an area which extends from the western coast of Turkey, up through the western coast of the Black Sea, through parts of the Italian peninsula, and then far into the valley of the Danube River (recall the goddess, Danu).* Perhaps the Neolithic ceremonial mounds of England and Ireland are associated with this civilization. Minoan Crete seems to have been its last surviving remnant. A wealth of female figures and figurines, apparently goddess images, and ceremonial sites associated with them, has been uncovered. An improved technology of dating has placed these artifacts at a much earlier time than "classical" civilization, and, as I said, throws this into a revealing, and somewhat humbling, new perspective. Perhaps even our marvelous classical Greece is not the acme of civilization, for if an unquestioning male bias is a formidable limitation, then this afflicts Greece, for assuredly its bias in body and world is male. Harry Redner writes perceptively,

The main symbolic bearer of classical civilization is the Apollonian body, the body depicted in all the classical plastic arts and enshrined in the classical symbolic conception of man. It is a whole body, all of rounded surfaces with no interiors, perfect in harmony and balance of its limbs and motion. It represents pure form in action. Whether it be the actual body of a god or a man, it is changeless and immortal. For Spengler this body is the symbolic vehicle for the "soul" of classical culture. We have argued that it is the sublimated form of actual changes carried out in the body by the Polis regimen of training and education. It was a very strict gymnastic discipline, directed to the athletic-military arts, to which the young male body was subjected. In addition, the male body was segregated from women and encouraged to desire itself in the mirror image of another male who is both a lover and a potential rival with whom to strive in public action and speech. *Paedeia* is the educational continuation of this total bodily discipline carried out in a quasi-erotic relationship between a young man and his elderly tutor. All this is the bodily foundation for the Greek cultivation of Reason. Through what psychic repressions was such a body further sublimated to produce the pure abstract form of intelligence, *Nous* or pure mind? This is the key psychoanalytic question about classical civilization.**

---

*Marija Gimbutas, *The Goddesses and Gods of Old Europe: 6500–3500 B.C.: Myths and Occult Images*, ed. (Berkeley and Los Angeles: 1982).
**Harry Redner, *The Ends of Philosophy: An Essay in the Sociology of Philosophy and Rationality* (New York: 1986), pp. 350–351.

In discovering an alternative to this imperious male paradigm, one discovers new possibilities for living. We find in these truly ancient—goddess oriented—civilizations an archetypal circle, not a pyramid, not a counterpart of the erect male body enclosed magisterially in itself—all hard surfaces with no appreciable interior, head ruling imperiously the lower and baser portions. In striking contrast to the pyramid, we find circular chambers dug in the earth, caves dwelt in and adorned, round mounds with vegetable matter at the core, vast waves of earth heaped up around brows of hills. The impression on the senses is utterly different from that made by the pyramid; different as well is the inducement to feel and behave. Instead of a dominating transcendence, purity, aridity, rigid determination, unambiguous clarity, imposition and exclusion, one sees—and feels—immanence, communality, irregularity; and flexibility, vague demarcation, darkness, fecundity, egalitarian relationships, and inclusion—a wholly different form of meaning-making and transcendence.

As with the body, so with the world experienced by it. For over four thousand years thinking has been mainly a male activity, and the thinking has been done, of course, by body-selves which are male. What new insights into the powers and limitations of this thinking can we gain when we fix on this fundamental fact? The paradigmatic human individual has been pictured as the paradigmatic male, all hard surfaces with no appreciable interior, erect, sharply cut out from the surrounding field and other individuals, self-standing, in control. Even the Greek goddesses were similarly pictured, and never as pregnant. But they were sculpted by males, we recall, as female characters in the theatre were enacted by males. What if we attend carefully to the numerous figures and figurines recovered from Neolithic sites, probably depicting the pregnant goddess, and attend to women portraying and enacting women? What if we regard the female body as also paradigmatically human? How would this change our thinking about ourselves as body-selves, as thinkers, and change our thinking itself?

What if a human can be soundly individual, and yet conceive and gestate another individual within that same body? What if human individuation is perfectly compatible with engulfment in others, with appropriate dependency, and with caring? What if males' thinking typically exaggerates what differentiates at the expense of what is shared, because of their anxiety that they will not succeed in establishing what distinguishes them from their birthing source—something as contingent as that?

Much more than does the female, the male tends to equate his individual self with a separate, radically unitary, self-enclosed body, and tends to think of all individual things on this model. It is true, after all, that things known are processed through the body-self which knows. Why shouldn't these things take on some of body-self's gender characteristics, but so automatically and unthematically that the knower does not know this, since all his "clarity" and "distinctness" emerges from shadowy mimetic engulfment in other males and their world? Thus the classical conception of any "substance," any individual reality, would take on the character of the male individuals who do the thinking: separate, self-enclosed, self-sufficient, able to have attributes. Nothing would remain in the known world to contrast with the male body-self and to question its hegemony.

In questioning gender we question the deepest assumptions about what things are. We redefine definition and reconceive individuation. Notice that typically the male tends to respond anxiously to engulfment in another, and to anything which threatens the "integrity" of his bodily envelope. But if the pregnant female body were also regarded as paradigmatically human, the engrained masculine notion of individuation and individual integrity would change some, and the dread of engulfment as violation would diminish. Probably the male's fear of pollution is greater than the female's, other things being equal. Probably his need to control others and to subordinate them is likewise greater. Recall that the mistake I made in teaching Current Moral and Social Issues was that I monopolized the authority, and could not resist the temptation to perform, and thereby to control the students. The teacher can make an important contribution to guidance without having to control everything in the classroom.

This new—and apparently very old—way of thinking which we learn from Women's Studies alters the way we think and feel about ourselves and the world. As one is open to the cavities and caves of the earth, and accepting of their darkness, so one is open to the cavities and caves of one's own body—whether male or female.* The person is not "all rounded surfaces with no interior." As one loves one's own soft, fertile belly, so one loves the ceremonial burial and fertility mounds heaped up on the earth for communal worship. Opening to the dark inwardness of the body encourages opening to the boundless world. The visceral sense of interdependence and communality of all things begins indeed in the viscera—if it is soft, vulnerable, unthreatening, and unthreatened. The open body and open world are field phenomena of reciprocity, a unique transcendence. To feel a vital part of the vast world is cause for rejoicing.

Like answers to like, sensibly and insensibly. Instead of the sharply cut out, detached, illuminated object in the focus of vision, we find the inclusive whole with which we identify in the darkness of kinesthetic involvement (the remarkable Biblical metaphor, "Bowels of mercies," seems appropriate). Definition is being redefined. Perhaps it need not lean so heavily on the exclusion of the individual-being-defined from what is not itself. In softening the contours of beings and strengthening their communal centers of relatedness in the field, don't we decrease their defensiveness and their fear of being violated and polluted, hence the incidence of fear and aggression?

We grope to discern an identity of inclusion rather than exclusion. Perhaps individuality need not be a defended cell, hard-edged, obdurate, and well lit, but just the experienced uniqueness of one's own place in the encircling, interdependent, reciprocal world. One is a unique body-self uniquely placed, but also a field being existing in mimetic resonance. One human being is *not* another, but need this be an *aversive* exclusion? And

---

*If both men's and women's affinity to the mother is not an explicit theme, it remains as blind, repressed mimetic engulfment, involving either thoughtless rebellion or just uncritical involvement in whatever inertial system one happens to be caught up in. For example, recall my students "sucking somnolently on the immense tit," mentioned in chapter I.

one must identify with and become mimetically engulfed in certain local groups that mold and confirm one's humaness; but need each group *aversively* exclude other groups? Definition and individuation of both individual and local group require negativities, but need these be destructive? We begin to fathom cruelty, I think, as a response by the isolated ego and isolated group to the threat of annihilation.* But we grope for self beyond this ego, and maybe find it in the darkness of the Earth and its Earthlings open to each other—or all opened to the night sky, or to the dawning or darkening sky. I believe Einstein's call to a new way of thinking is a summons to a new way of being bodyselves—ec-static, field beings.

All the hierarchical dualisms are attended by another, a silent pair: light as coming from "up there" and as superior to darkness; light as equated with illumination and knowledge, and darkness as equated with baseness, ignorance, and superstition. What if this bias must be undermined along with the others? What if the features which so sharply differentiate things from each other, and which are lit in the hard, sharp, dry, pure light, are not more fundamental than the features which are shared in the warm darkness of background fusion and engulfment? What if the male child's biological and physiognomic difference from the mother has been exaggerated by a "rationalist," patriarchal culture beyond all reason, so as to become a vastly misleading and damaging archetype of the human condition? What if the inner, kinesthetic sense of the body attuned empathically to others is at least as important as what we can visually discriminate?

In the patriarchal age, what is *up* and *top* and *over* is given preeminent status: as the head, the capital of reason in the erect male body, is given this. The watchful head is the high seat of reason and the locus of human "essence, " "rational animal," in both singular and corporate bodies. Hierarchical mentality has structured our behavior for millennia. There is so little to con-

---

*Eli Sagan, *At the Dawn of Tyranny* (New York: 1985). See also Renée Weber, "Field Consciousness and Field Ethics," *Re-Vision*, Summer/Fall, 1978. She speaks of "psychological atom smashing." What would happen if the vast energy expended in holding together the ego were to be released for other purposes?

trast it with that we take it for granted dumbly; practically no human group is immune to it. Recall the earlier description of the American Philosophical Association and its ingrained (and I think desperate) habit of ranking its members, the "minds." We have learned to identify ourselves with a number of local groups pyramidally structured which define themselves through rigidly segregated levels, and as other than, and typically better than, other pyramidally structured groups. Since our identity is fashioned in the identity of these groups, and since each group becomes the model of humanity for its members—thus the top and best—we will experience other groups as potential replacers of ourselves, as threats to our being, as powerful pollutants. Racial groups are particularly lethal in this regard, but it is not only they. What if, however, there is no apex position to be lost? What if the best configuration of human relationships is not a pyramid of pyramids?

We find in the ancient circles, mounds, and caves of goddess worship a radically different model of human being and identity. If we all occupy different positons in a vast, all-inclusive circle, rather than occupying different levels in different pyramids which are themselves at different levels, then it is impossible to fall from a height and more difficult for movement to be experienced as mortal threat. There is movement, but this means simply that different positions are assumed by its members at different times in the great circle. Nor is one part of the circle up, and the other down, nor need the circle define itself as other than anything else, because there is nothing else. Nor need we assume that there must be an autocratic figure at the center dictating what must happen at the periphery. If in the deepest way we identified ourselves as members of such a circle, our identities would be very different.

Change must occur on this primal level of body-self as spatio-spiritual, as field phenomenon, in the very way it defines and individuates itself and other things (and we should recall that part of Einstein's genius consisted in his thinking this way about some topics). True, there is danger in getting lost in utopian thinking, and we probably deceive ourselves if we imagine that some change in our living and upbringing could eliminate all threat of pollution. Inescapably, we are separate organisms with private, immediately lived fluids and processes, who must guard against intrusions from the public world.

But this guarding need not be as watchful and fearful as it is. The other need not be so dominantly the *other* other, the alien, outcaste, or ruler as super-caste—the other as the counterpart of the self as defended cell and isolated ego. I think that sources of pollution can never be wholly eliminated and child-like innocence regained—that would be another form of totalitarian thinking—but it may be realistic to suppose that sources of pollution and disturbance can be diminished; also spread around and thinned a bit, so that they are not concentrated in a few spots as scapegoats, negative polarities, targets.

We are adding content to Dewey's call for reverence for the body. There is much more to the body-self than its ability to say "I" of itself at any moment and to assert itself as ego. My whole self is a field being, involved in some way in the cycles of the self-regenerating, interdependent universe. At every instant more flows through me than I can ever acknowledge or calculate, and, as Girard put it, the sacred consists in that which dominates us in direct proportion to our efforts to control it.

So at some point the efforts should cease, just as Dewey allowed his body to take the lead at certain points so that his consciousness could catch up with and recognize its own conditions in body and environment. He found blockages and split-off states, instantaneous shunnings and exclusions, a panicky effort to form a tight little self through what, in effect, is purification ritual. If freedom is to be expanded and solid autonomy achieved, this individuating response must be reconditioned, auto-conditioned. Needed is a visceral image of inclusion in a non-hierarchical whole, that which is set off from nothing else. There is otherness, but not split off and threatened. And *if*, as James implied, there must be some opponent with whom we are "morally at war," why can't it be the parochialism which has held us in its frightened grip?

I have tried a thought experiment. What does this vast sweep of history and the new possibilities for us which it suggests, have to do with the multiversity here and now, and its pretension to being an educational institution? In presenting this ancient, contrasting way of being and thinking, we are not indulging a historical interest merely (as important as that is). There is some evidence that the Neolithic way of life was pre-patriarchal, and much more peaceful than that which has replaced it to this day.*

But even if the evidence were conclusive we would not know enough to apply it to our own situation. How can a way of living, dimly surmised in the stone age, and agricultural time, be recovered and used in an urban, post-technological world? Isn't this an invitation to a pipe dream?

Not quite. For I have argued repeatedly that archaic modes of experiencing survive practically unchanged, and that we have ignored them at our peril. Moreover, in glimpsing the Neolithic we see alternatives to current patriarchal, hierarchical, and divisive structures embedded in the twentieth-century university—alternatives we would probably not have dreamed of otherwise, so in the grip of the metaphor of time's "arrow" and inevitable scientific progress are we. Looking backwards puts patriarchal structures into sudden relief, and suggests a different ideal of life.

It is this *ideal*—this *image*, this *story*—which might be embodied in contemporary university life, if we are inventive and resolute enough. Only despair of the intellect leads us to think that ideals and ideas are ineffectual. Over the long term of human evolution, they have altered the very shape of our bodies,

---

*The rapidly emerging body of evidence involves several parameters: absence of fortifications around cities dating between 6500 and 4000 B.C.; more nearly egalitarian living quarters than is typical of later times; the infrequency of sumptuous royal burials, particularly the burials of kings, replete with weaponry and wealth; the absence of battle-mutilated bodies; the absence of art commemorating battle and victory; the profusion of statuary of the goddess. The sites include the remarkable civilizations of Crete, and what Gimbutas calls Old Europe, a vast area. An excellent source of information is Riane Eisler, *The Chalice and the Blade: Our History, Our Future* (New York: 1987). Eisler builds on the work of Gimbutas (and on that of James Mellaart on Çatal Hüyük), and provides a good, easily accessible bibliography. The latter portion of her book deals with possibilities of partnership between men and women, and is intriguing.

and our modes of reproducing and training ourselves.* In the life of the moment, properly focused ideals and ideas open the possibility of reconditioning basic responses. To think that we can detach ourselves from ourselves and view ourselves with pure neutrality and objectivity is absurd. As James pointed out in "The Will to Believe," it sounds scientific to say, "Withhold belief until the evidence is in." But in matters pertaining to our education, to what we make of ourselves, the evidence that comes in depends in large part upon the beliefs we *choose to hold* and to act upon.

Doubtless an essential part of Freud's genius was his ability to discern archaic urges and tendencies, such as those he termed the Oedipus Complex. But it is an essential part of his limitations that he did not see alternatives to patriarchal structures. We must get beyond Freud if we would reconceive the human relations that constitute the university. For I am convinced that the current neglect of students can be traced, in large part, to the survival of archaic patriarchal biases which construe students as subordinate, base, "women's work," threatening to the identity of the professional academic, polluting.

In an inspired chapter of *The Mermaid and the Minotaur,* "The Dirty Goddess," Dorothy Dinnerstein reveals how profoundly formative of self and educational are gender relations within the home, particularly as they affect child-rearing. As the twig is bent, so bends the tree. She traces the grave consequences for all human life of psycho/physical dualism, and its close attachment to male/female dualism. These crude realities mold our lives regardless of how up-to-date our technology is. Indeed, insofar as technology has, for hundreds of years now, drawn the father out of the home and out of the neighboring lands, it contributes to the effects of the dualism. For that is the point: the father is "spirited away" from the home nearly every day, leaving the mother to handle the inescapable material realities of the

---

*Regarding the role of ideals and ideas in the upright posture of humans, the effect of this on the anatomical structure of women, and, finally, the consequences of this for the "pre-mature" birth of infants of our large-headed species, see Alison Jaggar, *Feminist Politics and Human Nature* (Totowa, N.J.: 1983), pp. 109-110.

body-selves needing to be toilet-trained, washed, fed, clothed, weaned, and raised. The ancient patriarchal association of mother with *mater* and matter is still in force.* All the vulnerability, the threats of humiliation and pollution, associated with the flesh get associated with mother, while father tends to be seen as a winged pure intellect, who employs technology to escape it all and to achieve power and skill in the vastly more important outer world. This dualism of mind and body tends to split all the selves involved, and to turn them into eccentric fragments who constantly shore up a beleaguered, ill founded existence.

Dinnerstein has a proposal to ameliorate the malaise. It is simple and profound: if both male and female parents had a nearly equal hand in raising the children, then it would be unlikely that males would get characterized as mainly pure mind and females as mainly (im)pure body. There would be less likelihood of women being targeted as the sole source of body miseries and pollution. There would be a much better chance for all persons to live fully and openly, unburdened of the task to defend against the *other*. Possibilities of pollution, never fully eradicable I believe, would nevertheless be spread around and thinned. In the objectively relative reciprocating field, each gender is deeply identified with the other anyway. Why, then, mangle ourselves with some perversely constricting notion of identity as *purely* this or *purely* that? We should have learned from the Underground Man that we would not really like this kind of purity even if we could find it, and from twentieth-century physics that the sharp lines between subject and object, observer and observed, self and other, individual and group, can no longer apply even in physics. How much less can they apply in human relations!

The relevance of all of this to the university setting is clearly evident. The Oedipal situation in the patriarchal home reproduces itself in the professionalized university, the messy work of caring for students and "staying at home with them" being con-

---

*Dorothy Dinnerstein, *The Mermaid and the Minotaur* (New York: 1977), particularly chapter seven.

strued as "women's work." The prestige of the professionalized professor is directly proportional to the duration and profitability of travel beyond the university, to getting established in the more important outside world of publishing and conventioneering, of pure research and exclusive relationships with peers. And it is a clear sign of the primitive power of these purist, intellectualist drives that the biological gender of the professor is often irrelevant. Those who are biologically female, but who have been educated within patriarchal institutions, can at times be the most ferocious proponents of what we have defined as masculine habits of thinking and being. These are the "Athenas" of academia, those who—as in Aeschylus' *Oresteia*—think that father-murder is a more serious crime than mother-murder, and who side with Orestes instead of Electra.

Indeed, so aggressive and domineering did patriarchal thinking become in "classical" Greece, that Aristotle could argue that only the father supplies the distinctive human form to the child; hence only the father is the true parent, and since female children ("mutilated males") do not receive the fully intact form or essence of the true parent, they are "monters, even if natural ones."*

Who would "stay home" and "hold a student's hand" and "nurse" him or her through emotional crises attendant upon a new depth of learning when the professor might be off lecturing outside the university? Particularly if it is before a group of professional peers who authorize one's status as a penetrating, hard, rigorous mind? Who would share one's presence with perhaps a single student, be available and vulnerable, when I, the professor, might be standing before those significant others who note everything I say and look only at me as I display "astonishing erudition"? Unless there is a radical shift in thinking, only a "fool" would opt to "stay at home" when he or she could be off "starring" on the world-wide academic scene.

Professionalism is a world-orientation, and it tilts, pervades, and structures the whole culture as a mode of self-formation, individual and corporate. Its impact on all the professions aimed

---

*Quoted in Catherine Keller, *From a Broken Web: Separation, Sexism, and Self* (Boston: 1986) pp. 48–50.

at caring for human beings is particularly dubious; indeed, the very notion of care tends to be defined out of existence. Take nursing, for example. Who would rather be the caregiver if he or she could be the administrator? Who wants to endure "soiling" encounters with the patient? This distancing from fellow human beings occurs also in social work: wards tend to be experienced as objects with problems to be calculated, rather than persons in dire need of the sustaining presence of fellow humans.*

What we are striving for is fundamental, humane knowledge. If the university can do nothing to discover it, then it should stop pretending to educate human beings. We face the challenge of redefining definition and individuation, and of salvaging the best of a patriarchal past without swallowing it whole. If each can grow to understand his or her uniqueness without overemphasizing this (and the uniqueness of one's corporate or social organism as well), that is, without feeling radically other than the other, then much humane and ethical knowledge would already be ours. If we do not think that this is possible, it will surely be impossible, for we will not try to achieve it.

Just the slightest progress along these lines would be beneficial for the university. If we cease to think of the world's work as done by pure, male intellects, then that aspect of educating the young which is caring for them, will not be stigmatized as "women's work," sissy and polluting. Administrators will not be obsessed with staffing their knowledge factories with "star" professors, each with a string of trophies.

Much of the most important work in the university is unrecorded and unrecordable: listening, and sitting with another's fear, pain, or joy, and knowing silently that one exists in solidarity with that other person, no matter how lowly; knowing that each of us derives from a common source in the earth, and that each will rejoin it at some unknown but inevitable moment. Despite the educator's special authority, that person can be drawn out to confront the question of what to make of his or her own life. Not to identify with what is young, lowly, uncertified, un-

---

*Roberta Imre, *Knowing and Caring: Philosophical Issues in Social Work* (Lanham, MD.: 1983).

formed, mortal in the student is not to identify with all this in oneself. It is to lose contact with the regenerating life of the species, hence with oneself. Beyond all particular corporate bodies within which we participate, lies the Earth and the rest of reality with which we can identify, the matrix which is opposed to nothing, for all contrasts occur within it.

The question is, can we identify deeply with what we all have in common: the Earth as it turns in space, and our shared status as Earthlings? Or, will humans continue to lean heavily on differences between nations, races, genders, groups of all kinds in the formation of identity? We are all "naturally" inclined toward chauvinism, because we are raised in groups which are more or less local, and these tend to figure for their members as the paradigmatic samples of humanity; other groups are *other.* The question becomes, then, can we fix on an image of the whole of humanity which is sufficiently powerful to recondition the chauvinistic response? This is the supreme challenge to our ability to substitute moral and rational values for irrational ones. The time is ripe to face the challenge, for never has there been a stronger reason to do so: survival. It is not clear that enough humans will succeed in this to tip the balance, for any threat to the current chauvinistic response is a threat to our being, and arouses deep anxiety and hostility.

The egotism and shallowness and overbearing mein of many in the university is shameful and appalling. It is, among other things, the culmination of a long patriarchal and hierarchical tradition. We can see it in the obsessive preoccupation with individual rights at the expense of responsibility and caring—living fully and emotionally. There are now opportunities to speak "in a different voice," and to listen to it.* If we do, the horizon will open up, and possibilities of knowing and being will open up that we would not otherwise have dreamed to be possible. If we do, we will at least hesitate a moment before closing our horizons in neat sets of dualistic, hierarchic, and "exhaustive" alternatives. As William James believed, philosophical study

---

*Carol Gilligan, *In a Different Voice* (Cambridge, Mass.: 1982).

is the habit of always seeing an alternative, and as his father, Henry, put it, love cannot have a contrary, but must em-
brace what is most opposed to it. The Earth encompasses all
Earthlings.

It is only the most savagely professionalized professors who
squirm and raise their backs and respond to talk of love as if it
were polluting. It is surely confirming evidence of the excesses of
professionalism that there are many professors who think they
can neatly divide their personal lives from their professional
roles. There can and ought to be distinctions, but need they be
ones which alienate? What is the point of hanging on to the simplistic polarization of personal and professional life? The most
archaic, personal habits mold the ways we relate to students and
to fellow teachers every day. The reciprocating field of interactivity never releases us.

Writing on the eve of his ninetieth year to his friend and
sometime collaborator, Arthur Bentley, John Dewey wrote sev-
enty words that sum up much of what I want to say. Dewey
answers criticism of his logic made by two analytic philosophers,
Alonzo Church and Arthur Smullyan:

Church and Smullyan don't realize, in the first place, that logical *form*,
instead of being set over against subject-matter, is itself a distinction in
subject-matter, and in the second place, in consequence, they translate
what we say over into what it would be *if they* held it—it is as if we're
part of their system—a kind of criticism I've received most of my life
from my professional colleagues.*

Dewey is saying that these professional intellectuals will not
listen, cannot listen—will not, cannot, stand open to another
person's life and thought. It's as if their heads were fists frozen
shut that crash against another's text and deposit their own seed
within it and criticize it on that basis. The suggestion here of
purely male—hence incompletely human—sexual activity is de-

---

*Letter of April 26, 1948, in *John Dewey and Arthur F. Bentley: A Philosoph-
ical Correspondence*, ed. S. Ratner, J. Altman, and J. E. Wheeler (New Brunswick, N.J.: 1964), p. 590.

liberate. Aggressive habits of thought are patterns of activity frozen and concealed in our bodies, and the need to define and constitute identity through exclusion is so impulsive and powerful that we ourselves misunderstand and pollute the other in order to provide a pretext for regarding it *as* other and for excluding it. These professional intellectuals, Dewey is saying, cannot tolerate or even imagine the truth as another has discerned it. They project their demons.*

---

*In writing this chapter I am particularly indebted to Donna Wilshire, and to her article, "The Uses of Image, Myth, and the Female Body in Re-Visioning Knowledge,"in *Gender/Body/Knowledge: Feminist Reconstructions of Knowing and Being,* ed. Alison Jaggar and Susan Bordo (New Brunswick, N.J.: 1989).

EPILOGUE

But where there is peril, deliverance too gains in
strength.

—Friedrich Hölderlin

Professionalism emerges as a quasi-religion, our only way, apparently, of holding ourselves together after the disintegration of religious myths and pre-industrial traditions. It permeates the
culture. Take a too-frequent experience in refurbishing a house.
One watches the painters carefully as they paint the structure,
for they trample the plants and have scant regard for what the
gardener has done. The gardner plants his vines which cling to
the painted walls of the house and damage them and has little or
no regard for what the painter has done. Dare one have a plas-
terer come to fix the hole in the ceiling? Will he ruin the newly
finished floor in the process? The electrician's work leaves a bit
of carpentry to be finished, but the carpenter has completed his
job and will not come back.

When this happens the gaps left between professional specialties never quite get filled and the whole job never quite gets
finished. What professional can one call to fill in the gaps left by
all the recognized professionals when each has finished what
each considers his or her field? One would need a meta-
professional, and they don't exist, apparently. (Will handymen
and "girls-friday" push for professional status, or will they continue to endure the stigma of amateurism?)

But when professionalism disintegrates the university, as it
has, a much graver situation results. It is not houses we are dealing with, but human beings. No one exists in the university to
fill the gaps left by the departments—surely not philosophers,
who have spent decades isolating themselves in highly technical,
arcane projects. And what filters in through the gaps in a uni-

versity student's "education" is not plaster dust, or paint drops on the flattened plants and bushes, but an archaic and sacred background which is unrecognized, undisciplined, wild. Purification rituals and exorcisms as wild and dark as any "savage" culture—wilder, darker, but less obvious—sift through the gaps and leave everything an eerie color. There is a dream-like atmosphere permeating the twentieth-century research university. Something at work is never acknowledged, and what Max Weber feared has pretty well come true: a race of highly trained barbarians is produced, "specialists without spirit, sensualists without heart."

The temptation is strong to shrug one's shoulders, throw up one's hands, and drift off. Either this or to propose wild plans for dismantling universities, or at least departments and professional associations. None of this will happen by fiat, and there are no institutions ready to take their place. Only chaos would result, even if these units could be dismantled at once. After recognizing what is going on, and what is not said in the university about the university—perhaps cannot be said in our impoverished secular vocabularies—we teachers have no alternative, I believe, but to work patiently within the universities.

Brooding around all our efforts to revitalize the university is the demoralizing threat of meaninglessness. The obsessive concern with the ego's immediate interests—both individual and corporate egoism—threatens now to terminate human history. This would not be end as fulfillment and meaning-making, but as termination. It threatens us, the co-creators of history, with meaninglessness. It is not merely that we cannot precisely predict the consequences of even a limited nuclear exchange, say. The very meaning of our inherited concepts threatens to dissolve. What is the meaning of "war," for example, if neither side can win, were the available nuclear weapons to be used?

But since the meaning of ourselves cannot be dissociated from the meaning our world and our activities have for us, the meaning of ourselves threatens to dissolve. As we assess our prospects for survival, it is not as if we were solid beings stepping into a foggy field. It's as if we had started to merge with the fog itself. Who are we that we have brought this about?

What might we be? Perhaps this threat of our own problematical meaning, or our own immanent meaninglessness, is a blessing in disguise, for now we have some motive to *think*.

If we would follow a thread of meaningfulness and survive, we must dilate our attention and grasp the archaic background of our experience in its present obscurity, turbulence, and jumble. We can no longer mindlessly reenact purification rituals that humans have used to define themselves up to now, but which if continued would probably prove fatal, for friction between individuals and between groups might touch off the final blasts. But it is secular, hierarchical, and linear nonsense to think that all purification ritual can be jettisoned. Some rituals are both unavoidable and valuable. Acknowledged purification ritual can powerfully assist us in leaving past stages of development behind and getting on to new ones. Each of us is ineluctably a body which experiences immediately its own internal processes, and these are not to be mixed indiscriminately in the public world if we are to have sound identities as individuals. Moreover, our corporate bodies, our societies, must be defined, *in part,* in terms of what they are *not*.

But everything depends upon what is excluded and why, upon the meaning that *not* has. There are sensible and constructive negativities and nonsensical and destructive ones. We can define ourselves by excluding ourselves from stagnation and despair, for example. "*I* am the being who need *not* be depressed every time I happen to feel tired or 'off my feed'." Or, "*We* are the beings who need *not* revel in ignorance and prejudice and deify ourselves at the expense of others who become for us polluted and base thereby." Individually and collectively we can be defined in terms of our place on the vast circle of the family of human beings. Each person's and each group's place is theirs, and *not* another's, but it does not follow that one's familiar place is better than another's. Vital individuality requires vital participation in a field recognized to be reciprocal. The tyrant's power over others is ultimately debilitating for the tyrant himself, because it cuts him off from the freely given gifts of informed, intelligent, and respected others. Fear—and its child, greed—constricts our attention to short runs of events and consequences.

The traits dividing the genders seem to be the most charged and difficult to keep in balance. I, a male, am *not* female. Of course. But the big question remains to be asked and answered: how significant are these differentiating traits? For some males they constitute their most significant ones. This way leads to the model of the dominating, eccentric male. Deeply trapped in the patriarchal scheme of definition through opposition, he thinks that the only alternative to this emphasis upon masculinity must be non-differentiation, re-engulfment in the mother and obliteration of his identity as an individual. Behind the tyrant lies the fearful child.

But there are any number of ways of differentiating differentiation itself, and securing thereby a sound identity as an individual. A trait can differentiate without separating or opposing. Simply because each of us occupies a unique place within the reciprocating and boundless field—that is enough to individuate us soundly, *if* we can deeply experience it, that is, if we can *recondition* ourselves to respond to this newly imaged place; in other words, if we can be *morally* centered. Only outmoded mechanistic views infer fallaciously from finitude and dependency to automatism, futility, and abasement.

I am not asking that the university become another Esalen or Omega Institute, only that it address the persons within it as beings who are immeasurably more than their professional roles. I am asking that it leave room for listening, ruminating, and silence, and that it not drive young professors into mania if they would hope to have an academic career. For what we have now in the university is, I believe, a purity unto death. It is not the case that all death is physical. According to Plato, Socrates thought that unrighteousness runs faster than death. There can be a death of the soul—by that I mean a death of body-self, the "dreaming animal," as Kierkegaard described us.

I think that we have a chance to avert this death if we see that beyond all our calculations along all our linear metrics lies the never-ending cycle of Nature—birth, death, rebirth—and also the possibility of continued cycles of the human generations—birth, death, rebirth. There is a priceless purificational ritual of rebirth in which we acknowledge what we are doing in leaving a past stage of development behind us and preparing the ground for the new. The ritual energizes and empowers. If the university is an educational institution it acknowledges this, and engages wholeheartedly in the intergenerational task of teaching.

In 1948, the year Dewey wrote to Bentley complaining of the constricted lives and thinking of professional philosophers, the astrophysicist, Fred Hoyle, remarked that once a photograph of the Earth taken from the outside becomes available, a new idea as powerful as any in history will emerge. We now have such photographs of our blue planet—with its thin and delicate membrane of air, its different seasons in its different hemispheres—and there is evidence that these photographs have furthered the ecological movement. They provide a powerful image which we can use in our attempt to recondition our chauvinism and our point-instant egotism and absolutism. They pose the challenge of freely redefining our being, and that is the ultimate educational challenge.

There is as yet only little evidence, however, that the university-become-multiversity grasps the intergenerational and interdisciplinary nature of this challenge to its existence. Typically, its administrative and faculty leaders have lacked the imagination, courage, and organizational skills to face it. They keep the bureaucratic machinery running day after day—a difficult job, to be sure!—and then on the morning of graduation intone, or whine, or belt out a few philosophical slogans to the departing students and their dutiful parents.

It is sad to realize that all this has to be set out and argued, as I have tried to do in this book. But it is certainly necessary to do so, because we have been caught up so long in what can be called the patriarchalist myth: the hero sets himself off decisively and contemptuously from mother and matter and progresses inexorably toward total domination and control. We dimly expect, I think, that death itself will someday be conquered. Death is merely current medical failure.

This is the ultimate ego trip, and when death halts such a trajectory it is mere terminus and absurdity. If we grasp ourselves as we are, however, in the reciprocating and regenerating field, then death is a fulfillment—strange and beautiful and sad as it is—because it prepares the matrix and leaves room for the next births.

For the academic who equates self with the point-instant ego, the student is a mere distraction or a pollutant. For the one who links self with the reciprocating and regenerating field, the student is a fulfillment.

Simple recognition of finitude and mortality, simple recognition of fact, is called for. But nothing seems to be more difficult for us professors, caught up as we are in our thrusts of intellect and momentary honors. When the professional life presumes to totalize, it becomes a closet lined with mirrors, and against its walls we can beat our heads and die in a way as persons without ever knowing why.*

The key point is that there is no substitute for human relationship and presence, for listening, for sharing silence and wonderment, and for caring. There is no expert knowledge of the human self which can be claimed by any particular academic field. There are merely insights here and there which must be tested through experience to see if they contribute to a more sane and vital life, or to a more empty, insane, and boring one. Our common task is to achieve just enough behaviorally effective humane knowledge to avert disaster—atomic war, toxic events, meaningless lives. If threat of disaster is not enough to mold us into minimally adequate educational community in the university, then nothing will work, I think, and we deserve whatever fate we get.

> So teach us to number our days, that
> we may apply our hearts unto wisdom.

---

*See William Barrett, *Death of the Soul: From Descartes to the Computer* (Garden City, New York: 1986)

INDEX

Please remember that this is a library book,
and that it belongs only temporarily to each
person who uses it. Be considerate. Do
not write in this, or any, library book.